DATE OF MAGAZINE	BORROWER'S NAME	TIME DUE

WEALTH & POVERTY

Four Christian Views of Economics

Edited by
Robert G. Clouse
with
contributions by

William E. Diehl
Art Gish
John Gladwin
Gary North

InterVarsity Press
Downers Grove
Illinois 60515

InterVarsity Press is the book-publishing division of Inter-Varsity Christian Fellowship, a student movement active on campus at hundreds of universities, colleges and schools of nursing. For information about local and regional activities, write IVCF, 233 Langdon St., Madison, WI 53703.

Distributed in Canada through InterVarsity Press, 860 Denison St., Unit 3, Markham, Ontario L3R 4H1, Canada.

Cover illustration: Greg Wray

Acknowledgment is made to the following for permission to reprint copyrighted material:

All Scripture quotations, unless otherwise indicated, are from the Revised Standard Version of the Bible, copyrighted 1946, 1952, © 1971, 1973.

Scripture quotations marked TEV are from the Good News Bible— Old Testament: Copyright © American Bible Society 1976: New Testament: Copyright © American Bible Society 1966, 1971, 1976.

Scripture quotations marked NEB are from The New English Bible. © The Delegates of the Oxford University Press and The Syndics of the Cambridge University Press 1961, 1970. Reprinted by permission.

Other Scripture quotations are from the King James Version (KJV).

The poem on page 152 by Peter Maurin is taken from The Catholic Worker (1 April 1934). Used by permission.

The quotation on pages 209-10 is from "U.S. and Soviet Agriculture: The Shifting Balance of Power" by Lester R. Brown, Worldwatch Paper 51 (Oct. 1982). Used by permission.

The quotation on pages 224-25 is from I Believe in the Second Coming of Jesus by Stephen Travis. Used by permission of William B. Eerdmans Publishing Company.

ISBN 0-87784-347-3

Printed in the United States of America

Library of Congress Cataloging in Publication Data
Main entry under title:

Wealth and poverty.

    Includes bibliographies.
    1. Economics–Religious aspects–Christianity–
Addresses, essays, lectures.   2. Church and the poor–
Addresses, essays, lectures.   I. Clouse, Robert G.,
1931-   II. Diehl, William E.
BR115.E3W36   1984   261.8'5   84-3808
ISBN 0-87784-347-3

17	16	15	14	13	12	11	10	9	8	7	6	5	4	3	2	1
96	95	94	93	92	91	90	89	88	87	86	85	84				

To my wife Bonnidell and my friends
J. Robert Constantine
Richard Pierard
Don & Madonna Yates
who have encouraged me to work
for justice for the poor
and the oppressed.

Robert G. Clouse

Acknowledgments

Wealth and Poverty: Four Christian Views *joins* The Meaning of the Millennium: Four Views *and* War: Four Christian Views *as the third volume I have edited for InterVarsity Press. Many people have helped me prepare these books, and I would like to thank them for their efforts. They include Herbert Rissler, Virginia Banfield, Woodrow Creason and the inter-library loan staff at the Cunningham Memorial Library at Indiana State University, particularly Karen Chittick, Mary Ann Phillips, Carol Chapman and Richard Collins. This book also benefits from the criticisms and questions of President Ted Mercer and the faculty and student body of Bryan College in Dayton, Tennessee. In April 1983 I presented some of the ideas and interpretations contained in this work in the Staley Lectures at that institution. Their gracious and stimulating response aided in the preparation of the manuscript.*

Robert G. Clouse
Indiana State University
Terre Haute, Indiana

Despite ... progress, the existence of absolute poverty for many hundreds of millions of people involving malnutrition, illiteracy, disease and starvation is a fact of today's world. Robert McNamara, President of the World Bank, defined absolute poverty "as a condition of life so characterized by malnutrition, illiteracy, disease, squalid surroundings, high infant mortality and low life expectancy as to be beneath any reasonable definition of human decency." Regardless of whether we are capitalist or Marxist, Christian or Hindu, or whether the colour of our skin is black, brown, white or yellow, absolute poverty remains a disturbing fact. In the early seventies the international Labour Office estimated that the very poor amounted to 700 million. More recently the World Bank puts the figure at 800 million. The number of undernourished and hungry is put at somewhere between 500-600 million and one billion.

Most of us in the West have no idea of what it must be like to live in such a situation of total deprivation with no or very little work, no adequate sanitation or clean water, economic insecurity, little if any formal education, inadequate health services, overcrowded housing, without either running water or electricity.

Brian Griffiths
Director, Centre for Banking and International Finance,
City University of London,
taken from his London Lecture in Contemporary Christianity, 1980

Introduction
Robert G. Clouse

The Bible portrays God as concerned with the affairs of this world. His spokespersons, the Old Testament prophets, repeatedly emphasized the need for justice in human affairs. Jesus never distinguished between the "religious" and "social" aspects of service to others. He fed the hungry, healed the sick and raised the dead. In Matthew 25 he commanded Christians to provide food for the starving, care for the sick, aid to prisoners, clothes for the naked and housing for refugees. Caring for the needy was so important, he said, that it was equivalent to caring for him. In numerous situations, including his defiance of Sabbath customs and his treatment of the woman taken in adultery, he placed human needs before religious and ceremonial considerations (Mk 2:23-28; Jn 8:3-11).

The Call to Social Involvement
Those who followed Christ were to be salt and light in the world and servants to others (Mt 5:13-16; Mk 10:43-44). Jesus directed them to love their neighbor as themselves. In response to the question "Who is my neighbor?" Jesus told the story of the good Samaritan, which taught that all people fall into the category of neighbor (Lk 10:29-37).

Although a few years ago it may have been necessary to amplify this case for social involvement, thanks to a number of excellent books, statements and conferences, this is no longer needed. Now we must discuss the direction this social and political activity ought to take. Some wish to bolster conservative influences in society. Others emphasize a more liberal approach, and still others believe that radical change is necessary to help our neighbors. Global problems present a massive challenge. Some twenty years ago a nationally known speaker might have pointed out that society must deal with war, poverty and racism. Rather than bringing solutions to these difficulties, the passage of time has witnessed the growth of more crises relating to environmentalism and sexism.

Those who wish to serve Christ must deal with people who identify many of these problems, especially poverty, with capitalism. It is not a simple matter to either defend or condemn modern industrial capitalism from the Scriptures. One economist explains this dilemma for the Christian:

> The economy of Biblical times was agrarian, not industrial. People of that time knew nothing of our applied technology, economic machinery, or complex investment schemes. Output came from land and labor, with minimal capital for investment.
>
> Consequently, productive savings was irrelevant in that system. People could consume, hoard, or give, but productive investment was hardly an option.
>
> Scripture clearly condemns sumptuous living, non-productive accumulation, and hoarded wealth. "Come now, you rich," wrote James, "weep and howl for the miseries that are coming upon you. You have laid up treasure for the last days. Your gold and silver have rusted, and their rust will be evidence against you and will eat your flesh like fire" (James 5:1, 3).
>
> But what of productive investment? The Bible is not explicit on wealth accumulation of this kind. Unfortunately, the church has done little to deal with issues of wealth accumulation in the form of productive capital.[1]

It is the purpose of this book to confront the reader with issues of prosperity and poverty created by modern forms of wealth accumulation and to give some indication of the variety of current evangelical opinion on these matters. A Christian must remember that the gospel is not a natural or necessary ally of capitalism. For centuries the church existed with medieval manorialism, but that economic arrangement passed and the cause of God continued. It is dangerous to identify the gospel with any social or political system.

Capitalism

Exactly what is meant by *capitalism*? It can be defined, in an abstract sense, as "an economic system based preponderantly on the private ownership and use of capital for the production and exchange of goods and services with the aim of earning a profit. In this sense, the system is theoretically not limited by time and place and can be described and analyzed in the abstract language of the economist."[2]

Capitalism is also an historical phenomenon. It is an institutional order that developed gradually in Europe during the Middle Ages, spread to the Western Hemisphere and other parts of the world during early modern times, and reached its peak development in the later nineteenth century. The introductory comments which follow will deal with the historical growth of capitalism.

The Era of Expansion

Medieval Europe was dominated by a series of decentralized units called manors. These estates or village communities produced all or at least most of what they used. In reality, few estates could satisfy either the volume or variety of needed products. Basic commodities, including salt and iron as well as luxury goods such as spices, wine and fine cloth, were bought from traders.

The transition from an economy of self-sufficiency to one of exchange for profit took several centuries. Certain periods of European history stand out as important in the process of change. The first was the era of expansion during the twelfth through the fourteenth centuries, which witnessed the birth of capitalism. The cities of northern Italy were the center for this early development, but it soon spread to other parts of Europe. City life revived as merchants gravitated to these centers of commerce. Estates began to concentrate on the growth of cash crops and to buy their industrial needs from the cities. Water power and wind power were harnessed for the grinding of grain and fulling of cloth. The "commercial revolution" which resulted led to new trading and business practices such as the partnership, the bill of exchange, double-entry bookkeeping and certain forms of marine insurance. East Asian goods were brought to Europe by the Italians and traded at fairs such as those in Champagne.

Commercial prosperity led to growth in population and to geographical expansion through colonization and conquest. Within the settled areas of Europe, land-hungry peasants cleared the forests, drained the marshes and reclaimed land from the sea. On the periphery of the continent (east of the Elbe, south of the Pyrenees, and in the eastern Mediterranean), frontiers were opened for the colonists. A growing population and war combined to increase the demand for goods and services. Experiences on the frontier of Europe in such activities as the Crusades changed European tastes and created new wants. Then, during the fourteenth century, a pause came to medieval expansion. It has been attributed to the effects of the Black Death (1353), the Hundred Years' War between France and England, and the closing of the European frontier because of defeats in the East.

The Era of Commercial Activity
By the early sixteenth century the economy had recovered from its slump, and the second wave of capitalistic growth began. This period lasted until the early seventeenth century. Stimulated by overseas discoveries, the economic improvement was based on vast quantities of gold and silver brought from America. The new wealth made possible an unprecedented expansion of commercial credit. As direct trade routes were established, Asia was also exploited to provide greater quantities of spices, cotton and silks at lower costs.

In this enlarged commercial arena, leadership passed from the Italian maritime cities to the Iberian countries and finally to the states of northern and western Europe. Sixteenth-century Antwerp and seventeenth-century Amsterdam became the financial and mercantile centers of world trade. In the Low Countries the new-found wealth of America was traded for the grain, fish, timber, metal, textiles and hardware of Europe. The "riches of the Indies" slipped through the fingers of the Spanish and Portuguese into the hands of northwestern Europeans. Although the output of goods increased during this phase, the money supply grew at an even faster rate. The result was inflation. Many workers were unable to secure high enough wages to match inflation.

Some historians have argued that this gap between wages and costs favored the growth of capitalism by permitting a high rate of profit and a more rapid increase of wealth.[3] Attention has also focused on a possible spiritual cause for the impressive expansion of capitalism in early modern Europe. This so-called Weber thesis links the rise of Protestantism and the encouragement it gave to hard work, thrift and honesty with the growth of the capitalistic spirit. Max Weber (1864-1920) argued that Calvinism, with its doctrine of election, caused great anxiety in the mind of the believers about salvation. Instead of leading to fatalism, this caused Calvinists to seek reassurance in lives of order, restraint and diligence to their calling—traits which would characterize the elect. Such a lifestyle favored capital accumulation, rational behavior and success in business. Weber also taught that for many later Calvinists these means became ends in themselves, apart from any belief in predestination. Consequently the Protestant ethic, in a secularized form, was able to survive the decline of religious enthusiasm.[4]

By the late seventeenth century the first two waves of capitalism had subsided. These early centuries have been called the era of commercial activity. There was some industrial growth in these years, such as textile manufacturing in medieval Italy and Flanders, but it was exceptional. These early capitalists made their profits from trade and finance rather than manufacturing. But even trade and finance were only a small part of the larger economy.[5] Most goods exchanged in commercial transactions came from traditional sources, such as home production, craft work and agriculture. So capitalists engaged in trade had most of their investment in stocks of raw material, cash or commodities for trade, not in plants and equipment for production.

The commercial aspects of European life declined as part of the "general crisis" of the seventeenth century. The recession which had started about 1610 was more pronounced after 1640. It was caused at least in part by a decline in the quantity of precious metals arriving from the New World. By the 1640s, imports of gold were only eight per cent of what they had been in the 1590s, and silver thirty-nine per cent. Many of the mines were exhausted, and those that did remain productive lacked adequate laborers. To cope with the emergency brought on by the decline in the supply of gold and silver, the Spanish began minting large quantities of copper coins. These drove out the more valuable coins and led to violent price fluctuations that disrupted trade.

In spite of these problems there were some bright spots in European economic life. Sweden, the Low Countries and England were able to gain a greater share of commerce. The Dutch developed a large merchant fleet and became the main carriers of goods for Europe. But England challenged the Netherlands through a series of Navigation Acts, and in the Anglo-Dutch Wars it succeeded in taking over much of the sea trade. British colonies also aided mercantile development by providing raw materials and markets for finished goods. During the eighteenth century, with the defeat of the French, the English held a significant portion of global leadership.

Industrial Capitalism

The third period of capitalistic expansion, which began in the eighteenth century, differed from previous stages for several reasons. Worldwide competition and pressure to supply an even larger market encouraged that fundamental technological breakthrough called the industrial revolution. The scientific revolution also helped distinguish the period from preceding examples of capitalistic expansion. Among the key elements science provided were a climate of opinion that encouraged experiment and innovation, a linkage of learned persons and artisans, and an interest in practical and profitable activities on the part of scholars.

It is interesting to note that the industrial revolution came first to England rather than to a nation like France, even though the French were in many ways more advanced than the English. A reason for this can be found in the differing religious situations of the two countries. As Walt Rostow explains,

> Students of British invention and innovation in the eighteenth century have long noted the disproportionate role in the germinal inventive and innovational activities of the English Nonconformists and Scottish Presbyterians. . . .
>
> There is a considerable literature that sought to find in the somewhat paradoxical theology of the Protestant Reformation the clue to the Nonconformists' ardent pursuit of economic ends.

But William Petty early perceived what subsequent economic history would confirm about the role of creative minorities in traditional societies—from English Nonconformists to Japanese samurai. Blocked in routes to the top, but not denied access to education and money, they found modernizing activities congenial.

Thus the problem of religion in early modern history and all that lay behind Britain's Revolution of 1688 (and the French revocation of the Edict of Nantes in 1685) become directly relevant to the locus of the first industrial revolution. In the creative processes of invention and innovation—where the number of men engaged was inherently small, but where numbers mattered greatly—Britain had, for noneconomic reasons, stumbled upon a solution to its religious problem and to the problem of Scotland that substantially strengthened its hand in the race to the takeoff barrier.... The British Nonconformists contributed a scale and a thrust to the generation and application of new technology that larger France could not match. They were, in my view, the critical margin France denied herself in 1685.[6]

Thus it was Britain that led the world in the industrial revolution and in the era characterized by industrial capitalism. The basis was found in a new technology consisting of a cluster of innovations which led to "the substitution of machines for human skill and strength; of inanimate for animate sources of power (the water wheel, but even more, the steam engine); and the new, more abundant raw materials for those traditionally used (thus, the replacement of charcoal by coke in iron smelting); and the organization of work in compact units under supervision—the factory system."[7]

The earliest examples of factories, or "mills" as the British called them, produced textiles. A series of relatively simple and inexpensive inventions had reduced the cost and increased the output of cotton goods. Because of these changes, production could be centered in one place. In the 1780s the steam engine, perfected by James Watt, began to supply the power for factories. By 1820 the cotton industry occupied first place among British manufactures, accounting for half of all English exports. It was the forerunner of later industrial development. Through increased production and lower costs, the cotton industry created new markets and demonstrated how capital could be invested in new enterprises with great reward for the entrepreneur.

A more impressive example of material advance was the mechanization of transportation. By 1829 a locomotive was demonstrated that could travel twenty-nine miles per hour while carrying a load of several tons. The railroad system which resulted from this discovery was a product of several innovations, including high-pressure engines, iron for rails, machine tools for fabrication and better lubrications for ease of operation. The whole process was a constantly changing, self-sustaining system. During the 1830s and '40s coal and iron replaced cotton as king and opened a new phase of industrialization. By the early twentieth century electrical equipment, chemicals and automobiles were the leaders in production.

Industrialization and Its Impact on People

The technological advances produced widespread social and institutional changes. It is to these that most people refer when they use the term *capitalism*. Modern industry grew at the expense of older forms of production. Skilled artisans of earlier times had had few physical comforts, but they had the satisfaction of making items for which they alone deserved the credit. This was manufacturing in the original sense of the word, meaning to make by hand (from Latin, *manus* for "hand" and *facere* for "to make"). The industrial revolution redefined the term to mean "made by machine," a change which led to the deterioration of the creative human spirit.

Industrialization also created a growing gulf between the employer and the employee. Ever since medieval times they had been referred to as "master" and "man," terms indicating a personal relationship which was doomed by the advent of the machine age. Before the development of the factory system most production had been on a small scale. A young boy would become an apprentice to a master craftsman, who would treat him as one of his own family. In due time the apprentice could become a master worker and then a master with apprentices working for him. The tools of the trade were comparatively inexpensive, permitting widespread ownership and facilitating the transition to a leadership role. But with the coming of expensive, power machinery it became impossible for a worker to become an owner. Centralization of production also led to greater misery for the workers because they were forced to live in expanding industrial cities known for their crowded, jerrybuilt, unsanitary and thoroughly disagreeable housing. The *proletariat,* as they came to be called, were packed together into class-conscious groups.

A new class. Most of the new wealth went to the middle class, or *bourgeoisie.* In Britain this group had fought for Cromwell against Charles I and had struggled with a minority status during the eighteenth century. In the nineteenth century, however, their business acumen and entrepreneurial spirit supplied the drive for Victorian prosperity. They were liberals in the classical sense of the term; that is, they wanted freedom of speech and the press, religious liberty, freedom from arbitrary arrest and imprisonment, no restraint on trade or commerce, the right to make a fortune, and the privilege to vote. Government, they believed, should limit its activities to enforcing contracts and preserving peace. They were optimistic, believing that innovation and growth would eliminate age-old human problems. In their view people were poor because they were extravagant or lazy, and it was wrong for government to intervene on their behalf. During the nineteenth century people sharing their views gained control of the major governments of western Europe, and their ideas spread to North America and central Europe.

Improved living conditions. The new techniques of industrialization which the middle class fostered resulted in a flood of useful articles which were formerly scarce. After initial hardships were overcome, working people had better houses, clothes and bed linens, and a more varied diet. With the passing of time, fewer babies in the industrialized nations died, life expectancy increased, and more capital was available for investment in schools, hospitals and factories. New power sources made it possible to reduce the length of the workday, although it was only through the growing power of the trade union movement that the number of work hours was actually lessened. By the end of the nineteenth century, the twelve-hour day had been reduced to ten, and after World War 1 it was down to eight. Without the introduction of power machinery and the factory system such improvement would probably have been impossible.

Problems. These gains were accomplished by a massive shift from variable capital invested in stocks of raw material and finished goods to fixed capital consisting of plant and equipment. The new form of investment resulted in a large increase in the scale of manufacturing. Enterprises founded at the beginning of the industrial revolution were small and grew primarily through reinvestment of earnings. But by the midnineteenth century new ventures in capital-intensive industries (those requiring more capital than labor), such as iron production and mining, were too large for the resources of a single entrepreneur or even a small partnership. Industrialists in these fields found it necessary to form limited-liability, joint-stock corporations. This trend was characteristic of continental European firms, especially in Germany where the pace of industrialization did not pick up until after 1850. Not only were the Germans late arrivals on the capitalist scene, but they had less wealth. Consequently, larger firms and investment banking arrangements were useful to them.

Industrial capitalism grew at an uneven rate. At times goods would be overproduced, and then factories would shut down, forcing the layoff of workers. Instead of the regular ups and downs of the preindustrial economy, determined largely by poor harvests, a complex series of factors based on investment, demand and interest rates led to recessions every seven to ten years. These business cycles have often been attributed to inflation and deflation. One of the more serious cycles was the Great Depression of the 1930s.

Capitalism Criticized and Championed

Criticism of capitalism sharpened during this era. The main ideas for the attack were furnished by one of the greatest of the nineteenth-century thinkers, Karl Marx (1818-83), and his followers. Marx believed that capital had a tendency to concentrate in a few hands. Capitalists would compete with each other, and as a result there would be fewer and fewer of them, and larger and more frequent depressions. Thus the condition of the workers would grow more desperate. Finally, the proletariat would rebel, seize power and abolish private property. This did not happen as Marx predicted, and consequently Lenin and some twentieth-century Marxists taught that imperialism had prolonged the life of capitalism. What seems to have interfered with the fulfillment of Marx's vision was the development of trade unions and government regulation of business.[8] Industrial capitalism proved to be a more flexible system than either its friends or foes thought it could be.

During the late nineteenth and early twentieth centuries the United States developed into the new industrial giant of the world. It became the physical and psychological center for capitalism. Many Christians championed the free enterprise system and urged others to struggle for prosperity. As one minister put it, "Godliness is in league with riches."[9] Russell Conwell, a famous nineteenth-century preacher, identified religion with business in his famous sermon "Acres of Diamonds," which he delivered over six thousand times—earning millions of dollars for himself in the process. In 1925 Bruce Barton published a book *The Man Nobody Knows*, which pictured Jesus as a successful businessman. Jesus, he claimed, was not a "man of sorrow," a weakling or a suffering martyr. On the contrary, he was a dynamic leader, a "man's man" who took twelve ordinary individuals and built a successful corporation that has lasted ever since. He was, like Henry Ford or J. Pierpont Morgan, a founder of modern business.

This uncritical acceptance of capitalism was shaken by the Great Depression of the 1930s with its political and social unrest. The spectacle of hungry, unemployed people and unused factories discredited traditional capitalist economics because it seemed unable to find solutions. Most Americans were satisfied on a concrete level with the response given by the New Deal policies of Franklin D. Roosevelt and on an ideological level by the adjustments to capitalism suggested by John Maynard Keynes and his supporters. The economic policy that resulted included an emphasis on steady growth in production and the adjustment of demand to supply through government manipulation. The mistakes that might occur in the new approach could be corrected before great harm was done to the general society. When unemployment grew because demand lagged, the economy could be revived by tax cuts and an increase in government spending. If inflation occurred because there was too much demand, monetary policies could restrict the available money to dampen the economy. Keynesian economics became the consensus.

During the 1970s, however, this economic policy seemed unable to deal with a series of crises that sent shock waves through the capitalistic systems of western Europe and North America. Heightening the economic problems were severe crop shortages, environmental pollution, and a growing gap between rich and poor. Certain influential scholars suggested that there were indeed limits to growth. Liberation movements in Third World countries indicated that Keynesian policies were inadequate as an overall approach for a global economy. Contrasting solutions from both right and left again became options for social action. Where did Christians stand on these issues?

Christians and Economics
Evangelical Christians have attempted to bring their insights to bear on these economic difficulties. The contributors to this volume feel that they have solutions for our current problems. They represent a broad range of political and social outlooks. The conservative view is explained by Gary North, the guided market or mixed system by William Diehl, the decentralized approach by Art Gish, and the centralized solution by John Gladwin.

Each writer reviews the biblical basis for his position, surveys economic theory and assumptions, describes the appropriate role of the government in economic life, and discusses the proper Christian lifestyle in the face of staggering poverty and human degradation. Notes and an annotated bibliography of literature on wealth and poverty follow each major essay. Then the other contributors respond from their respective viewpoints.

I hope the discussion contained in this book will lead each of us to work and pray for the establishment of a better economic order. As Brian Griffiths challenged his listeners:

Christianity starts with faith in Christ and it finishes with service in the world. Although not its object, it is nevertheless, its inevitable consequence. . . . Obedience to Christ demands change, the world becomes his world, the poor, the weak and the suffering are men, women and children created in his image; injustice is an affront to his creation; despair, indifference and aimlessness are replaced by hope, responsibility and purpose; and above all selfishness is transformed to love.

I believe that more than anything else this is what people the world over are looking for. It will not be found in either capitalism or Marxism but only through humility and obedience to Christ. But having found it in the most personal and intimate of all encounters, [I find] the most remarkable thing is that it is relevant to the social, political and economic problems even of the late twentieth century.[10]

Notes

[1]James Halteman, "The Christian Use of Money," InForm, Bulletin of Wheaton College 59, no. 4 (July 1982): 1.

[2]David S. Landes, *The Rise of Capitalism* (New York: Macmillan, 1966), p. 1.

[3]Earl J. Hamilton, *American Treasure and the Price Revolution in Spain 1501-1650* (1934; reprint ed., New York: Octagon Books, 1965). For criticism of Hamilton's ideas see John U. Nef, "Prices and Industrial Capitalism in France and England, 1540-1640," *Economic History Review* 7 (1936-37): 155-85; and David Felix, "Profit Inflation and Industrial Growth: The Historic Record and Contemporary Analogies," *Quarterly Journal of Economics* 70 (1956): 441-63. The full story of the growth of capitalism can be traced in Shepard B. Clough and Charles W. Cole, *Economic History of Europe* (Boston: D. C. Heath, 1968); and Shepard B. Clough and Richard T. Rapp, *European Economic History: The Economic Development of Western Civilization,* 3rd ed. (New York: McGraw-Hill, 1975).

[4]See Max Weber, *The Protestant Ethic and the Spirit of Capitalism* (New York: Scribner, 1958). Although the Weber thesis has not been accepted by many historians, other disciplines seem to be impressed by it. Works treating the thesis from a sociological and psychological perspective are listed in the bibliography which follows.

[5]For an interesting treatment of the growth of international trade and of the persistence of local exchange, see the volumes by Fernand Braudel, *Civilization and Capitalism,* vol. 1, *15th-18th Century: The Structures of Everyday Life* (New York: Harper & Row, 1981), and *Civilization and Capitalism,* vol. 2, *15th-19th Century: The Wheels of Commerce* (New York: Harper & Row, 1982).

[6]Walt W. Rostow, *How It All Began: The Origins of the Modern Economy* (New York: McGraw-Hill, 1975), pp. 184-88.

[7]Landes, *Rise of Capitalism,* pp. 13-14. Also see his history of the industrial revolution, *The Unbound Prometheus: Technological Change and Industrial Development in Western Europe from 1750 to the Present* (London: Cambridge Univ. Press, 1969).

[8]On Marx see R. N. Carew Hunt, *The Theory and Practice of Communism* (New York: Macmillan, 1951); and David Lyon, *Karl Marx: A Christian Assessment of His Life and Thought* (Downers Grove, Ill.: InterVarsity Press, 1981).

[9]Quoted in J. Philip Wogaman, *The Great Economic Debate: An Ethical Analysis* (Philadelphia: Westminster Press, 1977), p. 2.

[10]Brian Griffiths, *Morality and the Market Place* (London: Hodder and Stoughton,

1982), pp. 154-55. The debate over liberty and equality, integral to the Christian desire to help the poor and admonish the rich, is being carried on among several groups. For a survey of one of the more interesting aspects of this discussion, see Randall Rothenberg, "Philosopher Robert Nozick vs. Philosopher John Rawls," *Esquire* 99, no. 3 (March 1983): 201-9.

Select Bibliography
Recent evangelical thought on political and social justice

Campolo, Anthony, Jr. *The Success Fantasy*. Wheaton, Ill.: Victor Books, 1980.

Clouse, Robert G.; Linder, Robert D.; and Pierard, Richard V., eds. *The Cross and the Flag*. Carol Stream, Ill.: Creation House, 1972.

Cotham, Perry C. *Politics, Americanism, and Christianity*. Grand Rapids, Mich.: Baker, 1976.

Dayton, Donald W. *Discovering an Evangelical Heritage*. New York: Harper & Row, 1976.

Dunn, James M. *Politics: A Guidebook for Christians*. Dallas: Christian Life Commission, Baptist General Convention of Texas, 1970.

Frazier, Claude A., ed. *Politics and Religion Can Mix*. Nashville: Broadman, 1974.

Griffiths, Brian. *Morality and the Market Place*. London: Hodder and Stoughton, 1982.

Griffiths, Brian, ed. *Is Revolution Change?* Downers Grove, Ill.: InterVarsity Press, 1972.

Grounds, Vernon C. *Revolution and the Christian Faith*. Philadelphia: Lippincott, 1971.

Hatfield, Mark. *Between a Rock and a Hard Place*. Waco, Tex.: Word, 1976.
———. *Conflict and Conscience*. Waco, Tex.: Word, 1971.

Lapp, John A. *A Dream for America*. Scottdale, Pa.: Herald, 1976.

Linder, Robert D., ed. *God and Caesar: Case Studies in the Relationship between Christianity and the State*. Longview, Tex.: Conference on Faith and History, 1971.

Linder, Robert D., and Pierard, Richard V. *Politics: A Case for Christian Action*. Downers Grove, Ill.: InterVarsity Press, 1973.
———. *Twilight of the Saints: Biblical Christianity and Civil Religion in America*. Downers Grove, Ill.: InterVarsity Press, 1978.

Menendez, Albert J. *Religion at the Polls*. Philadelphia: Westminster, 1977.

Miguez Bonino, José. *Christians and Marxists: The Mutual Challenge to Revolution*. Grand Rapids, Mich.: Eerdmans, 1976.

Moberg, David O. *The Great Reversal: Evangelism and Social Concern*. 2d ed., rev. Philadelphia: Lippincott, 1977.

Mott, Stephen C. *Biblical Ethics and Social Change*. New York: Oxford Univ. Press, 1982.

Monsma, Stephen V. *The Unraveling of America*. Downers Grove, Ill.: InterVarsity Press, 1974.

Motter, Alton M., ed. *Preaching on National Holidays*. Philadelphia: Fortress, 1976.

Mouw, Richard J. *Political Evangelism*. Grand Rapids, Mich.: Eerdmans, 1973.

———— . *Politics and the Biblical Drama.* Grand Rapids, Mich.: Eerdmans, 1976.
Padilla, René C., ed. *The New Face of Evangelicalism.* Downers Grove, Ill.: Inter-Varsity Press, 1976.
Perkins, John. *A Quiet Revolution.* Waco, Tex.: Word, 1976.
———— . *Let Justice Roll Down.* Ventura, Calif.: Regal Books, 1976.
———— . *With Justice for All.* Ventura, Calif.: Regal Books, 1982.
Pierard, Richard V. *The Unequal Yoke: Evangelical Christianity and Political Conservatism.* Philadelphia: Lippincott, 1970.
Schaeffer, Francis. *A Christian Manifesto.* Westchester, Ill.: Crossway Books, 1981.
Sider, Ronald J. *Rich Christians in an Age of Hunger.* Downers Grove, Ill.: Inter-Varsity Press, 1977.
Sider, Ronald J., ed. *The Chicago Declaration.* Carol Stream, Ill.: Creation House, 1974.
Simon, Arthur. *Bread for the World.* Grand Rapids, Mich.: Eerdmans, 1975.
Valentine, Foy. *Citizenship for Christians.* 2d ed. Nashville: Broadman, 1974.
Wallis, Jim. *Agenda for Biblical People.* New York: Harper & Row, 1976.

On capitalism
Clough, Shepard B., and Cole, Charles W. *Economic History of Europe.* Boston: D. C. Heath, 1968.
Clough, Shepard B., and Rapp, Richard T. *European Economic History: The Economic Development of Western Civilization.* 3d ed. New York: McGraw-Hill, 1975.
Felix, David. "Profit Inflation and Industrial Growth: The Historic Record and Contemporary Analogies." *Quarterly Journal of Economics* 70 (1956): 441-63.
Nef, John U. "Prices and Industrial Capitalism in France and England, 1540-1640." *Economic History Review* 7 (1936-37): 155-85.

On the Weber thesis
Catherwood, Sir Frederick. *The Christian in Industrial Society.* 3d ed. Leicester, England: Inter-Varsity Press, 1980.
Green, Robert W., ed. *Protestantism and Capitalism: The Weber Thesis and Its Critics.* Boston: D. C. Heath, 1959.
Hammond, Phillip E., and Williams, Kirk R. "The Protestant Ethic Thesis: A Social-Psychological Assessment." *Social Forces* 54, no. 3 (March 1976): 379-89.
Ives, E. W. "The Economic System: The Capitalist Connection." In *God in History,* pp. 154-70. Tring, England: Lion Pub., 1979.
Kitch, M. J., ed. *Capitalism and the Reformation.* New York: Barnes & Noble, 1968.
Razzell, Peter. "The Protestant Ethic and the Spirit of Capitalism." *British Journal of Sociology* 28, no. 1 (March 1977): 17-35.
Reid, W. Stanford. "John Calvin: The Father of Capitalism?" *Themelios.* Vol. 8, no. 2 (January 1983): 19-25.

Free Market Capitalism

Free Market Capitalism
Gary North

Ye shall do no unrighteousness in judgment: thou shalt not respect the person of the poor, nor honour the person of the mighty; but in righteousness shalt thou judge thy neighbour" (Lev 19:15 KJV).

"I have been young, and now am old; yet I have not seen the righteous forsaken, nor his seed begging bread" (Ps 37:25 KJV).

The topic of wealth and poverty should not be discussed apart from a consideration of the law of God and its relationship to the covenants, for it is in God's law that we find the Bible's blueprint for economics. Biblical justice, biblical law, and economic growth are intimately linked. The crucial section of Scripture which explains this relationship is Deuteronomy 28. There are external blessings for those societies that conform externally to the laws of God (vv. 1-14), and there are external curses for those societies that fail to conform externally to these laws (vv. 15-68).

And it shall come to pass, if thou shalt hearken diligently unto the voice of the LORD thy God, to observe and to do all his commandments which I command thee this day, that the LORD thy God will set thee on high above all nations of the earth: And all these blessings shall come on thee, and overtake thee, if thou shalt hearken unto the voice of the LORD thy God. Blessed shalt thou be in the city, and blessed shalt thou be in the field. Blessed shall be the fruit of thy body, and the fruit of thy ground, and the fruit of thy cattle, the increase of thy kine, and the flocks of thy sheep. Blessed shall be thy basket and thy store.... The LORD shall establish thee an holy people unto himself, as he hath sworn unto thee, if thou shalt keep the commandments of the LORD thy God, and walk in his ways. And all people of the earth shall see that thou art called by the name of the LORD; and they shall be afraid of thee. And the LORD shall make thee plenteous in goods, in the fruit of thy body, and in the fruit of thy cattle, and in the fruit of thy ground, in the land which the LORD sware unto thy fathers to give thee. (Deut 28:1-5, 9-11 KJV)

Deuteronomy 28 is an extension and expansion of chapter 8, in which the relationship between law, blessings and the covenant is outlined. God was about to bring his people into the Promised Land, as the fulfillment of the promise given to Abraham. The "iniquity of the Amorites" was at last full (Gen 15:16 KJV). The Canaanites' era of dominion over the land was about to end. On what terms would the Hebrews hold title to the land and its productivity? Deuteronomy 8 spells it out: *covenantal faithfulness.* This meant adherence to the laws of God.[1]

Deuteronomy 8 reveals to us the foundations of economic growth. First, God grants to his people the gift of *life.* This is an act of grace. He sustained them in the years of wandering in the wilderness, humbling them to prove their faith—their obedience to his commandments—and providing them with manna, so that they might learn that "man doth not live by bread only, but by every word that proceedeth out of the mouth of the LORD doth man live" (vv. 2-3 KJV). A 40-year series of miracles sustained them constantly, for their clothing did not grow old, and their feet did not swell (v. 4). He also provided them with chastening, so that they might learn to respect his commandments—the way of life (vv. 5-6). Second, God provided them with *land,* namely, the land flowing with milk and honey (vv. 7-8): "A land wherein thou shalt eat bread without scarceness, thou shalt not lack any thing in it;

a land whose stones are iron, and out of whose hills thou mayest dig brass" (v. 9 KJV). This also was an act of grace.

Life and land: Here are the two fundamental assets in any economic system. Human labor, combined with natural resources over time, is the foundation of all productivity. The third familiar feature of economic analysis, *capital,* is actually the combination of land plus labor over time. (The time factor is important. From it stems the economic phenomenon of the rate of interest: the discount of future goods against the identical goods held in the present.)[2] (*Warning:* I use notes to add explanatory material, to keep from cluttering up the text too much.) The original sources of production are land and labor.[3] If the Hebrews were willing to dig, the land would produce its fruits.

So much for the gifts. What about the conditions of tenure? They were not to forget their God. They were not to "accept the gift but forget the Giver," to use a familiar expression.

The very fullness of the external, visible, measurable blessings would serve as a source of temptation for them:

> When thou hast eaten and art full, then thou shalt bless the LORD thy God for the good land which he hath given thee. Beware that thou forget not the LORD thy God, in not keeping his commandments, and his judgments, and his statutes, which I command thee this day: Lest when thou hast eaten and art full, and has built goodly houses, and dwelt therein; and when thy herds and thy flocks multiply, and thy silver and thy gold is multiplied, and all that thou hast is multiplied; Then thine heart be lifted up, and thou forget the LORD thy God. (Deut 8:10-14 KJV)

God provides gifts: life and land. He also provides a *law*-order which enables his people to expand their holdings of capital assets (the implements of production) and consumer goods. But these assets are not held by men apart from the ethical terms of God's covenant. The temptation before man is the same as the temptation before Adam: to forget God and to substitute himself as God (Gen 3:5). It is the assumption of all Satanic religion, the assumption of *humanism,* the sovereignty of man. God warned the Israelites against this sin—the sin of presuming their own *autonomy:*

> And thou say in thine heart, My power and the might of mine hand hath gotten me this wealth. But thou shalt remember the LORD thy God: for it is he that giveth thee power to get wealth,

that he may establish his covenant which he sware unto thy
fathers, as it is this day. (Deut 8:17-18 KJV)

These words lay the foundation of all sustained economic growth
—and I stress the word *sustained*. While it is possible for a society
to experience economic growth without honoring God's law,
eventually men's ethical rebellion leads to external judgment and
the termination of economic growth (Deut 28:15-68). It is this
concept of God as the giver which underlay James's announce-
ment: "Every good gift and every perfect gift is from above, and
cometh down from the Father of lights, with whom is no variable-
ness, neither shadow of turning" (Jas 1:17 KJV).

If men whose society has been (and therefore is still) covenanted
with God should fall into this temptation to forget God and to at-
tribute their wealth to the might of their own hands, then God will
judge them:

And it shall be, if thou do at all forget the LORD thy God, and walk
after other gods, and serve them, and worship them, I testify
against you this day that ye shall surely perish. As the nations
which the LORD destroyeth before your face, so shall ye perish;
because ye would not be obedient unto the voice of the LORD
your God. (Deut 8:19-20 KJV)

The Paradox of Deuteronomy 8

God has given us an outline of the covenantal foundations of a holy
commonwealth.[4] This is as close as the Bible comes to a universally
valid "stage theory" of human history or economic development.[5]
Long-term economic growth is based on men's honoring the explicit terms of God's law. The stages are as follows:

1. God's grace in providing life, land, and law
2. Society's adherence to the external terms of God's law
3. External blessings in response to this faithfulness
4. Temptation: the lure of autonomy
5. Response:
   a. Capitulation that leads to external judgment; or
   b. Resistance that leads to further economic growth

The covenant is supposed to be *self-reinforcing*, or as economists
sometimes say, it offers a system of *positive feedback*. Verse 18 is
the key: God gives his people external blessings in order "that he
may establish his covenant which he sware unto thy fathers" (KJV).

The promise would be visibly fulfilled by their entry into the Promised Land, thereby giving them confidence in the reliability of God's word. God's law-order is reliable, which means that men can rely on biblical law as a *tool of dominion*, which will enable them to fulfill (though imperfectly, as sinners) the terms of God's dominion covenant: "And God blessed them [Adam and Eve], and God said unto them, Be fruitful, and multiply, and replenish the earth, and subdue it: and have dominion over the fish of the sea, and over the fowl of the air, and over every living thing that moveth upon the earth" (Gen 1:28 KJV). This covenant was reaffirmed with Noah (Gen 9:1-7). It is still binding on Noah's heirs.[6]

The paradox of Deuteronomy 8 is this: Blessings, while inescapable for a godly society, are a great temptation. Blessings are a sign of God's favor, yet in the fifth stage—the society's response to the temptation of autonomy—blessings can result in comprehensive, external, social judgment. Thus, there is no way to determine simply from the existence of great external wealth and success of all kinds—the successes listed in Deuteronomy 28:1-14 —that a society is facing either the prospect of continuing positive feedback or imminent negative feedback (namely, destruction). The ethical condition of the people, not their financial condition, is determinative.

Visible success is a paradox: It can testify to two radically different ethical conditions. Biblical ethical analysis, because it recognizes the binding nature of revealed biblical law, is therefore a fundamental aspect of all valid historiography, social commentary, and economic analysis. An index number of economic wealth is a necessary but insufficient tool of economic analysis. The numbers do not tell us all we need to know about the progress of a particular society or civilization. We also need God's law as an ethical guide, our foundation of ethical analysis.

Ethics and Economic Analysis
A great debate has raged for over a century within the camp of the economists: "Is capitalism morally valid?" Marxists and socialists ask this question and then answer it: *no.* "But capitalism is efficient," respond the defenders of the free market. A few of the defenders also try to muster ethical arguments based on the right of individuals to control the sale of their property, including their

labor services, without interference from the civil government.[7]

This sort of ethical analysis has not convinced many critics of capitalism. They reject the operating presupposition of free market economic analysis: *methodological individualism.* As *methodological collectivists,* they deny the right of men to use their property against the "common good." Problem: Who defines the common good? (The Christian answers that the Bible defines the common good, and sets forth the institutional arrangements that will achieve it. The Bible teaches neither collectivism nor individualism; it proclaims *methodological covenantalism.*)[8] Another problem: Even if the common good can be defined by humanistic social commentators, who has the right to enforce it? Finally, can the State, through its bureaucracy, enforce the common good in a cost-effective manner?[9] Will the results resemble the official ethical goals of the planners? What kinds of incentives can be built into a State-planned economy that will enable it to perform as efficiently as a profit-seeking, free market economy?[10]

The fundamental issue is *ethical.* The question of efficiency is a subordinate one. Few Marxists or socialist scholars seriously argue any longer that the substitution of socialist ownership of the means of production will lead to an increase of per capita output beyond what private ownership would have produced. The debates today rage over what kinds of economic output are morally valid. Also, who should determine what "the people"—whoever they are—really need? The free market, with its system of private ownership and freely fluctuating prices? Or the civil government, with its system of political competition and lifetime bureaucratic funcionaries?[11]

The real debate is a debate over ethical issues, something that economists have tried to hide or deny since the seventeenth century.[12] Economist William Letwin, who is wholeheartedly enthusiastic about this supposed triumph of value-free economics, does admit that there are difficulties with this outlook: "It was exceedingly difficult to treat economics in a scientific fashion, since every economic act, being the action of a human being, is necessarily also a moral act. If the magnitude of difficulty rather than the extent of the achievement be the measure, then the making of economics was the greatest scientific accomplishment of the seventeenth century."[13] Apparently even more important than Newton's discoveries![14] This faith in analytic neutrality has been reaffirmed by the developers of the two most prominent schools of free market economic analysis, Milton Friedman and Ludwig von Mises.[15]

One reason why the critics have been so successful in their attack against the academic economists' hypothetically neutral defense of the free market is this: *Hardly anyone in the secular world really believes any longer that moral or intellectual neutrality is possible.* This is why Christian economics offers a true intellectual alternative: it rests on a concept of *objective* revelation by a true Person, the Creator of all knowledge and the Lord of history. The Bible affirms that neutrality is a myth; either we stand with Christ or we scatter abroad (Mt 12:30).[16] The works of the law—not the law, but the works of the law—are written on every human heart (Rom 2:14-15).[17] No man can escape the testimony of his own being, and nature itself, to the existence of a Creator (Rom 1:18-23).

Socialists deny the possibility of neutral economic analysis, and their criticism has become far more effective as humanistic scholarship has drifted from faith in objective knowledge into an ever-growing awareness that all human knowledge is relative. (Marxists still believe in objective knowledge for Marxists, but not for any other ideological group.)[18] Since all intellectual analysis is tied to a man's operating presuppositions about the nature of reality, and since these presuppositions, being pre-theoretical, cannot be disproven by logic, the socialist critic's logic is also undergirded by his equally unprovable presuppositions.[19] (There is a problem for non-Christian subjectivist thought, however: the breakdown of objective science.)[20] Even a few economists are slowly coming to face the implications of subjectivism with respect to objective, neutral analysis, but not many, and their books are not yet influential. These men tend to be associated with "new left" economics, and the "establishment" is not impressed.[21]

As Christians we must always maintain that *ethics is basic to all social analysis.* We must make clear what most professional economists prefer to ignore: It is never a question of analysis apart from ethical evaluation; it is only a question of which ethical system, meaning *whose* law-order: God's or self-professed autonomous man's? Because the Bible provides us with a comprehensive system of ethics, it thereby provides us with a blueprint for economics.[22]

Biblical Law and Exploitation

The prophets came before Israel and called the people back to the law of God. The people did not respond; the result was captivity. The law of God, when enforced, prevents exploitation. The case-law applications of the law are therefore to be honored. Even the supposedly obscure case laws often have implications far beyond their immediate setting. For example, "Thou shalt not muzzle the ox when he treadeth out the corn" (Deut 25:4 KJV). Paul tells us that this law gives us a principle: "The labourer is worthy of his reward" (1 Tim 5:18 KJV). Christ also said that the laborer is worthy of his hire (Lk 10:7). In short, if we must allow our beasts of burden to enjoy the fruits of their labor, how much more should human laborers enjoy the fruits of their labor!

Problem: Who decides how much to pay laborers? The church? The State? The free market? The Bible is quite clear on this point: Laborers and employers should bargain together. The parable of the laborers in the vineyard is based on the *moral validity of the right of contract*. The employer hired men throughout the day, paying each man an agreed-upon wage, a penny. Those hired early in the morning complained when others hired late in the day received the same wage. In other words, they accused their employer of "exploitation." This was an "unfair labor practice." His answer:

> Friend, I do thee no wrong: didst not thou agree with me for a penny? Take [that which] thine is, and go thy way: I will give unto this last [laborer], even as unto thee. Is it not lawful for me to do what I will with mine own? Is thine eye evil, because I am good? (Mt 20:13-15 KJV)

Wasn't he morally obligated—and shouldn't he have been *legally* obligated—to have paid more, retroactively, to those hired early in the day? No. When they were hired, he offered them the best deal they believed they had available to them. He was "meeting the market." Had a better offer been available elsewhere, they would have accepted it. Alternatively, should he have paid less to the men hired later in the day? No. He owed them the wage he had agreed to pay.

Those hired in the morning had not known that a job would be available later in the day at the same wage. They faced *economic uncertainty*. (Economic uncertainty about the future is an inescapable fact of human action in a world in which only God is omniscient. Any system of economics that in any way ignores or de-emphasizes the economic effects of uncertainty is innately, inescapably erroneous, for it relies on a false doctrine of man.) They took the best offer that any employer made. If they had been omniscient, they might have waited, lounged around for almost the whole day, and then accepted an eleventh-hour job offer. "A full day's pay for an hour's labor: what a deal!" (An analogous approach to salvation: refuse to accept the Gospel in your youth, so that you can "eat, drink, and be merry," and then accept Christ on your deathbed. "A full life's worth of salvation for a last-minute repentance: what a deal!") But men are not omniscient. So they act to benefit themselves with the best knowledge at their disposal.[23] The employer had done them no wrong. Their eye was evil.

Christ used this parable to illustrate a theological principle, the sovereignty of God in choosing men: "So the last shall be first, and the first last; for many be called, but few chosen" (Mt 20:16 KJV). The employer had a job opportunity to offer men; God offers salvation in the same way. The employer paid a full day's wage to those coming late in the day. If this action of the employer was wrong, then God's analogous action in electing both young and old ("late comers" and "early comers") to the same salvation is even more wrong. But this is the argument of the ethical rebel; Paul dismisses it as totally illegitimate. "What shall we say then? Is there unrighteousness with God? God forbid. For he saith to Moses, I will have mercy on whom I will have mercy, and I will have compassion on whom I will have compassion" (Rom 9:14-15 KJV).

One of the most important facts of economics is this: *Employers compete against employers, while workers compete against workers.* Employers do not want rival employers to buy any valuable economic factor of production at a discount. Those who hire laborers do so in order to use their services profitably. They have no incentive to pass along savings to their competitors. If a worker's labor is worth five shekels per hour to two different potential employers, and the worker is about to be hired by one of them for four shekels, the second employer has an incentive to offer him more.

He will offer him enough to lure him away from the competitor, but not so much that he expects to lose money on the transaction. The free market's competitive auction process therefore offers *economic* rewards to employers for doing the *morally correct* thing, namely, honoring the biblical principle that the laborer is worthy of his hire.

Similarly, workers compete against workers. They want jobs. If an employer is offering a job to one employee for more than another person is willing to work for, the second person has an incentive to step in and utter those magic words: "I'll work for less!" He underbids the competition. (When I say "underbid," I mean underbid in terms of money; I could also say that he overbids his competitors in terms of the hours of labor that he offers the employer for a given wage payment.) The free market's auction process offers an incentive to workers to offer employers "an honest day's labor for an honest day's pay." In short, the free market offers economic rewards to laborers for doing the morally correct thing, just as it offers employers.

Very, very rarely do employers and workers in a modern industrialized economy compete head to head. These instances take place when neither the worker nor the employer has a good idea of his own competition, or when one of the two is ignorant. Laborers may not know the going wage rate. Employers may not know if other workers are available for the money they are willing to pay. So it becomes a question of *negotiation*, the same kind of negotiation that Esau and Jacob transacted for Esau's birthright (Gen 25:29-34).

There is nothing wrong with competitive bargaining, as I explain in chapter eighteen of my economic commentary on the Bible, *The Dominion Covenant: Genesis*. Normally, competing offers are well known to all parties; advertising has made information on pricing and services widely available. "Help wanted" signs and classified ads do more for the income of the majority of laborers than all the trade unions in the land—legalized monopolies established by one group of workers to deny the legal right of other workers to compete against them.[24] Nevertheless, where there are gaps in men's information, men must pay to improve their knowledge. *Information is not a zero-cost good.* Any system of economic analysis which ignores or de-emphasizes this economic fact of life is innately, inescapably erroneous.

When a society guarantees men that they will be allowed to keep the fruits of their labor, it promotes the spread of information. Men can afford to invest in the expensive process of improving their knowledge. They are able to capitalize their efforts. If they are successful in improving their knowledge about competing economic offers, either as employers or laborers, they reap the rewards. Members of society are the beneficiaries, since better knowledge means less waste—fewer scarce economic resources expended to achieve given economic ends. The ends are set by competing bidders in the "auction" for consumer goods and services.[25] It should be recognized from the beginning that a deeply felt *hostility toward the moral legitimacy of the auction process* undergirds the socialist movements of our era.

Predictable Law
The Bible instructs a nation's rulers not to respect persons when administering justice (Deut 1:17). Both the rich man and the poor man, the homeborn and the stranger, are to be ruled by the same law (Ex 12:49). Biblical law is a form of God's grace to mankind; it is to be dispensed to all without prejudice. This is the implication of Leviticus 19:15, which introduced this chapter. The predictability of the judicial system is what God requires of those in positions of authority.

Predictable ("inflexible") law compels the State and the church to declare in advance just exactly what the law requires. This allows men to plan for the future more efficiently.[26] "Flexible" law is another word for *arbitrary* law. When a man drives his automobile at 55 miles per hour in a 55 m.p.h. zone, he expects to be left alone by highway patrol officers. The predictability of the law makes it possible for highway rules to be effective. Men can make better judgments about the decisions of other drivers when speed limits are posted and highway patrol officers enforce them. The better we can plan for the future, the lower the costs of our decision-making. *Predictable law reduces waste.*

The Hebrews were required by God to assemble the nation—rich and poor, children and strangers—every seventh year to listen to the reading of the law (Deut 31:10-13). Ignorance of the law was no excuse. At the same time, biblical law was comprehensible. It was

not so complex that only lawyers in specialized areas could grasp
its principles. The *case laws*, such as the prohibition on muz-
zling the ox as he treaded out the corn, brought the general principles down into concrete, familiar terminology. In this sense,
biblical faith is essentially a democratic faith, as G. Ernest Wright
argues, for

> it can be laid hold of with power by the simplest and most hum-
> ble. We are surrounded by mystery, and ultimate knowledge is
> beyond our grasp. Yet God has brought himself (Deut. 4:7) and
> his word to us. We can have life by faith and by loyal obedience
> to his covenant, even though our knowledge is limited by our
> finitude. One need not wait to comprehend the universe in order
> to obtain the promised salvation. It is freely offered in the cove-
> nant now.[27]

The law of God gives to men a tool of dominion over an otherwise
essentially mysterious nature, including human nature—not
dominion as exercised by a lawless tyrant, but dominion through
obedience to God and *service to man*.[28]

For example, consider the effects of the eighth commandment,
"Thou shalt not steal." Men are made more secure in the ownership of property. This commandment gives men security. They
can then make rational (cost-effective) judgments about the best
uses of their property, including their skills. They make fewer mistakes. This lowers the costs of goods to consumers through competition.

Christian commentators have from earliest times understood
that the prohibition of theft, like the prohibition against covetousness, serves as a defense of private property. *Theft is a self-con-
scious, willful act of coercive wealth redistribution, and therefore
it is a denial of the legitimacy and reliability of God's moral and
economic law-order.*

The immediate economic effect of widespread theft in society is
the creation of *insecurity*. This lowers the market value of goods,
since people are less willing to bid high prices for items that are
likely to be stolen. Uncertainty is increased, which requires that
people invest a greater proportion of their assets in buying protection services or devices. Scarce economic resources are shifted
from production and consumption to crime fighting. This clearly
lowers per capita productivity and therefore per capita wealth, at

least among law-abiding people. Theft leads to wasted resources.

The internal restraints on theft that are provided by godly preaching and upbringing help to reduce crime, thereby increasing per capita wealth within the society. *Godly preaching against theft* is therefore a form of *capital investment* for the society as a whole (what the economists call "social overhead capital"), for it releases scarce economic resources that would otherwise have been spent on the protection of private and public property. Such preaching also reduces the necessary size of the civil government, which is important in reducing the growth of unwarranted State power.

What is true about the reduction of theft is equally true concerning the strengthening of men's commitment to private property in general. When *property rights* are carefully *defined* and *enforced*, the value of property increases. Allen and Alchian, in their standard economics textbook, have commented on this aspect of property rights:

> For market prices to guide allocation of goods, there must be an incentive for people to express and to respond to offers. If it is costly to reveal bids and offers and to negotiate and make exchanges, the gains from exchange might be offset. If each person speaks a different language [as they did at the tower of Babel], if thievery is rampant, or if contracts are likely to be dishonored, then negotiation, transaction, and policing costs will be so high that fewer market exchanges will occur. If *property rights* in goods are weaker, ill defined, or vague, their reallocation is likely to be guided by lower offers and bids. Who would offer as much for a coat likely to be stolen?[29]

The authors believe that the higher market value attached to goods protected by strong ownership rights spurs individuals to seek laws that will strengthen private-property rights. Furthermore, to the extent that private-property rights exist, the power of the civil government to control the uses of goods is thereby decreased. This, unfortunately, has led politicians and jurists to resist the spread of secured private-property rights.[30]

There is no question that *a society which honors the terms of the commandment against theft will enjoy greater per capita wealth* than one which does not, other things being equal. Such a society rewards honest people with greater possessions. This is as it should be. A widespread hostility to theft, especially from the point of view of self-government (self-restraint), allows men to make more accurate decisions concerning what they want to buy and therefore what they need to produce in order to offer something of value in exchange for the items they want. Again, I cite Allen and Alchian:

> The more expensive is protection against theft, the more common is thievery. Suppose that thievery of coats were relatively easy. People would be willing to pay only a lower price for coats. The lower market price of coats will understate the value of coats, for it will not include the value to the thief. If the thief were induced to rent or purchase a used coat, the price of coats would more correctly represent their value to society. It follows that the cheaper the policing costs, the greater the efficiency with which values of various uses or resources are revealed. The more likely something is to be stolen, the less of it that will be produced.[31]

When communities set up "neighborhood watches" to keep an eye on each other's homes, and to call the police when something suspicious is going on, the value of property in the community is increased, or at least the value of the property on the streets where the neighbors are helping each other.

We want sellers to respond to our offers for goods or services. At the same time, we as producers want to know what buyers are willing and able to pay for our goods and services. The better everyone's knowledge of the markets we deal in, the fewer the resources necessary for advertising, negotiating, and guessing about the future. These resources can then be devoted to producing goods and services to satisfy wants that would otherwise have gone unsatisfied. The lower our transaction costs, in other words, the more wealth we can devote to the purchase and sale of the items involved in the transactions.

One transaction cost is the defense of property against theft. *God graciously steps in and offers us a "free good": a heavenly system of punishment.* To the extent that criminals and potential criminals believe that God does punish criminal behavior, both on earth and in heaven, their costs of operation go up. When the price of something rises, other things being equal, less of it will be demanded. *God raises the risks ("price") of theft to thieves.* Less criminal behavior is therefore a predictable result of a widespread belief in God's judgments, both temporal and final. When the commandment against theft is preached, and when both the preachers and the hearers believe in the God who has announced his warning against theft, then we can expect less crime and greater per capita wealth in that society. God's eternal criminal justice system is flawless, and it is also inescapable, so it truly is a free good—a gift from God which is a sign of his grace. This is one aspect of *the grace of law*.[32] It leads to increased wealth for those who respect God's laws.

Compulsory Wealth Redistribution

The Bible says, "Thou shalt not steal." It does not say, "Thou shalt not steal, except by majority vote." A society which begins to adopt taxation policies that exceed the tithe—ten per cent of income—thereby increases economic uncertainty, as do other types of theft, both public and private. This increase in uncertainty may be even more disrupting, statistically, than losses from burglary or robbery, because private insurance companies can insure against burglary and robbery. After all, *who can trust a civil government which claims the right to take more of a person's income than God requires for the support of his kingdom?* What kind of protection from injustice can we expect from such a civil government? The next wave of politically imposed wealth redistribution is always difficult to predict, and therefore difficult to prepare for, so the costs of production increase.

When Samuel came before the Hebrews to warn them about the evils of establishing a king in Israel, he thought he might dissuade them by telling them that the king would take a whopping ten per cent of their production (1 Sam 8:15). They did not listen. (And, for the record, neither have Christians listened to warnings against the forty and fifty per cent taxation levels of the modern welfare State.) The Pharaoh of Joseph's day imposed a tax of twenty per cent (Gen 47:24-26). Egypt was one of the great tyrannies of the ancient world.[33] It was probably the most massive bureaucracy in man's history until the twentieth century.[34] Yet every modern welfare State—meaning every Western industrial nation in the late twentieth century—would have to cut its total tax burden by at least *half* in order to return to the twenty per cent level of Egypt in Joseph's day.[35]

Foreign Aid: State to State

Foreign aid means an increase in taxes in one nation, so that money can go to other nations. State-to-State aid must go through official, bureaucratic channels. Only in major emergencies—famines, floods, earthquakes—do foreign governments allow Western nations to bring food and clothing directly to their citizens. They understand the obvious: The increasing dependence of citizens on goods from a foreign civil government increases their direct dependence on that foreign civil government. He who pays the piper is in a position to call the tune. Oddly enough, intellectual proponents of increased State welfare fail to recognize what leaders in Third World nations understand immediately, namely, "there ain't no such thing as a free lunch." With the benefits come controls and future political or diplomatic obligations.

When the United States sends food under Public Law 480 (passed in 1954), to India, the Indian government, not private business, allocates it—or whatever is left after the rats at the docks and in the storage facilities consume approximately half of it. (Rats and sacred cows in India consume half of that nation's agricultural output.[36] It would take a train 3,000 miles long to haul the grain eaten by Indian rats in a single year.[37])

There is a great temptation for government officials of under-developed nations to use this food to free up State-controlled capital which is then used to increase investments in heavy industry—investments that produce visible results that are politically popular—projects that cynics refer to as *pyramids*. These large-scale industrial projects are in effect paid for by the food subsidies sent by the West. Without the free food sent by the West, these uneconomical, large-scale projects would be out of the question politically. Even worse, foreign aid enables governments to spend heavily on military equipment that will be used to suppress political opponents or other Third World nations—themselves recipients of Western foreign aid.[38]

What would happen if the West were to stop shipping food at below-market prices? Local farmers in the recipient nations have been hurt—or in some cases, driven into bankruptcy—by the West's below-production-cost food, so they have reduced investments in the agricultural system. These nations have become increasingly dependent on the West's free food. If the subsidies were to cease, the agricultural base might be insufficient to provide for the domestic population, for agricultural output has been reduced as a result of taxpayer-financed cut-throat competition from Western governments that gave away the food. At the same time, if the subsidies were to cease, heavy industry projects could also go bankrupt (or, more accurately, may lose even more tax money than they lose already, and therefore become political liabilities).

Let us not be naive about the political impetus for shipments of American farm products under Public Law 480. The farm bloc and the large multinational grain companies are major supporters of the compulsory "charity" of foreign food aid, just as farmers favor the food stamp program. Farmers can sell their crops to the U.S. government at above-market prices, and then the government can give the food away to people who would not have bought it anyway. Politicians like the program also because the U.S. government uses the promise of free food as a foreign policy lever.[39]

Government subsidies to Agriculture have become a way of life in the United States, as have government controls on agriculture.[40]

We know that foreign governments are hostile to what they refer to as "Western control," when private foreign capital comes into their nations. Why this hostility? *Because pro-socialist political leaders in underdeveloped nations resent the shift of sovereignty from civil government to the private sector, both foreign and domestic.* Yet these same officials beg for more State-to-State aid from the West. Why? Because *they* control the allocation of this form of economic aid after it arrives. The question of foreign aid, like all other forms of compulsory economic redistribution, raises questions of sovereignty.

Should we recommend increased taxes in Western nations in order to "feed the starving poor" in foreign nations? Is this what Christ meant by loving our neighbors? Are Western tax revenues really feeding the starving poor, or are they financing the bureaucratic institutions of political control that have been created by pro-socialist, Western-educated political leaders who dominate so many of the Third World's one-party "democracies"? Are poor people in the West being taxed to provide political support to wealthy politicians in the Third World? Does the Bible teach that State-to-State wealth transfers are ethically valid? Or does the

Bible require *personal* charity, or church-to-church charity—
charity which is not administered by foreign politicians?

These are fundamental questions regarding sovereignty, authority, and power. In the construction of the kingdom of God on earth,
should we promote the increased sovereignty of the political State?
Samuel's warning is clear: *no* (1 Sam 8). Any discussion of government "charity"—compulsory wealth redistribution—must deal
with this issue of sovereignty.

Other questions, closely related to the preceding ones, are these:
Is the poverty of the Third World the fault of the West? Is the Third
World hungry because people in Western industrial nations eat
lots of food? Does the West, meaning Western civil governments,
owe some form of reparations (restitution) to Third World civil
governments?

"We Eat; They Starve"

Consider the words of theologian-historian Ronald Sider, whose
best-selling book, *Rich Christians in an Age of Hunger*, has become
one of the most influential books on seminary and Christian college campuses all over the United States. His introduction to the
book sets forth the problem:

> The food crisis is only the visible tip of the iceberg. More funda-
> mental problems lurk just below the surface. Most serious is the
> unjust division of the earth's food and resources. Thirty per cent
> of the world's population lives in the developed countries. But
> this minority of less than one-third eats three-quarters of the
> world's protein each year. Less than 6 per cent of the world's
> population lives in the United States, but we regularly demand
> about 33 per cent of most minerals and energy consumed every
> year. Americans use 191 times as much energy per person as the
> average Nigerian. Air conditioners alone in the United States
> use as much energy each year as does the entire country of
> China annually with its 830 million people. One-third of the
> world's people have an annual per capita income of $100 or less.
> In the United States it is now about $5,600 per person. And this
> difference increases every year.[41]

I can remember reading textbooks written in the 1950s that affirmed
the wonders of American capitalism, and that pointed with pride
to the fact that 6 per cent of the world's population *produced* 40

per cent (or 33 per cent, or whatever) of the world's goods. But that argument grew embarrassing for those who proclaimed the supposed productivity of socialism. Socialist nations just never caught up. So capitalism's critics now complain that 6 per cent of the world's population (Americans) annually uses up one-third of the world's annual production, as if this consumption were not simultaneously a process of production, as if production could take place apart from the using up of producer goods. This is *word magic*. It makes productivity appear evil.

It is true that Westerners eat a large proportion of the protein that the world produces each year. This has been used by vegetarian socialists to create a sense of guilt in Western meat-eating readers of socialist literature. You see, our cattle eat protein-rich grains. "Corn-fed beef" is legendary—or notorious, in the eyes of the critics. Because of this, argues Dr. Sider, the "feeding burden" of the United States is not a mere 210 million (the number of human mouths to feed), but 1.6 billion.[42] "No wonder more and more people are beginning to ask whether the world can afford a United States or a Western Europe."[43] (Outside of college and seminary campuses, not many people seem to be asking this question, as far as I can see. Certainly the Haitian boat people and Latin American refugees aren't asking it. Neither are Jews who are emigrating from the Soviet Union.)

The psalmist proclaimed a poetic truth about God's ownership of the world by identifying these words as God's: "For every beast of the forest is mine, and the cattle upon a thousand hills" (Ps 50: 10 KJV). But "liberation theologians" are not impressed. Dr. Sider informs us:

> The U.S. Department of Agriculture reports that when the total life of the animal is considered, each pound of edible beef represents seven pounds of grain. That means that in addition to all the grass, hay and other food involved, it also took seven pounds of grain to produce a typical pound of beef purchased in the supermarket. Fortunately, the conversion rates for chicken and pork are lower: two or three to one for chicken and three or four to one for pork. Beef is the cadillac of meat products. Should we move to compacts?[44]

Must we rewrite the words of the psalm (with the seven-to-one ration in operation): "For every chicken of the forest is mine, and the soybeans upon seven thousand hills"? Perhaps the greatest irony of all is that a 1982 study by the U.S. Department of Agriculture indicates that low-income Americans—the people who liberation theologians supposedly want to deliver from "oppressive institutions"—eat more meat per capita than high-income Americans. Blacks consume more meat per capita than other racial groups.[45] Thus, the "less meat" program would reduce one of the prime pleasures of the poor in America.

Unquestionably, Third World populations sometimes suffer protein deficiencies. But any program of "social salvation through protein exports" is going to encounter problems that the wealth-redistributionists seldom consider. *People's food is fundamental to their culture.* Trying to stay on a diet has confounded millions of Americans. Eating habits are very difficult to alter, even when the eater knows that he should change. An education program to get Third World peasants to change their diets is going to be incredibly expensive, and probably futile. "Rice-eating people would often rather starve than eat wheat or barley, which are unknown to them," writes biologist Richard Wagner.[46]

This problem goes beyond mere habits. Sometimes we find that people's diets have conditioned their bodies so completely that the introduction of a new food may produce biological hazards for them. This is sometimes the case with protein. Wagner comments:

Another even more bizarre instance was seen in Colombia, where a population was found with a 40 percent infestation of *Entamoeba histolytica,* a protozoan that generally burrows into the intestinal wall, causing a serious condition called amoebiasis. However, despite the high level of *Entamoeba* infestation, the incidence of amoebiasis was negligible. The answer to this puzzle was found in the high-starch diet of the people. Because of the low protein intake, production of starch-digesting enzymes was reduced, allowing a much higher level of starch to persist in the intestine. The protozoans were found to be feeding on this starch rather than attacking the intestinal wall. If this population had been given protein supplements without concurrent efforts to control *Entamoeba* infestation, the incidence of amoebiasis would probably have soared, causing more problems than the lack of protein.[47]

Cultures Are "Package Deals"

When a foreign culture introduces a single aspect of its culture into the life of another, there will be complications. This single change serves as a sort of *cultural wedge*. As the historian Arnold Toynbee puts it, "In a cultural encounter, one thing inexorably goes on leading to another when once the smallest breach has been made in the assaulted society's defenses."[48] Changing people's eating habits, apart from changing their understanding of medicine, costs of production, agricultural technology, risks of blight, marketing, and an indeterminate number of other contingent aspects of the recommended change, is risky when possible, and frequently impossible.

Third World peasants often recognize the implications of a particular "cultural wedge" perhaps better than the Western "missionary" does: It may have a far-reaching impact on the culture as a whole—an impact which traditional peasants may choose to avoid. Unless the opportunity offered by the innovator is seen by the recipient as being worth the risks of unforeseen "ripple effects," the attempt to force a change in the recipient's buying or eating habits may lead to a disaster. Or, more likely, it will probably lead to a wall of resistance. Missionaries, whether Christian or secular, whether sponsored by a church or the Peace Corps, had better understand one fundamental principle before they go to the mission field: *You cannot change only one thing.*

One of the classic horror stories that illustrates this principle is the Sub-Sahara Sahel famine of the 1970s. This arid and semiarid area is vast. It stretches across the African continent, and it includes the nations of Senegal, Mauritania, Mali, Chad, Ghana, Niger, Upper Volta, Sudan, Ethiopia, Somalia, and part of Kenya. For 15 years, from the early 1960s through the mid-1970s, the West's civil governments poured hundreds of millions of dollars into this region. Yet between the late 1960s and 1974, hundreds of thousands of people starved, along with twenty million head of livestock. They are still starving. Why? As with most agricultural tragedies, there was no single cause. The area gets little rain: perhaps twenty-five inches in its southernmost regions, tapering off to an inch per year closer to the Sahara. The nomads needed water for their herds, as they had from time immemorial. The West gave them the water. Here was a totally new factor in the region's ecology. It destroyed them. This was one major cause.

The other cause was the absence of enforceable property rights in land. The nomads did not assign specific plots to specific families. No one was made personally and economically responsible for the care of the land. "All trees, shrubs, and pasture are *common*-access resources, so no *individual* tribesman has an incentive to conserve them, or add to their stock. No individual can reap the returns of planting or sowing grass, which hold the soil together and prevent 'desertification.' "[49]

Beneath the rock and clay and sand, there is water. A subterranean lake of half a million square miles underlies the eastern end of the Sahara. Drilling rigs can hit water at one thousand or two thousand feet down. These boreholes were drilled with Western foreign aid money at $20,000 to $200,000 apiece. About ten thousand head of cattle at a time can drink their fill. Therein lies the problem. Claire Sterling describes what happened:

> The trouble is that wherever the Sahel has suddenly produced more than enough for the cattle to drink, they have ended up with nothing to eat. Few sights were more appalling, at the height of the drought last summer [1973], than the thousands upon thousands of dead and dying cows clustered around Sahelian boreholes. Indescribably emaciated, the dying would stagger away from the water with bloated bellies to struggle to fight free of the churned mud at the water's edge until they keeled over. As far as the horizon and beyond, the earth was as bare and bleak as a bad dream. Drought alone didn't do that: they did.
>
> What 20 million or more cows, sheep, goats, donkeys, and camels have mostly died of since this grim drought set in is hunger, not thirst. Although many would have died anyway, the tragedy was compounded by a fierce struggle for too little food among Sahelian herds increased by then to vast numbers. Carried away by the promise of unlimited water, nomads forgot about the Sahel's all too limited forage. Timeless rules, apportioning just so many cattle to graze for just so many days within a cow's walking distance of just so much water in traditional wells, were brushed aside. Enormous herds, converging upon the new boreholes from hundreds of miles away, so ravaged the surrounding land by trampling and overgrazing that each borehole quickly became the center of its own little

desert forty or fifty miles square.[50]
In Senegal, soon after boreholing became popular (around 1960), the number of cows, sheep, and goats rose in two years from four million to five million. "In Mali, during the five years before 1960, the increase had been only 800,000. Over the next ten years the total shot up another 5 million to 16 million, more than three animals for every Malian man, woman, and child."[51] It is not just Americans and West Europeans who raise and eat "protein on the hoof."

The traditional nomad way of life is dead. Western specialists know it; the nomads know it. They live in tent camps now, dependent on handouts from their governments, which in turn rely heavily on the West's foreign aid programs. The West and the nomads forgot to honor (and deal with) this principle: *You cannot change only one thing.*

Cultural Transformation

The goal of charitable organizations that deal in foreign aid should be to bring the culture of the West to the underdeveloped nations. By "the culture of the West," I mean the law-order of the Bible, not the humanist, secularized remains of what was once a flourishing Christian civilization. This means that these organizations cannot be run successfully by cultural and philosophical relativists. Missionaries should seek to impart a specifically Western way of looking at the world: future-oriented, thrift-oriented, education-oriented, and responsibility-oriented. This world-and-life view must not be cyclical. It must offer men hope in the power of human reason to understand the external world and to grasp the God-given laws of cause and effect that control it. It must offer hope for the future. It must be *future-oriented.* To try to bring seed corn to a present-oriented culture that will eat it is futile. With the seed corn must come a world-and-life view that will encourage people to grow corn for the future.

It does little good to give these cultures Western medicine and not Western attitudes toward personal hygiene and public health. It does little good to send them protein-rich foods if their internal parasites will eat out their intestines. The naive idea that we can simply send them money and they will "take off into self-sustained economic growth" cannot be taken seriously any longer.[52] To at-

tack the West because voters are increasingly unwilling to continue to honor the tenets of a naive faith in State-to-State aid—faith
in the power of political confiscation, faith in the power of using
Western tax revenues to prop up socialist regimes in Third World
nations—is unfair.[53]

P. T. Bauer of the London School of Economics has made the
study of economic development his life's work. He has emphasized what all economists should have known, but what very few
acknowledged until quite recently, namely, that in the long run,
people's *attitudes* are more important for economic growth than
money. His list of what ideas and attitudes *not* to subsidize with
Western capital is comprehensive. No program of foreign aid,
public or private, should be undertaken apart from an educational
program to reduce men's faith in the following list of attitudes:

> Examples of significant attitudes, beliefs and modes of conduct
> unfavourable to material progress include lack of interest in
> material advance, combined with resignation in the face of pov-
> erty; lack of initiative, self-reliance and a sense of personal re-
> sponsibility for the economic future of oneself and one's family;
> high leisure preference, together with a lassitude found in trop-
> ical climates; relatively high prestige of passive or contempla-
> tive life compared to active life; the prestige of mysticism and of
> renunciation of the world compared to acquisition and achieve-
> ment; acceptance of the idea of a preordained, unchanging and
> unchangeable universe; emphasis on performance of duties and
> acceptance of obligation, rather than on achievement of results,
> or assertion or even a recognition of personal rights; lack of sus-
> tained curiosity, experimentation and interest in change; belief
> in the efficacy of supernatural and occult forces and of their in-
> fluence over one's destiny; insistence on the unity of the organic
> universe, and on the need to live with nature rather than con-
> quer it or harness it to man's needs, an attitude of which reluc-
> tance to take animal life is a corollary; belief in perpetual rein-
> carnation, which reduces the significance of effort in the course
> of the present life; recognized status of beggary, together with a
> lack of stigma in the acceptance of charity; opposition to women's
> work outside the home.[54]

A long sentence, indeed. If the full-time promoters of Western
guilt understood the implications of what Bauer is saying, there

would be greater hope for both the West and the Third World. What he describes is essentially the very opposite of what has come to be known as "the Protestant Ethic."[55] What is remarkable is the extent to which *ideologically motivated guilt-manipulators have adopted so many of the very attitudes that Bauer says are responsible for the economic backwardness of the Third World.*

Yes, the West continues to eat. The Third World finds it difficult to grow sufficient food. But Christians in the West are supposedly complacent. They are well-fed, while their "global neighbors" go hungry.[56] It appears that the ancestors of "rich Christians" and rich Westerners in general were very smart: They all moved to those regions of the world where food is now abundant. The Plains Indians, before Europeans came on the scene, experienced frequent famines. There were under half a million of them at the time.[57] Yet, somehow, European immigrants to the Plains arrived just in time to see agricultural productivity flourish. They now consume more than their "fair share" of the food, and their only excuse is that they produce it. This, it seems, is not a good enough answer—certainly not a morally valid answer. The West needs to come up with a cure for the hungry masses of the world, but not the one that worked in the West, namely, *the private ownership of the means of production.*

Ronald Sider has a cure—if not for the world's hungry masses, then at least for the now-guilty consciences of his readers, not to mention the not-yet-guilt-burdened consciences of the American electorate. "We ought to move toward a personal lifestyle that could be sustained for a long period of time if it were shared by everyone in the world. In its controversial *Limits to Growth*, the Club of Rome suggested the figure of $1,800 per year per person. In spite of the many weaknesses of that study, the Club of Rome's estimate may be the best available."[58] And which agencies should be responsible for collecting the funds and sending them to the poor in foreign lands? United Nations channels.[59] Private charity is acceptable—indeed, it is better than the United States government, which sends food and supplies to "repressive dictatorships"—but not preferable.[60] We need State-enforced "institutional change," not reliance on private charity, because "institutional change is often morally better. Personal charity and philanthropy still permit the rich donor to feel superior. And it makes the recipient feel inferior and dependent. Institutional changes, on the other hand, give the oppressed rights and power."[61]

But if the United States government is not really a reliable State to impose such institutional change, what compulsory agency is reliable? He neglects to say. The one agency he mentions favorably in this context is the United Nations—the organization which has formally indicted Israel as a "racist" nation, and which welcomed the Palestine Liberation Organization's Yasir Arafat, pistol on his hip, to speak before the membership.[62]

It is interesting that the Club of Rome drastically revised its no-growth position in 1976, [63] and in 1977, the year *Rich Christians* was published, the Club of Rome published a pro-growth, pro-technology study.[64] As William Tucker observes, "When you're leading the parade, it's always fun to make sudden changes in direction just to try to keep everyone on their toes."[65] Of course, it was favorable to vast State-to-State foreign aid programs.

A Zero-Sum Economy?

A zero-sum game is a game in which the winners' earnings come exclusively from the losers. But what applies to a game of chance does not apply to an economy based on voluntary exchange. Unfortunately, many critics of the free market society still cling to this ancient dogma. They assume that if one person profits from a transaction, the other person loses proportionately. Mises objects:

... *the gain of one man is the damage of another; no man profits but by the loss of others.* This dogma was already advanced by some ancient authors. Among modern writers Montaigne was the first to restate it; we may fairly call it the *Montaigne dogma.* It was the quintessence of the doctrines of Mercantilism, old and new. It is at the bottom of all modern doctrines teaching that there prevailed, within the frame of the market economy, an irreconcilable conflict among the interests of various social classes within a nation and furthermore between the interests of any nation and those of all other nations. . . .

What produces a man's profit in the course of affairs within an unhampered market society is not his fellow citizen's plight and distress, but the fact that he alleviates or entirely removes what causes his fellow citizen's feeling of uneasiness. What hurts the sick is the plague, not the physician who treats the disease. The doctor's gain is not an outcome of the epidemics, but of the aid he gives to those affected. The ultimate source of profits is always the foresight of future conditions. Those who succeeded better than others in anticipating future events and in adjusting their activities to the future state of the market, reap profits because they are in a position to satisfy the most urgent needs of the public. The profits of those who have produced goods and services for which the buyers scramble are not the source of losses of those who have brought to the market commodities in the purchase of which the public is not prepared to pay the full amount of production costs expended. These losses are caused by the lack of insight displayed in anticipating the future state of the market and the demand of the consumers.[66]

The "Montaigne dogma" is still with us. The economic analysis presented by Ronald Sider assumes it. He can be regarded as a dogmatic theologian, but *his dogma is Montaigne's.* Consider for a moment his statistics, such as the Club of Rome's assertion that $1,800 a year would just about equalize the living standards of the world. The Club of Rome assumes tremendous per capita wealth in the hands of the rich—so much wealth, that a program of compulsory wealth-redistribution could make the whole world middle class, or at least reasonably comfortable. But the capital of the West—roads, educational institutions, communications networks, legal systems, banking facilities, monetary systems, manufacturing capital, managerial skills, and attitudes toward life, wealth, and the future—cannot be divided up physically. Furthermore, there is little evidence that it would be sufficient to produce world-wide per capita wealth of this magnitude, even if it could be physically divided up and redistributed.[67]

If we divided only the *shares of ownership* held by the rich— stocks, bonds, annuities, pension rights, cash-value life insurance policies, and so forth—we would see a market-imposed redistribution process begin to put the shares back into the hands of the most efficient producers. The *inequalities of ownership* would rapidly reappear.

The important issue, however, is the Montaigne dogma. It views the world as a zero-sum game, in which winnings exactly balance losses. Then how do societies advance? *If life is a zero-sum game, how can we account for economic growth?* A free market economy is not a zero-sum game. We exchange with each other because we expect to gain an advantage. Both parties expect to be better off after the exchange has taken place. Each party offers an opportunity to the other person. If each person did not expect to better himself, neither would make the exchange. *There is no fixed quantity of economic benefits. The free market economy is not a zero-sum game.*

We understand this far better in the field of education. For example, if I learn that two plus two equals four, I have not harmed anyone. In the area of knowledge, we all know that the only people who lose when someone gains new, accurate knowledge are those who have invested in terms of older, inaccurate knowledge. Could anyone seriously argue that the acquisition of knowledge is a zero-sum game (except, perhaps, in the case of a competitive examination)? Would anyone argue that we should suppress the spread of new, accurate knowledge in order to protect those who have made unfortunate investments in terms of old information?

What should we conclude? The Third World needs what all men need: *faith in Jesus Christ and his law-order.* The Third World needs the increased economic output that is the inevitable product of true conversion to Christ. It needs a new attitude toward the future (optimism). It needs a new attitude concerning the power of biblical law as a tool of dominion. It needs to abandon the bureaucratic State agricultural control systems that pay farmers only a fraction of what their agricultural output is worth, with the difference going into State treasuries. It is not uncommon for West African governments to pay producers as little as *fifty per cent* of the market value of their crops.[68]

What the Third World needs is what we all need: less guilt, less civil government, lower taxes, more freedom, and churches that enforce the tithe through the threat of excommunication—not a "graduated tithe," but a fixed, predictable ten per cent of income. (A "graduated tithe" means a graduated ten per cent, which is contradictory. It is a political slogan, not a theological concept. It certainly is not a standard for State taxation: 1 Sam 8.)

Land Reform

We are told endlessly that Latin American nations need land reform. The government is supposed to intervene, confiscate the landed wealth of the aristocracy, and give it to the poor. This is a variation of Lenin's old World War 1 slogan, "peace, land, bread." Is such a program legitimate? Is it practical?

The Bible has a standard for land tenure: private ownership. First, how can we respect this principle and still expand the holdings of land by the peasants? Second, how can we keep agricultural output from collapsing when unskilled, poor peasants take over land tenure?

The answer to the first question is relatively simple in theory: We need to adopt the biblical principle of inheritance. All sons receive part of the inheritance, with the eldest son obtaining a double portion, since he has the primary responsibility for caring for aged parents. Rushdoony's comments are important:

> The general rule of inheritance was limited primogeniture, i.e., the oldest son, who had the duty of providing for the entire family in case of need, or of governing the clan, receiving a double portion. If there were two sons, the estate was divided into three portions, the younger son receiving one third.... The father could not alienate a godly first-born son because of personal feelings, such as a dislike for the son's mother and a preference for a second wife (Deut. 21:15-17). Neither could he favor an ungodly son, an incorrigible delinquent, who deserved to die (Deut. 21:18-21). Where there was no son, the inheritance went to the daughter or daughters (Num. 27:1-11).... If there were neither sons nor daughters, the next of kin inherited (Num. 27:9-11).[69]

By instituting the biblical mode of inheritance, the great landed estates of the Latin American world would be broken up. The civil government would immediately gain the support of the younger sons of the aristocracy. Land holdings would get smaller. Those sons who choose not to farm can sell their land to productive peasants, or if the poor people have no capital initially, hire them as sharecroppers. (In a capital-poor society, such as the American South immediately after the Civil War, sharecropping proved to be an economically sound arrangement.)[70] The sons can buy the necessary capital, assuming they do not inherit it.

With each death, the land holdings get smaller. Will this lead to the destruction of productive, large-scale agriculture? Not if it is really productive. The size of land holdings could be increased by purchase by productive farmers. Also, corporations could be set up that would issue shares of stock to owners. The holders would leave shares of stock to their heirs, not the actual land. Then heirs could sell these shares to other people, including members of the rising middle class. Without single-inheritor primogeniture, there could be a rising middle class.

One of the preludes to the American Revolution, especially in southern colonies, was the abolition of the English version of eldest-son primogeniture.[71] Puritan New England never did adhere to eldest-son primogeniture. Historian Kenneth Lockridge writes:

> The leaders of the [Massachusetts Bay] colony reflected a general awareness of the unique abundance of the New World in the novel inheritance law they created. In England, the lands of a man who left no will would go to the eldest son under the law of primogeniture, whose aim was to prevent the fragmentation of holdings which would follow from a division among all the sons. The law arose from a mentality of scarcity. It left the land-less younger sons to fend for themselves. In New England the law provided for the division of the whole estate among all the children of the deceased. Why turn younger sons out on the society without land or perhaps daughters without a decent dowry, why invite social disorder, when there was enough to provide for all?[72]

There was never a landed aristocracy in the New England because of this policy. Primogeniture and entail (prohibiting the family from selling the land) disappeared in all but two colonies prior to the American Revolution.

I offer this example of one possible social and economic reform to demonstrate how relevant biblical law is for all societies, and how a deviation from biblical law has led, over centuries, to the creation of a ticking time bomb in Latin American nations. Instead of broadly based private property in land, and the development of a responsible middle class, Latin American nations now face the likelihood of Marxist revolution, with the State, not the people, gaining control over the land. As Rushdoony remarks, "The state, moreover, is making itself progressively the main, and in some countries, the only heir. The state in effect is saying that it will receive the blessing above all others. It offers to educate all children and to support all needy families as the great father of all. It offers support to the aged as the true son and heir who is entitled to collect all of the inheritance as his own. In both roles, however, it is the great corrupter and is at war with God's established order, the family."[73]

Conclusion

God's law is clear enough: *The family is the primary agency of welfare*—in education, law enforcement (by teaching biblical law and self-government), care for the aged. The church, as the agency for collecting the tithe, also has social welfare obligations.[74] The civil government has almost none. Even in the case of the most pitiable people in Israel, the lepers, the State had only a negative function, namely, to quarantine them from other citizens. The State provided no medical care or other tax-supported aid (Lev 13 and 14).[75]

The balance of earthly sovereignties between the *one* (the State or church) and the *many* (individuals, voluntary associations) is mandatory if we are to preserve both freedom and order. The Bible tells us that God is both one and many, one Being yet three Persons. His creation reflects this unity and diversity. Our social and political institutions are to reflect this. We are to seek neither total unity (statism) nor total diversity (anarchism).[76] Biblical law provides us with the guidelines by which we may achieve a balanced social order. We must take biblical law seriously.[77]

The most effective social movements of the twentieth century's masses—Marxism, Darwinian science, and militant Islam—have held variations of the three doctrines that are crucial for any comprehensive program of social change: *providence, law,* and *optimism.* The Christian faith offers all three of these, not in a secular framework, but in a revelational framework. The failure of Christianity to capture the minds of the masses, not to mention the world's leaders, is in part due to the unwillingness of the representatives of Christian orthodoxy to preach all three with uncompromising clarity. *The world will stay poor for as long as men cling to any vision of God, man, and law that is in opposition to the biblical outline.*

We need faith in the meaning of the universe and the sovereignty of God. We need confidence that biblical law offers us a reliable tool of dominion. Finally, we need an historical dynamic: Optimism. We need a positive future-orientation for our earthly efforts, in eternity of course, but also in time and on earth. People need to surrender unconditionally to God in order to exercise comprehensive dominion, under God and in terms of God's law, over the creation.[78] There is no other long-term solution to long-term poverty. God will not be mocked.

Notes

[1]On the question of Old Testament law in New Testament times, see Greg L. Bahnsen, *Theonomy in Christian Ethics* (Nutley, N.J.: Craig Press, 1977).

[2]Ludwig von Mises, *Human Action*, 3rd ed. (Chicago: Regnery, 1966), chap. 18. Let me give an example of the "discount for time." If I were to announce that you have just won a new Rolls-Royce, and that you have a choice of delivery date, today or one year from today, which delivery date would you select (other things being equal)? You would want immediate delivery. Why? Because present goods are worth more to you than the same goods in the future. You might accept the Rolls-Royce a year from now if I paid you a rate of interest, in addition to the car. In fact, at some rate of interest you *would* accept the later date, unless you have a terminal disease, or an unquenchable lust for a Rolls-Royce.

[3]Murray N. Rothbard, *Man, Economy, and State*, 2 vols. (1962; reprint ed., New York: New York Univ. Press, 1979), 1:284-87, 410-24. See esp. chap. 6.

[4]On the holy commonwealth ideal in early American history, see Rousas J. Rushdoony, *This Independent Republic* (1964; reprint ed., Fairfax, Va.: Thoburn Press, 1978), esp. chap. 8.

[5]Daniel's interpretation of Nebuchadnezzar's dream about the great image was *historically specific*: four human empires (Babylon, Medo-Persia, Macedonia, and Rome), followed by the fifth Empire, God's (Dan 2:31-45). This was not an "ideal type," to use Max Weber's terminology, nor was it a developmental model. Hesiod's seemingly similar construction (Greece, 8th century B.C.)—from the Age of Gold to the Age of Iron—was, in contrast, an attempt at constructing a universal model of the process of decay in man's history. Hesiod, *Works and Days*, trans. Richmond Lattimore (Ann Arbor: Univ. of Michigan Press, 1959), ll. 109-201. The Bible's developmental model is based on *ethics*—conformity to or rebellion against God's covenant—not *metaphysics*, meaning some sort of inescapable aspect of the creation.

[6]Gary North, *The Dominion Covenant: Genesis* (Tyler, Tex.: Institute for Christian Economics, 1982).

[7]Murray N. Rothbard, *The Ethics of Liberty* (Atlantic Highlands, N.J.: Humanities Press, 1982).

[8]Gary North, "Methodological Covenantalism," *Chalcedon Report* (Oct. 1977), published by the Chalcedon Foundation, Box 158, Vallecito, California, 95251.

[9]I capitalize the word *State* where I am referring to the new god of twentieth-

century socialism. I distinguish this from "state," meaning a regional agency of civil government in the United States.

[10]One of the finest books ever written in economics covers these questions in detail: Thomas Sowell, *Knowledge and Decisions* (New York: Basic Books, 1980). Sowell is an ex-Marxist, so he knows the arguments well. See also Ludwig von Mises, *Socialism: An Economic and Sociological Analysis* (1922; reprint ed., Indianapolis, Ind.: Liberty Press, 1981). This was first published in the United States by Yale University Press in 1953.

[11]Gary North, *An Introduction to Christian Economics* (Nutley, N.J.: Craig Press, 1973), chap. 20: "Statist Bureaucracy in the Modern Economy."

[12]"The distinction between moral and technical knowledge is elusive.... From the standpoint of any science the distinction is absolutely essential. A subject is not opened to scientific enquiry until its technical aspect has been sundered from its moral aspect.... [T]here can be no doubt that economic theory owes its present development to the fact that some men, in thinking of economic phenomena, forcefully suspended all judgments of theology, morality, and justice, were willing to consider the economy as nothing more than an intricate mechanism, refraining for the while from asking whether the mechanism worked for good or evil. That separation was made during the seventeenth century.... The economist's view of the world, which the public cannot yet comfortably stomach, was introduced by a remarkable *tour de force*, an intellectual revolution brought off in the seventeenth century." William Letwin, *The Origins of Scientific Economics* (1963; reprint ed., Garden City, N.Y.: Doubleday/Anchor, 1965), pp. 158-59.

[13]Ibid., p. 159.

[14]Letwin does not actually say this. Perhaps he forgot about Newton. Or perhaps he was referring solely to social science when he named economics as "the greatest scientific accomplishment of the seventeenth century." Or possibly he really meant what he wrote, which boggles the mind.

[15]Mises writes: "In considering changes in the nation's legal system, in rewriting or repealing existing laws and writing new laws, the issue is not justice, but social expediency and social welfare. There is no such thing as an absolute notion of justice not referring to a definite system of social organization. It is not justice that determines the decision in favor of a definite social system. It is, on the contrary, the social system which determines what should be deemed right and what wrong. There is neither right nor wrong outside the social nexus.... It is nonsensical to justify or to reject interventionism from the point of view of fictitious and arbitrary absolute justice. It is vain to ponder over the just delimitation of the tasks of government from any preconceived standard of perennial values." Mises, *Human Action*, p. 721.

Milton Friedman, in a classic essay on epistemology, writes: "Positive economics is in principle independent of any particular ethical position or normative judgment." Friedman, *Essays in Positive Economics* (Chicago: Univ. of Chicago Press, 1953), p. 4. For a critique of the hypothesis of neutrality in economics, see Gary North, "Economics: From Reason to Intuition," in North, ed., *Foundations of Christian Scholarship* (Vallecito, Calif.: Ross House Books, 1976).

[16]On the impossibility of neutrality, see the writings of Cornelius Van Til, espe-

cially *The Defense of the Faith,* rev. ed. (Phillipsburg, N.J.: Presbyterian and Reformed, 1963).

[17]For a discussion of the similarities and differences between "the law" and "the works of the law" written on human hearts, see John Murray, *The Epistle to the Romans,* 2 vols. (Grand Rapids, Mich.: Eerdmans, 1959), 1:74-76.

[18]Marxists believe in objective truth—proletarian truth—but they hold that all other approaches are intellectual defenses of a particular class perspective. All philosophy is *class* philosophy—a weapon used by one class against its rivals. Since history is objectively on the side of the proletariat, there can be objective truth for Marxists only. See Gary North, *Marx's Religion of Revolution: The Doctrine of Creative Destruction* (Nutley, N.J.: Craig Press, 1968), pp. 61-71.

[19]Compare Thomas Kuhn, *The Structure of Scientific Revolutions,* rev. ed. (Chicago: Univ. of Chicago Press, 1970). See also Imre Lakatos and Alan E. Musgrave, eds., *Criticism and the Growth of Knowledge* (Cambridge: At the University Press, 1970). The works of Herman Dooyeweerd, the Dutch legal philosopher, deal extensively with the pre-theoretical presuppositions of all philosophy: *In the Twilight of Western Thought* (Phillipsburg, N.J.: Presbyterian and Reformed, 1960); *A New Critique of Theoretical Thought,* 4 vols. (Presbyterian and Reformed, 1954).

[20]Stanley L. Jaki, *The Road of Science and the Ways to God* (Chicago: Univ. of Chicago Press, 1978), chap. 15.

[21]See, for example, Walter A. Weisskopf, *Alienation and Economics* (New York: E. P. Dutton, 1971); Mark A. Lutz and Kenneth Lux, *The Challenge of Humanistic Economics* (Menlo Park, Calif.: Benjamin/Cummings, 1979). Lux is a clinical psychologist, not an economist, and Lutz taught at an obscure college. Benjamin/Cummings is not a familiar name in publishing. I am not berating these men, their publisher, or their employers, though I do not share their economic views. I am pointing to the difficulty of getting such views discussed within the normal channels of the economics profession. The economics profession has not adopted the forthright acceptance by these men of the obvious implications of subjectivism for the neutrality doctrine.

[22]David Chilton, "The Case of the Missing Blueprints," *Journal of Christian Reconstruction* 8 (Summer 1981).

[23]Again, consult Sowell's book, *Knowledge and Decisions,* for a detailed analysis of this issue. Also, see the classic study by Frank H. Knight, *Risk, Uncertainty and Profit* (1921; reprint ed., New York: Augustus M. Kelley, Pubs., n.d.).

[24]Gary North, "A Christian View of Labor Unions," *Biblical Economics Today* (April/May 1978), published by the Institute for Christian Economics.

[25]Gary North, "Exploitation and Knowledge," *The Freeman* (January 1982), published by the Foundation for Economic Education, Irvington, New York, 10533.

[26]Perhaps the most eloquent and scholarly work that argues for the connection between predictable law, human freedom, and economic productivity is the book by the Nobel Prize winner in economics, F. A. Hayek, *The Constitution of Liberty* (Chicago: Univ. of Chicago Press, 1960), esp. the first 15 chapters. See also his trilogy, *Law, Legislation and Liberty* (Chicago: Univ. of Chicago Press, 1973-80).

[27]G. Ernest Wright, "Deuteronomy," in *The Interpreter's Bible,* vol. 2, p. 509; cited by R. J. Rushdoony, *Institutes of Biblical Law,* vol. 2, *Law and Liberty* (Vallecito,

Calif.: Ross House Books, 1982), p. 413.

[28]Rushdoony, *Law and Society*, pp. 403-6.

[29]Armen A. Alchian and William R. Allen, *University Economics: Elements of Inquiry*, 3rd ed. (Belmont, Calif.: Wadsworth, 1972), p. 141. Italics in the original.

[30]Ibid.

[31]Ibid., p. 239.

[32]Ernest F. Kevan, *The Grace of Law: A Study in Puritan Theology* (1963; reprint ed., Grand Rapids, Mich.: Baker Book House, 1983).

[33]See the study by Karl Wittfogel, *Oriental Despotism: A Comparative Study of Total Power* (New Haven, Conn.: Yale Univ. Press, 1957).

[34]Lewis Mumford, "The First Megamachine," *Daedalus* (1966); reprinted in Lewis Mumford, *Interpretations and Forecasts: 1922-1972* (New York: Harcourt Brace Jovanovich, 1973). See also Max Weber, "Max Weber on Bureaucratization" (1909), in J. P. Meyer, *Max Weber and German Politics: A Study in Political Sociology* (London: Faber & Faber, 1956), p. 127.

[35]For a discussion of why Joseph's imposition of a twenty per cent tax in Egypt was not part of God's law for Israel, see Gary North, *Dominion Covenant: Genesis*, chap. 23.

[36]Robert M. Bleiberg, "Down a Rathole," *Barron's* (11 August 1975), p. 7. By 1975, the United States had sent to foreign nations agricultural assistance of about $25 billion.

[37]The estimate of Dr. Max Milner of the Massachusetts Institute of Technology. He says that in one recent year, rats in the Philippine Islands consumed over half the sugar and corn, and ninety per cent of the rice crop. "Over 40% of the World's Food Is Lost to Pests," *Washington Post*, 6 March 1977.

[38]P. T. Bauer, *Equality, the Third World and Economic Delusion* (Cambridge, Mass.: Harvard Univ. Press, 1981), p. 94.

[39]For background on the political support for Public Law 480 and the program's use as a tool of American foreign policy, see Dan Morgan, *Merchants of Grain* (New York: Viking, 1979), pp. 100-102, 122-28, 258-68.

[40]William Peterson, *The Great Farm Problem* (Chicago: Regnery, 1959).

[41]Ronald Sider, *Rich Christians in an Age of Hunger* (Downers Grove, Ill.: Inter-Varsity Press, 1977), p. 18. This book was co-published by the liberal Roman Catholic publishing house, the Paulist Press. Unquestionably, it represents an ecumenical publishing venture. Presumably, it reflects the thinking of a broad base of Christian scholars.

[42]Ibid., p. 152.

[43]Ibid., p. 152-53.

[44]Ibid., p. 43.

[45]Associated Press story, *Tyler Morning Telegraph*, 18 December 1982.

[46]Richard H. Wagner, *Environment and Man*, 3rd ed. (New York: Norton, 1978), p. 523.

[47]Ibid., pp. 518-19.

[48]Arnold Toynbee, *Civilization on Trial and the World and the West* (New York: World, 1958), pp. 286-87.

[49]John Burton, "Epilogue," in Steven N. S. Cheung, *The Myth of Social Cost* (San Francisco: Cato Institute, 1980), p. 66.

⁵⁰Claire Sterling, "The Making of the Sub-Sahara Wasteland,"*Atlantic* (May 1974), p. 102.

⁵¹Ibid., p. 103.

⁵²W. W. Rostow, *The Stages of Economic Growth: A Non-Communist Manifesto* (Cambridge: At the University Press, 1960). This was a best-seller on college campuses in the early 1960s. For a critique, see the essays by several economic historians in Rostow, ed., *The Economics of Take-Off into Sustained Growth* (New York: St. Martin's, 1963).

⁵³Examples of socialist (centrally planned) economies that have been propped up by U.S. government aid are Costa Rica, Uruguay, El Salvador, and Ghana. See Melvyn B. Krauss, *Development without Aid: Growth, Poverty and Government* (New York: New Press, McGraw-Hill, 1983), pp. 24-32. Another example is Zaire (formerly the Belgian Congo). Consider also that government-guaranteed loans, as well as below-market loans through such agencies as the Export-Import Bank, constitute foreign aid, for banks loan investors' dollars to high-risk socialist nations that would otherwise not have been loaned. The Soviet Bloc has done exceedingly well in this regard for decades. On this point, see Antony Sutton, *Western Technology and Soviet Economic Development*, 3 vols. (Stanford, Calif.: Hoover Institution, 1968-73).

⁵⁴P. T. Bauer, *Dissent on Development* (Cambridge, Mass.: Harvard Univ. Press, 1972), pp. 78-79.

⁵⁵Max Weber, *The Protestant Ethic and the Spirit of Capitalism* (New York: Charles Scribner's Sons, 1958). This book appeared originally as a series of scholarly journal articles in 1904 to 1905. See also S. N. Eisenstadt, ed., *The Protestant Ethic and Modernization* (New York: Basic Books, 1968).

⁵⁶Sider, *Rich Christians*, p. 30.

⁵⁷R. J. Rushdoony, *The Myth of Over-Population* (1969; reprint ed., Fairfax, Va.: Thoburn Press, 1978), pp. 1-3.

⁵⁸Ronald J. Sider, "Living More Simply for Evangelism and Justice," the Keynote Address to the International Consultation on Simple Lifestyle, England (17-20 March 1980), mimeographed paper, p. 17.

⁵⁹Sider, *Rich Christians*, p. 216.

⁶⁰Ibid.

⁶¹Sider, "Ambulance Drivers or Tunnel Builders" (Philadelphia: Evangelicals for Social Action, n.d.), p. 4.

⁶²For a critical analysis of Sider's views, see David Chilton, *Productive Christians in an Age of Guilt-Manipulators: A Biblical Response to Ronald Sider*, rev. ed. (Tyler, Tex.: Institute for Christian Economics, 1982).

⁶³*Time*, 26 April 1976.

⁶⁴Jan Tinbergen (coordinator), *RIO—Reshaping the International Order: A Report to the Club of Rome* (New York: New American Library, Signet Books, 1977).

⁶⁵William Tucker, *Progress and Privilege: America in the Age of Environmentalism* (Garden City, N.Y.: Anchor/Doubleday, 1982), p. 193.

⁶⁶Ludwig von Mises, *Human Action*, pp. 664-65. Italics in original.

⁶⁷Gary North, "Trickle-Down Economics," *The Freeman* (May 1982).

⁶⁸P. T. Bauer, *Dissent on Development*, pp. 401-3.

⁶⁹R. J. Rushdoony, *Institutes of Biblical Law* (Nutley, N.J.: Craig Press, 1973),

pp. 180-81.

[70]Blacks much preferred sharecropping to working for wages on White-owned farms: Roger Ransom and Richard Sutch, *One Kind of Freedom: The Economic Consequences of Emancipation* (New York: Cambridge Univ. Press, 1977), pp. 67-70.

[71]Robert Nisbet, the conservative American sociologist, concludes that the abolition of primogeniture and entail (fixing land to the family line) was an important symbol of the American Revolution. He admits, however, that few of the colonies in 1775 were still enforcing these laws. Nisbet, "The Social Impact of the Revolution," in *America's Continuing Revolution: An Act of Conservation* (Washington, D.C.: American Enterprise Institute for Public Policy Research, 1975), p. 80. Nisbet cites Frederick Le Play and Alexis de Tocqueville as sources for his opinion on the importance of the abolition of primogeniture and entail, pp. 82-83.

[72]Kenneth A. Lockeridge, *A New England Town, The First Hundred Years: Dedham, Massachusetts, 1636-1736* (New York: Norton, 1970), pp. 71-72.

[73]Ibid., p. 181. See also Gary North, "Familistic Capital," in *The Dominion Covenant: Exodus* (Tyler, Tex.: Institute for Christian Economics, 1984), forthcoming.

[74]James B. Jordan, "Tithing: Financing Christian Reconstruction," in Gary North, ed., *Tactics of Christian Resistance* (Tyler, Tex.: Geneva Divinity School Press, 1983).

[75]Gary North, "Quarantines and Public Health," *Chalcedon Report* (April 1977).

[76]R. J. Rushdoony, *The One and the Many: Studies in the Philosophy of Order and Ultimacy* (1971; reprint ed., Fairfax, Va.: Thoburn Press, 1978).

[77]Bahnsen, *Theonomy in Christian Ethics.*

[78]Gary North, *Unconditional Surrender: God's Program for Victory*, 2nd ed. (Tyler, Tex.: Geneva Divinity School Press, 1983). See also Roderick Campbell, *Israel and the New Covenant* (1954; reprint ed., Tyler, Tex.: Geneva Divinity School Press, 1982).

Select Bibliography

A question is being raised constantly in evangelical circles: "What is the Christian's responsibility to the poor?" Unfortunately, the people who tend to ask this question *really* are asking a very different question: "What is the *State's* responsibility to the poor?" A very different question requires a very different answer.

To answer both questions, Christians need information. I offer the following bibliography, so that Christians who get interested in the topic of the relationship between faith and cultural prosperity, or the related topic of ethical rebellion and cultural poverty, can follow through on their own.

There are always more books to be read than time to read them. Therefore, to save readers time and trouble, I will recommend the one book above all others—the Bible excepted, of course—that best answers the question: What does the Bible say concerning the Christian's responsibilities concerning the poor? The book is David Chilton's *Productive Christians in an Age of Guilt-Manipulators: A Biblical Response to Ronald J. Sider*, published by the Institute for Christian Economics, Box 8000, Tyler, TX 75711 ($4.95). Chapters include: "Biblical Law and Christian

Economics," "God's Law and the Poor," "The Exodus as a Liberation Movement," "Is God on the Side of the Poor?" "Foreign Aid," "Overpopulation," "The Jubilee Principle," "The Goal of Equality," "Statism," "The Prophetic Message," "The Basis for Economic Growth," and "The Conquest of Poverty." The book is well-documented and contains a three-page, four-column Scripture index. It also provides a lengthy bibliography.

The other book which is absolutely vital is Herbert Schlossberg's *Idols for Destruction: Christian Faith and Its Confrontation with American Society* (Nashville: Thomas Nelson, 1983; $8.95 soft cover, $14.95 hard cover). This is the finest presentation of Christian social theory ever written, period. It covers politics, inflation, taxation, poverty, foreign aid, the establishment of Christian alternatives to humanism, education, the evils of the corporate State—in short, *everything.* In my opinion, anyone who speaks in the name of Christ on social theory, and who has not mastered this book, need not be taken seriously.

The Jubilee Year (Lev 25) is no longer in force. It was a military spoils agreement governing the post-conquest dividing up of the land of Canaan. Every 50 years, the land of Israel reverted to the families that possessed each plot when they conquered the Canaanites under Joshua. Does this teach Christian socialism? Emphatically not. For an explanation, see my essay, "The Fulfilment of the Jubilee Year," in the newsletter published by the Institute for Christian Economics, *Biblical Economics Today* (April 1983).

The materials for developing a framework for economics (and other social sciences) are found in the book of Genesis. The Institute for Christian Economics has published my economic commentary on Genesis: *The Dominion Covenant: Genesis* ($14.95), which is volume 1 of *An Economic Commentary on the Bible*. The second volume, on Exodus, is scheduled to appear in early 1984. It deals extensively with the meaning of God's delivery of Israel from Egypt, a static, centrally planned, and highly bureaucratic civilization.

Theology

If Christ is God, then no human institution can claim comprehensive or final authority. All human governments, of which civil government is only one, are under God's sovereign power and are responsible to him. They are under his law. This law reduces the power of the civil government to a minimum. I have outlined this position in my book, *Unconditional Surrender: God's Program for Victory*, 2nd ed. (Tyler, Tex.: Geneva Divinity School Press, 1983; $9.95).

R. J. Rushdoony's book, *The Institutes of Biblical Law* (Nutley, N.J.: Craig Press, 1973), offers comprehensive studies of the contemporary relevance of Old Testament law. This set establishes the case for limited civil government under the rule of revealed law.

A simplified introduction to the perspective of these books is provided in the two-volume workbook by Gary DeMar, *God and Government: A Biblical and Historical Study* (Box 720515, Atlanta, Ga.: American Vision, 1982, 1983; $9.95 each).

Poverty

The best solution to poverty is productivity. This means capital investment, successful forecasting and planning (entrepreneurship), and future-orientation.

George Gilder's *Wealth and Poverty* (New York: Basic Books, 1981) demonstrates the crippling effects the State's welfare programs have had on the self-respect of the recipients. Compulsory welfare programs destroy the entrepreneurial spirit that is basic to an escape from the poverty trap.

Thomas Sowell, the ex-Marxist from Harlem, has provided a detailed study of Gilder's point in his book, *Race and Economics* (New York: David McKay, 1975). Sowell shows how immigrant groups before the New Deal raised themselves out of the ghetto, and how those farthest from government welfare (for example, Poles, Italians, Jews, orientals) did better economically within three generations than those that relied on politics for income and jobs (for example, the Irish). Walter Williams' book, *The State against Blacks* (New York: McGraw-Hill New Press, 1982), studies the barriers to Black Advancement that the government has created: minimum wage laws, occupational licensure, and so on.

The study of poverty in the United States by Harvard political scientist Edward Banfield, *The Unheavenly City Revisited* (Boston: Little, Brown, 1974), emphasizes the importance of attitudes, especially attitudes toward time, in the upward mobility of the poor, or absence thereof. He argues that one's class position is primarily a function of one's time perspective, not money.

Finally, there is sociologist Helmut Schoeck's study, *Envy: A Theory of Social Behavior* (New York: Harcourt, Brace, 1970), which analyzes the devastating effects on societies of the resentment of the poor against the rich.

A Guided-Market Response
William E. Diehl

I congratulate Gary North on making a heroic effort to present a biblical case for the free-market system. However, the arguments presented are flawed in so many instances that one senses the author is desperately grasping at straws. Nevertheless, North's viewpoint does represent the thinking of other Christians and therefore needs to be examined in some detail.

That the author is strong on "biblical law" is apparent. The essay provides us with thirty-nine Old Testament citations, of which twenty-three are from the book of Deuteronomy. Alongside these imposing Old Testament references the reader is given only nine New Testament citations, of which only four come from the mouth of Jesus. Notwithstanding one of North's concluding statements that we need "faith in Jesus Christ," this essay might more properly be entitled "Poverty and Wealth according to Deuteronomy." The teachings and parables of Jesus are rich with references to wealth, poverty and justice. Why has the author chosen to ignore these? Can it be that the words of the Master are an embarrassment to the advocates of a free-market system?

Before examining the author's Old Testament evidence, we need to remind ourselves that Jesus did have some strong words for legalists who neglect "the really important teachings of the Law, such as justice and mercy and honesty" (Mt 23:23 TEV). While Jesus did not claim that he came to abolish the law, he did clearly give them a new commandment. He said, "My commandment is this: love one another, just as I love you" (Jn 15:12 TEV). He demonstrated his dedication to the superior law of love by healing and gathering grain on the Sabbath in spite of Levitical laws to the contrary. Perhaps the sharpest words we ever hear from the lips of Jesus are directed at the hypocritical Pharisees who observed the letter of the law and ignored the spirit of it. "How terrible for you, teachers of the Law and Pharisees! You hypocrites! You are like whitewashed tombs, which look fine on the outside but are full of bones and decaying corpses on the inside. In the same way, on the outside you appear good to everybody, but inside you are full of hypocrisy and sins" (Mt 23:27-28 TEV).

The point is, of course, that since love is the "new commandment" of Christ we need to take care as we deal with Old Testament laws that we do not become so legalistic in our application to current situations that we prevent God's love from becoming manifest. It does seem necessary to point out some of the problems which arise when one selectively uses Old Testament references to support a position—no matter what that position may be.

The North essay makes frequent reference to private-property rights. The author does not indicate whether he sees this right to private property as a biblical teaching or a civil guarantee. Any implication that such a right was part of the Old Testament law needs to be clarified.

Implicit throughout Scripture is the understanding that "the earth is the LORD's, and the fulness thereof" (Ps 24:1), and that we as God's people are called to be stewards of creation. In fact, Leviticus 25:23 is very blunt about private property rights: "Your land must not be sold on a permanent basis, because you do not own it; it belongs to God, and you are like foreigners who are allowed to make use of it" (TEV).

The book of Leviticus lists quite a few restrictions on the ownership of private property. For example, when a farmer worked the land, he had to leave a border of the grainfield unharvested for the use of those who passed by. Or, if a man walked past a vineyard, he was allowed to take along as much as he could carry in his hands. In the context of North's essay, this would be called stealing.

The whole concept of the Jubilee year flies in the face of private-property rights as we know them. For, in the year of the Jubilee, which was every fifty years, all slaves were to be freed, all debts canceled, and all land returned to the original owners. William Lazareth in *Work as Praise* concludes from this, "Private property, therefore is never an absolute right in Holy Scripture. As an aid to personal freedom it is a relative civil right that is always conditioned by the will of God and the needs of the community. The need to serve justifies the right to possess in God's created order of life-in-community. Nowhere does the Bible sanction the accumulation of economic power and possessions as ends in themselves."[1]

Jesus' treatment of private-property rights was consistent with that of the Old Testament. One's holding of private property was for the purpose of fulfilling the will of God. He was quite outspoken about the accumulation of private property as an end in itself, as witnessed in his challenge to the rich young ruler or in his story of the wealthy farmer who tore down his old barns to make room for larger ones. When Jesus sent out the seventy, he instructed them to take no private property with them (Lk 10).

Much of North's defense of the free-market philosophy rests on the foundation of personal-property rights. However, when one conditions these rights by the biblical imperatives for the use of personal property, much of the author's position on such subjects as wealth redistribution and foreign aid simply does not hold water.

The essay offers few kind words about civil government. While all of us share in the disappointment with government which has failed to meet its potential for doing justice, it does not follow that less government is necessarily better. It is unfortunate that when the author addresses the issue of compulsory wealth redistribution he focuses on the *level of taxation* and says nothing about the *philosophy* of government being the means for a more equitable distribution of wealth.

For me it taxes all credibility to assume that in this highly complex society in which we live the needs of the poor can be met by Christians acting individually or through their churches on a voluntary basis. Even if all Christians had the commitment to care for the poor, how could I or my congregation possibly know where all the unmet needs were, and how could we be certain that there would be an equitable distribution of our benevolences? Some overall agency is needed for such a task, and it is obviously civil government.

Furthermore, North makes no mention of the basic impediment to a free-market system: human sinfulness. If all the people of this earth were Christians, which they are not, and if all Christians lived up to the biblical legalisms, which they do not, one might consider the possibility of the author's vision. But we are daily reminded of our basic self-serving nature, and we constantly turn to God for forgiveness. God's great gift of freedom carries with it the opportunity for his people to reject his laws, and past history offers little hope for a day in which all of us will be totally unselfish and truly servants to one another. From a biblical and theological standpoint, the free-market concept cannot be defended.

An interesting feature of the essay is the equating of taxation with stealing. Such a portrayal may be accurate in nations where there is taxation without representation. But our society is based on representative government, and we have seen many instances in which the people's views on taxation have caused policies to change or new faces to appear in Washington. Ronald Reagan claimed that his 1980 election was a mandate from the people to reduce taxes and "get government off the backs of the people." The historic Proposition 13 in California was another demonstration of the people's ability to change the system of taxation. The tax system in this country exists because the majority of our citizens are in support of it.

But the essay suggests that even though the majority may support taxation, it is still stealing from those who do not agree. From this one concludes that a free-market concept should permit people to pay only as much tax as they wish, regardless of the position of government as expressed through the majority vote of its citizens.

We need to note two places in the New Testament where the issue of taxes is presented. The first one involves Jesus. The three synoptic Gospels tell of the same incident: the enemies of Jesus seek to trap him with a question about the legality of paying taxes. He responds by pointing to the emperor's face on a silver coin and instructing that one should "pay to the Emperor what belongs to the Emperor, and pay to God what belongs to God" (Lk 20:25 TEV). He put no conditions on those instructions. In fact, he really gave the people a bit more than they asked about. In instructing the people to pay to the emperor the things which were the emperor's, he went beyond the matter of taxes and swept into his statement all responsibilities of citizens toward their government (Lk 20:19-25).

Paul gives clear and unmistakable instructions about taxes and the responsibility of the Christian to government. In Romans 13 he writes,

> Everyone must obey state authorities, because no authority exists without God's permission, and the existing authorities have been put there by God. Whoever opposes the existing authority opposes what God has ordered; and anyone who does so will bring judgment on himself. . . . That is also why you pay taxes, because the authorities are working for God when they fulfill their duties. Pay, then, what you owe them; pay them your personal and property taxes, and show respect and honor for them all. (Rom 13:1-2, 6-7 TEV)

There is nothing in either of these statements about "stealing" from the people. Nor is there any suggestion of a maximum tax rate of the tithe as suggested in the North essay.

Certainly we can agree with Paul that a government which ensures law and order is a gift of God. Without government we would have anarchy. As our society has become more complex, the role of government has necessarily increased. In the days of Moses there were no needs for paved highways. Today most of our highway systems are built and maintained by the government. Imagine the confusion we would have if all our roads were built and operated by private investors who collected tolls!

The North essay is critical of government inefficiency and bureaucracy. With this criticism all of us can agree. But in spite of potholes I support the philosophy of a public road system. In spite of problems in our schools I support public education available to poor and rich alike. In spite of bungling and red tape I support the principle that government should establish basic rules regarding how people and corporations treat each other and the environment. In spite of examples of fraud I support a system in which public assistance is given to those who are handicapped, sick, elderly or otherwise unable to care for themselves. Of course we must guard against overdomination by government at the expense of individual freedom. Of course we should be angry with government inefficiency and fraud. But to suggest, as some do, that all government is corrupt and that public agencies and programs have no rightful place in society is to reject one of the orders of God's creation.

In the section on foreign aid, North offers sweeping criticisms with little supporting evidence. Consider this statement: "There is a great temptation for government officials of underdeveloped nations to use this [gift of] food to free up State-controlled capital which is then used to increase investments in heavy industry—investments that produce visible results that are politically popular" (p. 42). If this statement is universally true, then why don't we see steel mills or automobile assembly plants in Sudan or Mali or Pakistan? Furthermore, the author neglects to mention that through the work of the United Nations, at its 1974 World Food Conference in Rome, there is an international plan for the distribution of food which is designed to prevent the very problems he outlines.

North asks, "Is the poverty of the Third World the fault of the West?" (p. 44). He proceeds to prove that Third World nations are responsible for their own poverty and that therefore we do not really help solve their basic problems by sending them food. While I am not as confident as North that Western society is not implicated in any way with Third World poverty, the question itself seems irrelevant. When one is born into poverty, one's hunger pains are not eased by knowing who is to blame.

The question "Is the Third World poverty the fault of the West?" is reminiscent of the question the disciples asked Jesus when they met a man blind from birth. They asked, "Teacher, whose sin caused him to be born blind? Was it his own or his parents' sin?" (Jn 9:2 TEV). Jesus points out that the blindness had nothing to do with his sins or his parents'. He explains, "He is blind so that God's power might be seen at work in him. As long as it is day, we must do the work of him who sent me; night is coming when no one can work" (vv. 3-4 TEV).

In the same way that Jesus had the power to give sight to one born blind, God has given us the power to eradicate hunger in those parts of the world where children are born into poverty. Notwithstanding all the cultural and dietary obstacles cited by North, the fact remains that it is within the ability of modern society to eliminate hunger from the face of the earth. The question is, are we committed to doing something about it? The author's observation that our ancestors "were very smart: they all moved to those regions of the world where food is now abundant" (p. 51) is an affront to human beings born into poverty. North's section devoted to foreign aid lacks any concrete suggestions as to how we should carry out Jesus' mandate to care for the poor. The reader is left hanging. The silence is ominous.

North's conclusion sums up our points of agreement and disagreement. Citing that "the church, as the agency for collecting the tithe, also has social welfare obligations," he adds, "The civil government has almost none" (p. 57). I agree with the first statement but not with the second.

The Bible is clear and consistent in its call for freedom, justice and responsibility for all God's people. The free-market philosophy as presented in this essay certainly addresses the issue of freedom. From my perspective the overriding attention to freedom shows little concern for issues of justice and therefore is not a position which can be supported by responsible Christians.

Notes

[1]Philadelphia: Fortress Press, 1979.

A Decentralist Response
Art Gish

Although I agree with North on a few basic points, I am left with the suspicion that he starts not with the Bible but with a conservative political and economic philosophy and then uses his concept of biblical law to legitimize that conservative ideology. I agree that society needs to be judged by biblical revelation, but North and I do not seem to be using the same Bible.

The center of North's faith seems to be in the book of Deuteronomy. He would come to different conclusions if he started with Jesus and the New Covenant and then looked at the Old Covenant law in that new light.

North tells us that God wants to bless us, and he calls us to covenantal faithfulness. Surely this is right. And it is true that faithfulness brings good while sin brings suffering. But we learn in the Bible that faithfulness also leads to suffering and the cross.

I like the concept of methodological covenantalism. That is the biblical alternative to both individualism and collectivism. North is right in saying that the real issue is ethical. We need to stand against ethical neutrality. If biblical ethics should be basic to any social analysis, however, then North's chapter leaves us with many questions.

Why does North so easily accept capitalist ideology? Where is his biblical critique of that ideology? Why should the style of the Christian's economic life be shaped by the market? Doesn't the biblical law against coveting argue against the capitalist system of institutionalized greed? Isn't "the lure of autonomy" a basic sin of capitalism?

It is not clear whether North favors a free market or a market controlled by biblical principles. If he favors the latter, who would enforce those biblical principles on the world? If we really let our economic lives be guided by biblical principles, wouldn't the market be so changed as to make it unrecognizable? It appears to me that North is more committed to the myth of the free market than to biblical authority.

Is competition part of God's intention for humanity, or is it an expression of the Fall? Will we be competing in heaven? Will there be winners and losers in heaven? I find the ideal of auctioning my labor to be morally repulsive, and North says nothing to show that it is not wrong. We are called to be sisters and brothers, not competitors. When I do carpentry for others, I try to take their needs and ability to pay into consideration and often lower my charge. Sometimes I even work for free. I have no interest in auctioning my labor to the highest bidder. I want to be a servant to God and to my neighbors. When I trade with a sister whom I love, I want to give her a value equal to or greater than she gives me because her welfare is as important as mine. How could I in love seek to maximize profit? Cooperation seems to be a more Christlike style than competition.

In capitalism workers and employers are competing most of the time. Employers are trying to squeeze as much as possible out of the workers, and the workers are trying to get by with doing as little as possible. Union/management contract negotiations are intensively competitive.

The parable of the laborers in the vineyard does not support capitalism but the biblical vision of equality and grace. Jesus' parable suggests that all should receive the same. Those who gathered much manna had nothing more than those who gathered little

(Ex 16:18; 2 Cor 8:14-15). Neither the Old Testament law nor the New Testament doctrine of grace is capitalistic.

The answer to our problems is not biblical law but God's grace, the saving grace of Jesus Christ expressed in a new order, God's kingdom. The law cannot bring salvation. Neither will the capitalistic doctrine of salvation by works lead to life. In the Old Testament the law was given to govern people's greed and anger. Revenge was limited to one eye for one eye, only two teeth for two teeth. Wouldn't it be wonderful if the world could just come up to this standard of morality?

In the New Covenant we are offered something much better, the grace of going beyond greed and revenge and therefore the need of law. Jesus invites us to be born again into a loving relationship with God, with our brothers and sisters, and even with our "enemies." As Christians, our lives can be governed by God's love and grace instead of law. For Christians there is one law, the grace we are given to love God and neighbor. Christians are called to something far beyond capitalism.

Why is North so selective in the laws he chooses to quote? Why does he not deal with Old and New Testament commands to share with the poor? His solution to poverty in the Third World is to impose Old Testament inheritance laws which are not continued in the New Testament. But he chooses to ignore the redistribution of wealth called for in the Jubilee (Lev 25), a call repeated in the New Testament.[1] North's "solution" to poverty is not only sexist and elitist, but it would not even begin to deal with the causes of poverty. The fourteen families who control El Salvador would continue to be in control, and the Indian peasants who had their land stolen from them would remain landless and poor. It has been more than fifty years since the land was stolen from them, and it is well past time for redistribution of that stolen wealth.

There is a catch in North's view of private property. The less thievery there is, the more the value of private property increases and the less able the poor are to buy it. In capitalism the more "moral" a people are, the more the poor are oppressed. My gain need not be the result of another's loss, but often it is. If the doctor overcharges the poor patient, who must struggle for years to pay the bill, then the doctor did gain at the loss of another. Did not John D. Rockefeller gain at the loss of others he drove out of business?

Do the banana companies not gain from the poor wages paid workers in Central America? There is no free-market economy. There is an international, managed economy in which people are compelled to sell their labor and land at unfair terms.

North shows a lot of concern about theft, but he says nothing of how the rich steal from the poor, how the multinational corporations rip off the people. "Is it not the rich who oppress you?" (Jas 2:6). My impression is that the Bible comes down much harder on the stealing done by the wealthy and the powerful than on the stealing which the poor do to survive.

Most of the stealing (and murder) in the world is legal and is done by those in power. Sometimes it is called a shrewd business practice, profitable investment or overpricing. It takes the form of some persons' receiving huge salaries while others barely survive. A poor person steals ten dollars and goes to jail. A rich person steals a million dollars, a few dollars at a time from the poor, and not only goes free but is praised for being successful. He may even be considered righteous, especially if a small percentage is then given back to the poor in the form of charity.

North seems to be unaware of the theft we commit when we withhold our goods from those who have need. The earth is the Lord's. It is not mine. Capitalism, that is, the system of private property and competition, is itself thievery; and it encourages theft by rewarding only winners and ignoring the needs of the losers. Competition encourages theft. But if I make all I have available to the poor, there is no reason for them to steal from me.

Thievery must be seen not only from the perspective of the property holder and producer, but also from the point of view of the oppressed, the exploited, the downtrodden. From their perspective theft is seen quite differently. It is ironic that our legal system is more concerned about property rights than human needs. We seem to think human worth derives from property instead of from God.

Just as important as the command to not steal is the command to not covet, which is the basis for both stealing and capitalism. Covetousness is the engine of the capitalist economy.

North should read the New Testament more carefully and discover that Jesus does not support defense of property against theft. "From him who takes away your coat do not withhold even your shirt. Give to every one who begs from you; and of him who takes away your goods do not ask them again" (Lk 6:29-30). Was Jesus a false teacher? Jesus also said something about turning the other cheek. To some that also sounds ridiculous. I agree with North that preaching and Christian witness are called for, but vengeance is to be left to God (Rom 12:19-21). True biblical preaching will be seen by those in power more as a threat to their privilege and power than as capital investment or a social asset.

Why is it that conservative Christians seem to have such difficulty with the New Testament? They either ignore it, as North does, or try to explain it away. The Old Testament clearly condemns the idea of a standing army, but most conservatives have little trouble supporting militarism. Why is it so difficult to recognize exploitation and injustice? Why is injustice only seen in socialist countries? It seems that, for many conservatives, if there is any seeming contradiction between the Old and New Testaments, they always go with the Old. This is particularly true on questions of war, violence and economics. If North insists on seeing Christianity as built on biblical law, at least he should include the Sermon on the Mount and the rest of Jesus' teachings. North even ignores the Old Testament prophets and many other important Old Testament laws.

North implies that taxation, at least above ten per cent, is theft. How can a Christian protest the taxes of the welfare state and be silent about the massive amount of taxes taken by the military? Yes, taxation is theft, but is North willing to give up his reliance on capitalistic relationships which cannot survive without police and military violence? Capitalism needs centralization, bureaucracy and taxes to survive. Is North open to a communal life in which all is shared and in which trust in God is the sole defense? Is North willing to give away all that he has, as the early Christians did, to join a church community that is caring for the poor, the unemployed, the mentally ill, the homeless, the alcoholic, the victims of the system?

I agree with most of North's critique of foreign aid. But why can't he see that poverty in the Third World and at home is related to Western exploitation? Yes, food aid is used primarily for political control, not humanitarian concern. And so is military aid, which constitutes the biggest bulk of foreign aid. The answer to needs in the Third World is not aid, but giving people control over their land and lives. The first thing we need to do for the Third World is to get off their backs. North dismisses subsistence agriculture because of periodic famines. But capitalism brings periodic wars and depressions. Maybe the cure has been worse than the disease. The answer is not charity or capitalism, but repentance, justice and the Jubilee.

Yes, there are Communists. And yes, they are as brutal and oppressive as capitalists. But the U.S. determination to "protect" the Third World from Communist domination causes much more pain than it cures. What peasant worker wouldn't rather live under Communism than the chaos of the war in El Salvador? If El Salvador and the whole Third World must go the way of Cuba, so be it. As Christians we are not commissioned to "save the world" with our strength. We are not sovereign. Rather we are called to preach Christ's gospel of repentance and peace, and to trust in God's ability to save the world.

We do not have all the answers for the world. We are not saviors. It troubles me then that North expresses the elitist, if not racist, view that Western values are superior to Third World values, that the Third World is poor because of its ignorance. This is not only arrogant; it is also unbiblical. I wonder why North quotes Bauer's long list of attitudes which are opposed to capitalistic development. He seems unaware of the extent to which Jesus and the biblical prophets stand condemned by that list. I wish North could see the demonic and destructive nature of Western values.

North seems more influenced by humanism (capitalism is a humanist ideology) than he recognizes. Apparently he believes that, as long as we follow certain laws, we can solve any problem, conquer any obstacle and create our own security. We don't need a Savior after all. We can save ourselves by obeying the laws of capitalistic development. North sounds more like a Pharisee than a New Testament Christian.

I am shocked that North would suggest that we go to the Third World and preach "the culture of the West." I thought we were to preach Jesus and him crucified. Or is capitalistic affluence the same as the way of the cross? Apparently, North believes thrift, education, development and responsibility will save. I don't. I believe the biblical vision stands in fundamental opposition to "the culture of the West."

I agree with North that there is little hope in increasing the power and sovereignty of the political state. But as long as the state preserves the ownership and control of resources and production by the few, the state will continue to have to decide between welfare handouts and letting people starve.

North makes a false dichotomy between unity (statism) and diversity (anarchism). In God's kingdom total unity is the communion of the Upper Room as recorded in Acts, a voluntary unity of the Spirit that is free of the law. It is the gift of God's Spirit, available to all who are willing to lay down everything. The answer is to be found in the redeemed and redeeming community of the church, not in the legal structures of the fallen world.

North too easily dismisses those who preach ecological stewardship and social justice as guilt manipulators. How much increased economic output does North think our ecosystem can support? He apparently thinks we can continue to consume, pollute and rape the earth and feel perfectly justified with no need for repentance. The issue is not guilt (although before God we are guilty), but living a redeemed life.

Finally, I am offended by North's sexist perspective and use of exclusively male language. This is hurtful to many of our sisters. North continually refers to men. I wonder if the gospel doesn't apply also to women. In Christ there is neither male nor female (Gal 3:28). A male-oriented view of the world is a big part of the reason for the world's mess.

Notes

[1]John Howard Yoder argues convincingly that Jesus proclaimed the Jubilee. See *The Politics of Jesus* (Grand Rapids, Mich.: Eerdmans, 1972), pp. 64-67. The common treasury and sharing of goods with the needy described in the book of Acts can also be seen as an implementation of the Jubilee.

A Centralist Response

John Gladwin

I would agree with the fundamental assertion in this paper that the debate is about ethical issues. While I find myself puzzled by aspects of this thesis and in profound disagreement with other parts of it, at least it makes the effort to base its discussion in ethical perspectives.

In terms of mood I was not sure whether the paper wanted us to return to the practice of Old Testament social life or to seventeenth-century Puritan ideals embodied in some of the early American experience.

The paper starts by asserting that Christians need to be *methodological covenantalists*. What exactly does this mean? Is this an assertion that God has made a covenant with the United States in like manner to the covenant he made with Israel? That, of course, was the muddle in the original Puritan position in some of its early forms. The crossover point of reference from the Israel of the Old Covenant to the world of the New Covenant is not to be found in the United States, but in the church. Is the paper asking for a new form of life in the church as distinct from the state? Is it sectarian in its understanding, or is it really saying that the principles of the covenant can be applied directly to national economic life as experienced in a body such as the United States?

Without in any sense questioning the personal commitment of the author to Jesus Christ, I am not convinced that the thesis he has presented to us is Christian. It appears to be founded in the religion of a fairly legalistic understanding of the Old Covenant. As Christians, however, we are called to live a new life and are to view the Old Testament in a new way in the light of the redemption experienced in Jesus Christ. The point of the gospel is not to call nations to copy Israel in the Old Covenant. The history of God's action with his people and the experience of the law and life of the nation of Israel lead us to Christ—not to some holy commonwealth instituted in the economic life of a revived, Puritan United States! In thinking about economics, we must learn from the story of Israel and from the principles of the law as we look for the life of the new age dawning on the world in Jesus Christ. Christ leads us forward in history, not backward!

It is for these theological reasons that questions must be asked about the way this thesis is worked out. For example, it moves from an assertion of covenant to an espousal of the values of competition, "employer versus employer," "worker versus worker." Does not the story of creation to the kingdom lead us to question a way of life in which we seek to get the better of one another? Is not cooperation a principle closer to the meaning of the gospel than competition?

Again, the thesis moves from some interesting insights concerning stealing to assertions about the integrity of private property. Yet the Bible views property as held in trust. There are no absolute rights over property in the Bible. "The earth is the LORD's" and given to us in trust. There is no endeavor in the essay to come to terms with the way, in a fallen world, that people and companies acquire property by the abuse of power. The Lord did not distribute the property rights of the United States in perpetuity to their present owners or until such time as they voluntarily decide to sell. Much property and ownership in the world is gained by conquest or by the abuse of people. By what right do people who acquired property through injustice (and the prophets knew all about such debased activity) say that God gave it to them and that no one has the right to forcibly take it away from them?

There is a charming commitment in this paper to natural or providential justice. Unfortunately, in a fallen world much that goes on is unjust. We are called to be vigilant to watch lest the owners of power in society turn to exploit others in their own self-interest. The providence of God does not preserve justice but rather the life of the world in which we are called to witness to the kingdom. The providence of God is gracious, not just. He allows his rain and sun to fall on the just and the unjust alike. At the opposite end of the same argument, the experience of people of poverty and abuse is not a consequence of their incompetence—a sort of natural or providential justice—but the arbitrary experience in which God subjects us to life in a fallen world. The people of God bear witness to their hope in Christ by their commitment to overcome such arbitrariness and so give visible expression to their conviction that the future kingdom will be one in which the present injustices will be overcome in the peace and harmony of the city of God.

Nevertheless, I believe that this thesis is right in asserting that our debate is about ethics. I would add that it is also and relatedly about theology. It is the understanding of Scripture, of God, of the world, of history and of the gospel that I would wish to pursue further in discussion with Gary North. I suspect we have some serious differences in these areas and would have to work hard to find common ground in our shared commitment to Jesus Christ.

II
The Guided-Market System

The Guided-Market System
William E. Diehl

T he scene is the poolside of the exclusive Hotel del Coronado at San Diego. Row after row of reclining lounges are filled with people soaking up the bright sun. Young men and women in gay red and white uniforms are busily delivering luncheon orders to their customers—petite sirloin steaks, Nova Scotia salmon, curried lamb or Dungeness crab legs. Nor far away, in a small pavilion, a group of middle-aged couples are gathered around a piano bar singing some of their old favorites from the 1940s. The bartender is busily mixing sangria with fruit in huge, chilled ceramic pitchers. A number of the loungers, listening to music on their own stereo headsets, are oblivious to everything around them. The air is filled with exotic scents as one by one they cover their bodies with expensive suntan oils. The scene can be duplicated from San Diego to Seattle, from Boothbay to Mobile Bay, from Palm Springs to Palm Beach.

Woe to those who lie on beds of ivory, and stretch themselves upon their couches, and eat lambs from the flock, and calves

from the midst of the stall; who sing idle songs to the sound of
the harp, and like David invent for themselves instruments of
music; who drink wine in bowls and anoint themselves with
the finest oils. (Amos 6:4-6)

If one divides the population of the world into thirds, it turns out
that the richest third get eighty per cent of the world's total gross
national product. North Americans consume more than twice as
much energy per person as western Europeans and 350 times as
much as the average Ethiopian. Because of a high diet of grain-fed
cattle, Americans consume 5 times as much grain per person as do
people in developing nations. The living standard of an average
American is far beyond the wildest dream of sixty per cent of the
people of this earth. "It is easier for a camel to go through the eye of
a needle than for a rich man to enter the kingdom of God" (Lk 18:25).

In the eyes of the world, the United States symbolizes a land of
great wealth, tremendous power, unbridled hedonism and profli-
gate consumption. It is also seen as a nation with strong Judeo-
Christian roots. In many ways the wealth of Americans can be challenged by the very Scriptures they hold sacred. Those who are em-
barrassed by the huge disparity between the haves and the have-
nots in this world can point to many places in the Old and New
Testaments where Holy Scriptures come down hard on the wealthy.
These people maintain, in fact, that the political and economic system of the United States is contrary to the will of God.

On the other hand, many Americans, using the same Bible as their
critics, can point to evidence that supports their belief that the
strength and prosperity of the United States is proof positive that
God rewards those who are faithful to his Word. They cite many Old
Testament verses to support this conviction, such as Deuteronomy
7:12-14:

If you listen to these laws and are careful to observe them, then
the LORD your God will observe the sworn covenant he made with
your forefathers and will keep faith with you. He will love you,
bless you and cause you to increase. He will bless the fruit of
your body and the fruit of your land, your corn and new wine
and oil, the offspring of your herds, and of your lambing flocks,
in the land which he swore to your forefathers to give you. You
shall be blessed above every other nation. (NEB)

While it is more difficult to find New Testament support for the notion that riches are the reward for faithfulness to God, many Christians do point to certain of Jesus' sayings. For example, in Mark 4:25 Jesus concludes the parable of the sower by saying, "For the man who has will be given more, and the man who has not will forfeit even what he has" (NEB).

With such texts to support their views, many Americans sincerely believe that the political and economic system which made this nation the wealthiest in the world is a system blessed by God.

Which way is it? Is our American structure of political, economic and social systems in accordance with God's will, or is it not?

The fact that our Scriptures can be used to support or condemn any economic philosophy suggests that the Bible is not intended to lay out an economic plan which will apply for all times and places. If we are to examine economic structures in the light of Christian teachings, we will have to do it in another way.

Are there certain principles which consistently carry through both the Old and New Testaments? If so, can we apply these basics as a way of evaluating economic structures? I believe we can. It seems to me that the principles of freedom, justice and responsibility can be found in the Bible from beginning to end, and that these themes are generally understood by all Christians in the same light. Let us look at each one briefly.

Freedom
In various ways God has been forever leading his children out of captivity into freedom. The Exodus event stands as a prime example in the Old Testament. Not only was God concerned about releasing his people from political captivity, but the vision of the Jubilee year as found in Leviticus 25:8-55 speaks of a freedom from economic and social captivity. The New Testament is filled with the good news that God does not want his children to be enslaved by a legalistic burden of the law. Jesus was constantly teaching the difference between the freedom of carrying out the spirit of God's laws and the slavery of trying to carry out the letter of these laws.

The apostle Paul writes frequently about the freedom which the gospel brings. When he wrote in Romans 3:28, "A person is put right with God only through faith" (TEV), Paul set forth a central doctrine of the Christian church. There is no way that we humans can earn God's acceptance of us. We constantly fall short of perfection. But God's acceptance of us is a free gift of love, totally without our merit.

Martin Luther told of his struggle to feel worthy of God's acceptance. He wrote, "My situation was that, although an impeccable monk, I stood before God as a sinner troubled in conscience and I had no confidence that my merit would assuage him." In the midst of his agonizing over his merit before God, the word *only* in Romans 3:28 suddenly pierced his mind with a stunning and liberating revelation. In that moment he realized that it was *only* through God's grace that he was put right with his Creator, not through anything he did. "Thereupon I felt myself to be reborn and to have gone through the open doors of paradise," Luther wrote. He later referred to this liberating verse in Romans as his "gate to heaven."

This good news is what Jesus was referring to when he said, "You will know the truth and the truth will set you free" (Jn 8:32). Not only does our Creator want us to be free from all forms of physical, economic and social domination by others, but he gives us a most liberating assurance that we are his without respect to what we do or how well we do it.

Justice

A second theme which runs throughout our Scriptures is God's call for justice. Not only would God have us be just in our treatment of one another, but he calls us to create political and social systems in which people are justly treated.

The prophet Micah is speaking of a code of individual behavior when he says,

God has told you what is good;
> and what is it that the LORD asks of you?
> Only to act justly, to love loyalty,
> to walk wisely before your God. (Mic 6:8 NEB)

The prophet Amos, on the other hand, is calling for justice in the nation when he demands, "Let justice roll on like a river and righteousness like an ever-flowing stream" (Amos 5:24 NEB).

Jesus also dealt with individual and corporate justice. His parables were full of examples of just and unjust people. But he also condemned the systemic injustice of his day. Addressing the lawyers and Pharisees, Jesus scolds, "You pay tithes of mint and dill and cummin; but you have overlooked the weightier demands of the Law, justice, mercy, and good faith" (Mt 23:23 NEB).

What are the biblical dimensions of justice? To care for the poor, the hungry, the sick, the lame, the orphans, the widow, the prisoner, the stranger and the children. How is justice distributed? By meeting people's immediate needs through charity and by ultimately eliminating the need for charity.

Responsibility

The third biblical theme which can be used to measure economic systems involves responsibility. In the Genesis story of creation God entrusts to man all the plants, fruit trees, animals, birds and reptiles and asks him to be fruitful. Throughout the Bible we are reminded that God is the owner of all creation; men and women are merely the stewards or managers. "The earth is the LORD's and all that is in it, the world and those who dwell therein" (Ps 24:1 NEB).

From Cain's initial rebuttal to God, "Am I my brother's keeper?" the Bible is filled with stories of God's people reluctant to assume responsibility—Moses, Gideon, Isaiah, Jonah and many others. Yet God persists in his call to responsibility.

The New Testament use of the word *steward* has provided contemporary Christianity with an understanding of our responsibility before God. We are to use the talents God has given us to care for his creation, to liberate his creatures and to provide justice in the land.

Freedom, justice and responsibility—by these three imperatives we will look at the guided-market system.

Guided-Market System

The term *guided-market system* can be defined in a number of ways, but for the purpose of this essay we will deal with a specific example, that of the United States in the 1980s.

Our economic system is built on several principles. The first is that there is private ownership of the means of production—a capitalistic system, if you will. Second, there is the principle that, given its freedom, the competitive market will decide what products are to be made (or what services are to be offered), how they will be produced (or offered), and who will get the benefit of the products (or services). This concept is called the market system, or free enterprise. The third element of the U.S. economic system is that it does not have unbridled freedom. It is subjected to some controls and limits. The controls are provided mostly by government which, in our case, is a democratic system. The citizens of our country, acting through the democratic process of government, determine the degree to which the capitalistic, free-enterprise market system will be "guided."

It must be recognized that none of the concepts referred to exist in an absolutely pure form in the United States. Not all means of production and services are privately owned. We do have public ownership of certain power plants, transportation systems, educational institutions and the like. Quasi-governmental units operate our turnpikes, bridges and ports. Not all our markets operate with complete freedom and, as a consequence, government does make some decisions on the "what, how and for whom" of certain markets. Efforts of the Carter and Reagan administrations to deregulate such industries as the airlines, trucking and natural gas are examples of a shift away from the government's making market decisions toward letting natural market forces decide on "what, how and for whom." Finally, we acknowledge that we do not have a pure democracy. Our citizens elect representatives who, presumably, act as their agents, but not always so. Nevertheless, the term *democratic, capitalistic free enterprise* is the closest one can come in defining the economic system of the United States.

One of the aspects of a debate between advocates of a relatively uncontrolled economic system and those favoring a rather tightly controlled economic structure involves a balance between freedom and justice. At one end of the range, a totally unbridled free-enterprise system does permit the powerful to exploit the powerless. (For many years the American economy supported the institution of slavery and, in later years, child labor. Justice suffered.) At the other end of the range, a tightly controlled system directs who will produce what for whom—and freedom suffers.

Various forms of democratic capitalism have been around for years, and its critics have been vocal about its shortcomings on justice. It was argued that if society owned the means of production and if market decisions were made through the democratic process, there would be more justice with little loss of freedom. In a way it was a most unfair comparison, for the theoretical benefits of an untested system were being compared to the actual performance of a functioning one. But we now have about thirty years of experience with democratic socialistic economies, and we are now in a position to compare apples and apples.

It is my position that democratic capitalism as practiced in the United States not only offers the greatest potential for freedom, justice and responsibility but, in fact, already comes closer to maximizing all three biblical principles than any other operating system. Before presenting the supporting evidence for this statement, however, we need to define how freedom, justice and responsibility play out in an economic system.

People should be free to make their own choices, in terms of both what they put into the economic system and what they take out of it. All people should be free to develop their full potential as creatures of God. They should not be coerced directly or indirectly into doing that which they really do not want to do. They should have a free political structure in which they can decide the extent to which they wish to have their government curb their freedom.

For there to be justice in an economic system, there must be a concern for the welfare of all citizens. In an economy in which everyone is free to compete, it is not fair that some are burdened by handicaps not of their own making. Adjustments must be made for those with physical handicaps to have equal opportunity to compete in the economic system. Factors such as sex, race, religion or ethnic background can become barriers against free access to the economy, and must be guarded against. There also should be no exploitation of the young or old. All people should have access to quality education. The principle of justice demands that past inequities must not be passed along to innocent children; a child born into an environment incapable of nurturing its full potential must be helped to escape the shackles of institutionalized poverty. Those capable of working should have the opportunity of doing so.

Responsibility in the economic system demands that the concerns for freedom and justice be combined to produce optimum benefit to God's creatures and his creation. Where justice has been lacking, society must provide charity to meet basic needs of nutrition, shelter, health care, education and income. But charity can never be an acceptable substitute for justice. Responsible Christians must always be working toward the establishment of an economic system which minimizes the need for charity. A long-term dependency on charity can rob humans of self-respect, stifle the development of human potential and condemn people to be forever captives of the welfare system. Responsibility within a relatively free economic system requires that Christians exercise their own controls with respect to lifestyle and the stewardship of creation. We *are* free to reject hedonism, to limit our consumption and to challenge materialism. We *are* free to follow a modest lifestyle in which we accept for ourselves only what we really need to sustain our well-being and dignity; and in so doing we encourage others to follow.

The American Experience
As one looks back over the past fifty years of American economic history, a good case can be made that our democratic capitalistic system has done pretty well for us. Prior to the era of Franklin Roosevelt, our American economic philosophy had a heavy bias toward laissez faire. There was a romantic idealism that anyone who worked hard enough could succeed. Little attention was given to the handicaps which society had placed on Blacks, women and the disadvantaged. But the trauma of the Great Depression forced a change in which government began to assume a much more active role in dealing with economic and social life.

As America came out of the Second World War, it entered a period of thirty years of remarkable economic growth. But at the same time the nation was working hard at eliminating the injustices in the system. Although change did not come without pain, advances were made in reducing discrimination, reducing poverty and providing better education and health care for the underclass. At the same time, more programs appeared which were of direct social benefit to middle-class America. Increased government intervention in these areas involved larger public expenditures of money and, of course, increased taxes. Tax revenues increased with little effort since, as inflation pushed them into higher tax brackets, individuals' tax burdens inevitably became heavier. In addition to directing public funds into welfare programs, government intervention in the economic system took other forms. The private sector was subjected to a broad range of controls and directives as government dealt with environmental concerns, equal employment opportunity, occupational safety and health, consumer protection, private pension plans and the like. The dials had clearly been turned toward justice issues at the expense of a degree of freedom among the private sector.

Nevertheless, as the United States observed its two-hundreth birthday and took stock of itself, there was reason for a degree of celebration. Individual freedoms within the economic system were about the best in the world, and even private-sector organizations could not point to many other nations which offered greater freedom to businesses. While certain other welfare countries were doing better in such important areas as full employment, longevity and infant mortality, the United States was close to the top. Although there were still large numbers of people who fell below the defined poverty level, the rather robust American economy was helping all the boats to rise. Certainly the nation still had a long way to go in ensuring justice for all citizens; but, all in all, the factors of freedom, justice and responsibility within the economic structure were in better harmony here than anywhere else in the world.

Of greater concern to the nation were problems in the areas of world affairs and domestic politics. The Vietnam War and Watergate were wrenching events in American history, but the nation did survive.

Economic problems began to appear, however, in the mid-1970s and continued to grow. After decades of inflation rates less than five per cent, in a relatively short time they moved up to double-digit levels. At the same time, economic growth and productivity flattened out. Within the world markets many American products were no longer competitive. A gradual shift in the structural make-up of our economy began as industrial jobs declined and service jobs increased. Once-powerful U.S. automotive, steel and basic metal industries reeled and began contracting under the heavy pressure of foreign competition. On top of it all, energy costs soared as oil-producing nations finally were able to secure a more realistic price for their resources.

It is important to note how quickly the free market responded to these developments. Nonprofitable manufacturing plants closed and significant efforts were made to improve productivity. The energy crunch caused a dramatic change in the type of cars Americans wanted to buy. Smaller foreign cars became popular for all, and Detroit launched crash programs to produce similar types. In contrast to the rapid response of free-market economies to the energy situation, the planned economies, especially those in the Soviet bloc, were slow to adjust. For a number of years, the U.S.S.R. shielded its satellite nations from the impact of the situation by selling oil from Soviet wells at pre-OPEC prices. When a correction finally was made and Soviet subsidies were discontinued, the impact was more severe than in the free-market industrial nations, which had actually been more dependent on Middle Eastern oil.

In analyzing the American economic situation of the early 1980s, many economists concluded that the inflationary spiral really was triggered by President Lyndon Johnson's effort to have a "guns and butter" program during the Vietnam War years. High government expenditures for military purposes and for expanding Great Society programs demanded more from our economic system than it could deliver, goes the theory, and as a result inflation took off.

Presidents Nixon, Ford and Carter tried various ways to control inflation and rejuvenate the sputtering economy. President Nixon the titular leader of a political party which has opposed government interference in the market system, surprised everyone by invoking wage and price controls in an effort to dampen inflation. Although it appeared to be working for a while, shortages and abnormalities began to occur in the marketplace, and when controls were finally lifted in 1974, inflation roared onward.

Again it is important to note the flexibility of the American system of democratic capitalism. In an effort to correct some problems in the market system, government moved in with economic controls. When the market did not respond as hoped for, government withdrew the controls. Americans seem to be aware of the dangers of the extremes of an unbridled free-market system on one hand and of a totally planned and controlled economy on the other. They are perfectly willing to live with a blend of public- and private-sector responses to economic problems.

In 1980, Ronald Reagan campaigned for president on the economic philosophy that too much government spending had overloaded the resources of our capitalistic system to the point where growth had been stunted. Reagan's strategy was to reduce the share of gross national product which represented government spending and to make it available to the private sector for plant modernization and new investment. *Supply-side economics,* it was called. By stimulating economic growth, all citizens would benefit, he promised.

Whether the election of 1980 represented an endorsement of the Reagan philosophy or a repudiation of the Carter policies is still being debated. But Reagan won and immediately set into motion plans which would "get big government off the people's backs" and stimulate the economy. Cuts were made in the rate of increases in spending on social programs (justice issues), and some programs which directly affected the poor and disadvantaged were severly cut or eliminated. Liberals were aghast at the seeming callousness of the Reagan administration toward the needs of disadvantaged citizens. The president defended his approach with two arguments. First, he assured the American people that supply-side economics would get America moving again and that "a rising tide lifts all the boats," by which he meant that poor people would benefit from an improved economy as well as the rich. His opponents labeled this philosophy "trickle-down economics." Second, President Reagan called for private enterprise and America's long-standing system of volunteerism to play a more active role in helping meet some of the social needs of the nation. To this his opponents claimed that he was thinking only in terms of charity and not justice.

The Reagan call for the private sector to become more involved in social needs opened wide a debate which had been going on for decades. Fifty years ago corporate leaders were convinced that their sole responsibility was for the welfare of their shareholders through the maximization of profit. Corporate leaders themselves were free to give to charity, but they scorned suggestions that their companies should divert any assets for public good. Over the years that position has been changing. Today some corporate executives feel that private-sector organizations, like individuals, have a responsibility to contribute to the welfare of society. A more self-

serving stance is taken by other leaders in the private sector who
point out that the free-enterprise system itself is threatened in a
society where the social needs of citizens go unattended. And
there still remain a substantial number of corporate executives who
are convinced that their contributions to society lie in operating
an enterprise which is profitable and thereby provides benefits to
shareholders, work to employees and a viable economy for society.

Again we have a demonstration of the flexibility of the guided-
market system as practiced in the United States. President Reagan
caused all Americans to examine the extent to which the public
and the private sectors should contribute to the welfare of the nation. Is it true that excessive spending by government throttles a
nation's economy? If so, how much is too much? To what extent do
government regulations on business in the area of environmental
concerns, safety and health, consumer protection and the like
contribute to a drag on the economy? What are the responsibilities
of the private sector with regard to contributing to the common
good of a society? How can we be certain that the needs of all types
of citizens will be met unless government assumes that role? These
are the types of questions which President Reagan caused to be
raised. It again demonstrated the ability of the American system to
deal with issues of freedom, justice and responsibility.

There is another side to the issue of who is to provide welfare
services, one which is not directly related to the impact of these
services on the nation's economy. It is the matter of the effect and
means of delivering such services. One of the criticisms of elements of the American welfare programs is that they have created
a dependency among the people who were to have been helped.
The eligibility requirements for some programs were such that
people found it better for their own self-interest to become completely dependent on the system rather than to be only partially so.
For example, low-income working poor who do not have sufficient
personal financial resources to afford legal services or secure certain health assistance, but who at the same time earn too much to be
eligible for government programs which provide these services,
often find that it is to their advantage to stop working altogether
and go on full welfare. Moreover, dedicated social workers frequently become frustrated and disillusioned as they find themselves spending more time filling out reports, verifying eligibility

and writing funding proposals than in seeing the people who need their help. They find themselves serving some program rather than serving people. The reality of ineffective and inefficient delivery of welfare services also raises questions as to whether other methods might better serve the cause of justice.

Other nations have looked at these same questions and have approached them in different ways. We need now to look at a few of the methods by which other democratic capitalistic nations handle the issues of freedom, justice and responsibility.

Some Other Approaches
The two nations which come to mind whenever one talks about issues of welfare and national productivity are Sweden and Japan.

Although over ninety per cent of all industry in Sweden is privately held, government involvement in all aspects of that nation's economy is so pervasive that some people would question whether it could be classified as a democratic capitalistic system. Not only does government provide generous welfare benefits to individuals, but in recent years subsidies as high as ten per cent of costs have gone to Sweden's aging industries in order to keep them competitive in world markets.

Of all nations, Sweden is most commonly recognized as the paragon of the welfare state. Among the principal features of its welfare system are a national health insurance, a pension system, free prenatal care and child delivery, annual allowance to the mother until the child reaches the age of sixteen, free tuition at Swedish universities, home-furnishing loans for newly-weds and rent subsidies for large families. Under a national policy of full employment, the state operates a job service, moves unemployed persons to areas where work is available and offers retraining to those who lose jobs through automation or disability. As a result of all of these services, Sweden has been able to keep unemployment very low and has boasted of the longest life expectancy and lowest rate of infant mortality of any nation in the world.

In recent years, however, much has been written about Sweden's having exceeded the capacity of its economic system to support its extensive welfare structure. Back in the 1950s and 1960s, Sweden's public expenditures amounted to from 30 to 40 per cent of the gross national product (GNP), and the economy was purring along in good shape. However, by 1980 public expenditures had increased to about 65 per cent of GNP, and the economy was in trouble. (I must hasten to point out that in the early 1980s almost *all* world economies were in trouble.) Economists differ widely in their opinions as to how much of Sweden's economic distress can be blamed on its high allocation of GNP to government spending.

What is fairly clear, however, is the effect which high government spending has had on the incentives of individuals and corporations. Marginal tax rates for the average worker have moved to 60 per cent, and when reduced transfer payments for above-average incomes are considered, the marginal rate approximates 80 per cent. The effect of such a staggering tax rate is to remove any incentive for overtime and to increase absenteeism. Why work overtime if 80 per cent of what I earn goes to the government? Why not stay home today? I'll only lose 20 per cent of a day's pay anyway. According to a survey made by the Swedish Metal Trades Employers Association, the average Swedish production worker worked only twenty-four hours per week in 1979.[1] Obviously such low productivity has hurt Sweden's ability to be competitive in world markets.

Moreover, there is little incentive to change jobs. Assar Lindbeck, professor of international economics at the University of Stockholm, writes, "The after-tax compensation for shifting to a new and higher paid job (before tax) would often seem too small to make a shift worthwhile. This effect has been accentuated by new legislation on job security, which makes the hiring of employees a very heavy investment for firms. Moreover, individual employees lose substantial capital assets in the form of 'seniority rights' when they shift from one job to another; the seniority rights system functions in fact like a tax on labor mobility."[2]

Might we conclude from all this that there comes a time in the functioning of an economic system when high government spending and the tax burden which follows reduce the likelihood that maximum human potential will be developed and, in fact, penalize the exercise of free choice of occupational shifts?

Lindbeck points to another consequence which to him is even more disturbing. In the present situation people resort to all kinds of means to reduce or evade paying high taxes—including dishonesty. He states, "In some business sectors that sell services to households, tax cheating seems at present to influence output prices so much that honest entrepreneurs have to decide either to quit or become dishonest themselves."[3] Since Lindbeck feels that honesty is a "collective good," he is disturbed that the system is destroying it.

In the early 1980s Japan stood out as the paragon of industrial productivity. For almost thirty years, following World War 2, Japan sustained a rate of economic growth which surpassed all other major nations. With some exceptions, notably the Japanese National Railroad, much of the country's industry is privately owned. The railroad has turned out to be an economic disaster of inefficiency, but the private-sector organizations have had dazzling success. Industrialists from all over the world have flocked to Japan to learn the secrets of high productivity and labor harmony.

Japan is still in an embryonic condition as a welfare state. Only about 15 per cent of its gross national product goes into government spending. With its high populational density and its rapid growth as an industrial nation, Japan faces tremendous social and ecological problems. Yet, surprisingly, Japan compares favorably with Sweden on certain key indicators of quality of life. Like Sweden, Japan has virtually no unemployment, running under 3 per cent for many years. But, unlike Sweden, which relies on government for maintaining full employment, Japan has developed an interesting cultural pattern in which many employers are expected to keep their workers on the payroll for a lifetime career, if that is the wish of the employee. This has been possible due to an aggressive marketing of Japanese products throughout the world. Working closely with government (through the Ministry of International Trade and Industry), Japanese producers have been able to take up any slack in their domestic economy by pushing exports.

But in another (and interesting) way Sweden and Japan need to be compared. The World Health Organization (WHO) frequently uses two criteria for measuring the performance of nations in the area of welfare: mean life expectancy and infant mortality. According to WHO data, in the period from 1960 to 1979 Sweden was able to increase its mean life expectancy from 73.5 years to 75.6 years. In that same period of time Japan's mean life expectancy went from 67.9 years to 76.2 years—actually surpassing Sweden. (Life expectancy in the United States in 1979 was 73 years.) From 1960 to 1979, Sweden was able to reduce its infant mortality rate from 16.6 deaths per 1,000 births to 7.5. In that same time Japan's rate dropped from 33.8 deaths per 1,000 births to 8.0—almost the equal of Sweden. (In comparison, the United States' rate in 1979 was 15.2.)

Japan's remarkable achievement was not accomplished through a massive public welfare program, a reality that Swedish citizens find hard to grasp. Japan has developed instead a family-centered, private welfare system.

Sven Rydenfelt, professor of economics at the University of Lund in Sweden, explains, "In Japan people obviously have been able successfully to adapt to life conditions in a state with little public welfare. They save extensively during their active years and then they are able to enjoy the good life even in old age. Whenever required, their children and relatives are prepared to support them." He continues, "In Japanese families, mothers as a rule leave the labor force and remain at home as soon as the first baby is born. Most of them stay at home for the rest of their lives. When the children have grown up and left home, the mothers very often take care of aged parents. In industry and trade, the human relationships between employers and employees are much better than in Sweden."[4]

Rydenfelt is critical of what he calls "hired love" in Sweden. He points to the irony that while many advocates of social welfare are critical of the evils of commercialism in the capitalistic free-enterprise system, the welfare state, in fact, commercializes love. He writes, "In spite of the official repudiation of street prostitution and 'hired love,' the welfare state is fundamentally based on the dogma that in child care, education, sick care and old age care, commercially 'hired love' is as good as love given and taken without payment between persons with intimate human relations."[5]

Nations and cultures are different. It is doubtful whether American citizens would ever agree to the extent of government involvement in social and economic matters found in Sweden. It is equally doubtful whether Americans could replicate the family-centered, private welfare system of Japan or to work under the paternalistic employer-employee relationship which exists there. What needs to be seen in these examples, however, is that all societies have a responsibility to care for the young, sick, handicapped, unemployed and aged, and that the means of providing such welfare can vary. Perhaps we need to be more innovative in finding ways to care for the disadvantaged and to help them become as self-sufficient as they possibly can. In any event we in America need to understand that we are responsible for those who cannot care for themselves and that our responsibility does involve some cost, whether in the form of taxes for public welfare or in personal involvement for private welfare.

Looking briefly at those nations which are closer to the classic definitions of socialism and communism, I find it difficult to see any evidence that the controlled societies, including totalitarian capitalistic countries, are doing a better job of providing freedom and justice within their economic systems than are the democratic capitalistic nations. Without exception, life expectancy is lower and infant mortality higher among these countries. Stories abound about the surprising harvests which result when the controlled societies permit citizens to keep the output of their own little plots of land. Private enterprise works.

China is experimenting with "economic zones" in which capitalism is being given a chance to prove its usefulness for the development of that Communist nation. Even with untrained labor the results are impressive, so much so that the zones will soon be physically cut off from the rest of the country, with guards patrolling their perimeters.

Because the controlled societies are less able to adjust to fast-changing world economic conditions than are the free-market societies, they are especially vulnerable to injury. The very concept of central planning discourages risk taking at all levels, and to suggest innovation is to question the wisdom of one's leadership. Of all the Soviet-bloc nations, Hungary is best weathering the worldwide economic slump. Hungary is the only Soviet-bloc nation in which central planning serves only as a guide, with local managers and leaders having the flexibility to respond to economic developments as they see fit. Then, too, Hungary does have a private sector and has built free-enterprise-type rewards into its state-controlled organization.

The Role of the Christian
There is no economic system which is inherently Christian in na-

ture. While the theory of a socialistic system may seem to have higher ideals than the self-interest motivations of the capitalistic philosophy, the history of the past thirty years raises serious questions about the attainability or desirability of the socialistic ideal. All systems fall short of expectations; they frequently defy the best efforts of good people who try to make them work.

If one agrees that the biblical principles of freedom, justice and responsibility are central elements of Christian life, then it does seem that the guided-market system, or the democratic-capitalistic system as we more commonly call it, offers the greatest potential for maximizing these virtues. However, the system will not deliver the qualities of freedom and justice by itself. Responsibility is needed, and that is where Christians enter the picture.

The comments which follow suggest things Christians should be doing in the 1980s in the United States to ensure freedom and justice for all. They may not be applicable to all guided-market systems in the 1980s since, as we have seen, these systems differ significantly. But they do apply here and now.

With respect to the issue of justice, Christians must speak out loudly and strongly. In particular, the word *welfare* has assumed negative connotations in this country. The word conjures up in the minds of many citizens a freeloading, shiftless, dishonest individual who is living off the taxes of others. Such is not the case. A major segment of our welfare clients consist of elderly women who are widowed and who are without any outside source of income. Christians need to set the record straight on just who exactly does benefit from welfare.

But there is a second problem connected with a disparagement of that word, and it has to do with our theology. As Christians, we believe that God accepts us without reservations. His love is for us without any merit of our own. God does not love the successful businessman more than the unemployed Black youth. Whatever is in store for us in eternity will not be based on whether or not we "deserved" it. Therefore, it is a denial of the gospel to proclaim that anyone does not "deserve" our help, and it is a scandal to project such thinking on disadvantaged people. It is bad enough to be poor; why should others say you are worthless? Welfare is *not* a dirty word, and Christians should speak out whenever that word is used demeaningly.

With whom do we work to ensure that we have a just society—individuals, private-sector organizations or government? The answer is, all three. All segments of society must contribute to the quality of life.

Our recent experience with the programs of the Great Society indicate that government may not always be the best provider of welfare services, even if it does supply the funds. It may be possible that in certain areas private-sector organizations can do a better job. Perhaps the next step in America's search for justice for all is to experiment more with direct subsidies or vouchers for people who need help. The concept of a negative income tax should be tried. Families below poverty-income levels would receive direct grants, depending on the size of the family and its actual income level. Such a family would then be free to make its own purchases of food, shelter, health services and the like. The private sector would be the providers, just as it now is for middle- and upper-class families. A modified approach to the negative income tax would be the issuing of vouchers for such specific items as food, shelter, health services and day care. The voucher system is more restrictive than the negative income tax since it deals with only specific areas of need. But, in either form, the private sector would be the provider of services. With many firms competing for the business, a more efficient use of federal money could be expected than that which we have experienced with a ponderous, bureaucratic system.

Instead of government agencies' training the unemployed or hard-to-train citizens, incentives, vouchers or subsidies should be offered to the private sector to do the job. Since the private sector is already in the business of training America's work force, why turn to government to train the unemployed?

If we as Christians respect freedom, we should be careful not to create dependency relationships among the poor. Every effort must be made to break dependency and to develop human potential and self-respect. We should carefully consider the implications of across-the-board welfare programs which apply to everyone. Will they tend to reduce initiative and freeze personal growth, as appears to be the case in Sweden? Should we not rather concentrate most of our programs on the severely disadvantaged underclass of some three million family units in which only one parent is present?

While we may place high importance on freedom, we cannot condone unbridled freedom which harms others. As Christians we expect law and order to prevail. Where it is reasonable to expect the private sector to contribute to society voluntarily, we should encourage that to happen. But we should not be so naive as to expect some economic organizations to commit scarce assets to social good when their competitors do not. Laws governing pollution control, waste disposal, occupational safety, product liability and the like are necessary to ensure that all the economic actors comply. Can we expect the private sector to erase sex discrimination voluntarily, or will some form of an Equal Rights Amendment ultimately have to be passed?

Christians have the responsibility to work hard on the issues of freedom and justice. Our problems are complex; the answers will not come easily. But we must be faithful to the call.

Lifestyle of Enough

There is yet another area in which Christians have an important responsibility. It has to do with lifestyle.

We have reason to be concerned about the wide gap between the haves and the have-nots in the world. In 1976 the per capita income in the United States was $7,933; in Bangladesh it was $123. Even within our own country there are vast differences in income levels between the top and bottom tenths of our population.

With large segments of the world's population having inadequate food and with millions of God's people being condemned to a life of perpetual poverty, why is it that Christians in America seem almost indifferent to these imparities? Is it because we look at problems with a cause-and-effect type of thinking? Do we think that, since we are not the cause of mass starvation in Africa and since we can do little as individuals to eliminate it, we are really unable to deal with the problem? Yes, we are concerned about people starving in other countries, but we know only too well that by refusing a second portion of food at a meal we are not going to add one bit to the available food supply in Bangladesh. We cannot see how our decisions to buy a large home or a more modest one has anything to do with the need for better housing in the South Bronx. The needs of the poor are so vast and our discretionary resources so small that we feel we are unable to make any difference. Our problem is that we are indeed looking at our living habits on a cause-and-effect basis.

Christians need to live a theology of enough, for it has no direct bearing on cause-and-effect relationships.

One of the earliest biblical references to a theology of enough is found in Exodus 16. This is the account of how God gave manna to the Israelites in the wilderness. Each person was instructed to gather as much manna as was needed for that day. Moses instructed the people not to gather any manna for the next day, since God would provide for each day. But some disobeyed and gathered more than they needed, planning to keep an extra share for the next day. On the next day, they discovered that this manna had bred worms and become foul. They had taken more than they needed.

One of the Old Testament wisdom writings says this:

Remove far from me falsehood and lying;
  give me neither poverty nor riches;
  feed me with the food that is needful for me,
lest I be full, and deny thee,
  and say, "Who is the LORD?"
or lest I be poor, and steal,
  and profane the name of my God. (Prov 30:8-9)

There are a number of Old Testament instructions on not collecting interest on money that is loaned to someone else (see Ex 22:25). Why? If we have money enough to lend to someone else, then we already have enough. Why should we extract interest from another who does not have enough?

Leviticus 25 contains many admonitions related to the philosophy of enough. Just as six days were enough to work and the seventh was a Sabbath, so also every seventh year the land was to be allowed to rest.

Paul expresses his thoughts on "enough" in a letter to the church at Corinth. He writes,

Provided there is an eager desire to give, God accepts what a man has; he does not ask for what he has not. There is no question of relieving others at the cost of hardship to yourselves; it is a question of equality. At the moment your surplus meets their need, but one day your need may be met from their surplus. The aim is equality; as Scripture has it, "The man who got much had no more than enough, and the man who got little did not go short." (2 Cor 8:12-15 NEB)

If we are to follow a theology of enough, it will mean that in whatever capacity we serve, our lifestyle will be a modest one. This does not mean that Christians who are bankers will walk around in worn-out blue jeans, that physicians will have antiquated equipment in their examining rooms, that homemakers will do laundry on scrubbing boards, or that lawyers will use orange crates for desks. In order to serve God in our roles in society we do need adequate tools to be effective. The banker must dress well enough to secure customer confidence, but that does not mean a wardrobe of fifteen hand-tailored suits and nine pairs of shoes. The physician must keep his or her office and equipment up-to-date enough to assure that patients will have adequate treatment. But that does not mean a large, fully carpeted suite of rooms with expensive furniture and redundant equipment. In order to assure that time can be spent with family, the homemaker will have enough labor-saving equipment to handle household chores efficiently. But that does not mean top-of-the-line appliances with elaborate controls and capabilities which really are not needed. Lawyers do need adequate desks, chairs and office equipment to carry out their work. But that does not mean that major law firms need huge, oak-paneled rooms with antique furniture, rare art, expensive desks and elegant private bathrooms with showers. By living modestly, as a banker, physician, homemaker or lawyer, as an electrician, assembler, bus driver or waitress, we will be demonstrating how Christians can live a theology of enough.

Such an approach to lifestyle may seem hopelessly idealistic. It certainly is fraught with all kinds of traps for Christians. How much is enough? Can we really measure the degree to which we need resources? Won't there always be the temptation to rationalize the acceptance of more than we need?

It probably would not be possible to achieve a lifestyle of enough if we try to do it alone. But we are not alone. Christians live in communities, and it is within our communities of faith that we can find help and support in trying to establish a lifestyle of enough. Within Christian congregations or small support groups we are now able to secure honest opinions and friendly counseling from our brothers and sisters on matters of the faith, family problems and ethical issues of life. Why cannot such communities of faith also help its members to be honest with themselves as they seek to develop a lifestyle of enough?

In this age of hedonism, crass materialism and excessive consumption, Christians can make a theological statement that, as God's stewards, we are to use for ourselves only what is necessary. We will conserve resources whenever possible and care for the environment around us. We will be modest in the selection of the homes we live in, the cars we drive, the clothes we wear and the food we eat. Of course, we can enjoy good restaurants, good music, the arts, travel and vacation. But for all these things, moderation and modesty should prevail. We live this style not because others have less than we do, but because as stewards of God's creation we should take only what we need.

By living the lifestyle of enough, we are making a witness to our own faith and challenging the value system of a hedonistic society. One who is constantly living at the low end of the range of his or her associates is constantly challenging their lifestyle. If we can operate in our calling effectively, living well below the average of our peers, then it would seem that the average is too high. Christians need constantly to challenge the conventional thinking and values of a hedonistic and excessively materialistic culture.

As a by-product to living a lifestyle of enough, we may well discover that we do have extra money to direct into causes which will help the disadvantaged of the world. If so, we can give thanks for that, too. But even if somehow, someday, all humans on this earth would have adequate food, shelter and health care, Christians would still need to follow a lifestyle of enough. It is the real-life demonstration of the meaning of Christian stewardship.

Conclusion

No one economic system has been ordained by God. While the Bible does challenge the economic misbehavior of individuals in areas such as stealing, cheating, exploitation of others, miserliness, the worship of wealth, indifference to the poor and lack of compassion, there are no economic structures which are clearly recommended for all time. Over the centuries it has been shown that Christians can live lives of faith within all kinds of economic structures. Therefore, it is important that Christians build into their economic systems those principles which are basic to the Christian faith.

If one agrees that the biblical principles of freedom, justice and responsibility are the most important ingredients of any economic structure, then the guided-market system comes closest to providing for all three. While the American system of democratic capitalism has its share of flaws, it is marvelously flexible and is capable of providing economic freedom and justice for all. For it to function properly, however, there must be responsible citizens who are constantly pressing for the system to do better. The role of Christians in a democratic-capitalistic society is to be working for freedom and justice through both the private and the public sectors and, at the same time, to be living lifestyles of enough, giving witness to the calling they have to be good stewards of God's creation.

Notes

[1]*American Metal Market*, 22 September 1980.
[2]Assar Lindbeck, "Sweden: The Limits to the Welfare States," *Wall Street Journal* 198, no. 49 (9 September 1981), p. 29.
[3]Ibid.
[4]Sven Rydenfelt, "The Swedish and Japanese Welfare States," *Wall Street Journal* 198, no. 64 (30 September 1981), p. 29.
[5]Ibid.

Select Bibliography

Beckman, David M. *Where Faith and Economics Meet*. Minneapolis: Augsburg, 1981. An economist at the World Bank looks at global economic agonies.
Benne, Robert. *The Ethic of Democratic Capitalism*. Philadelphia: Fortress Press, 1981. A Lutheran theologian argues that democratic capitalism best provides for justice within a market system of equitable arrangements.
Birch, Bruce C., and Rasmussen, Larry L. *The Predicament of the Prosperous*. Philadelphia: Westminster Press, 1978. The call for a radical change in lifestyle.
Boerma, Conrad. *The Rich, The Poor and the Bible*. Philadelphia: Westminster Press, 1978. A Dutch pastor shows how the Bible always challenges the oppression of poverty and how the church today has failed to meet the problem.
De Santa Ana, Julio. *Good News to the Poor*. Trans. Helen Whittle. Maryknoll, N.Y.: Orbis Books, 1979. A Third World theologian looks at the history of how the church has related to the poor.
Friedman, Milton. *Capitalism and Freedom*. Chicago: Univ. of Chicago Press, 1962. The Nobel Prize-winning book on economics. A nonreligious perspective.

Fuller, Reginald, and Rice, Brian K. *Christianity and the Affluent Society.* Grand Rapids, Mich.: Eerdmans, 1966. The responsibility of Christians in an affluent society.

Goudzwaard, Bob. *Aid for the Overdeveloped West.* Ontario, Canada: Wedge Pub., 1975. A Dutch economist looks at the problems of overdeveloped and underdeveloped nations.

————. *Capitalism and Progress.* Ontario, Canada: Wedge Pub.; Grand Rapids, Mich.: Eerdmans, 1979. A Dutch economist studies the history of capitalism, its problems and its possibilities.

Henderson, Hazel. *Creating Alternative Futures.* New York: Berkley Pub., 1978. A collection of provocative essays by one who scorns professional economists. In the style of E. F. Schumacher.

Hollis, Allen. *The Bible and Money.* New York: Dutton, Hawthorn Books, 1976. A United Church of Christ pastor writes on a theology of money.

Lee, Robert. *Faith and the Prospects of Economic Collapse.* Atlanta, Ga.: John Knox Press, 1981. A professor of social ethics deals with the economic crisis.

Lindsell, Harold. *Free Enterprise: A Judeo-Christian Defense.* Wheaton, Ill.: Tyndale, 1982. Proof that the Bible supports free enterprise.

Niebanck, Richard J. *Economic Justice.* Lutheran Church in America, 1980. How to grapple with the economic realities of our society. Written from an evangelical perspective.

Novak, Michael. *The Spirit of Democratic Capitalism.* New York: Simon & Schuster, 1982. A Roman Catholic theologian mounts a defense for democratic capitalism.

Rasmussen, Larry L. *Economic Anxiety and Christian Faith.* Minneapolis: Augsburg, 1981. A theologian looks at the changes in our economic structures and how the Christian faith can relate to them.

Schumacher, E. F. *Small Is Beautiful.* New York: Harper & Row, 1973. A popular book dealing with decentralist economics.

Sider, Ronald J. *Rich Christians in an Age of Hunger.* Rev. ed. Downers Grove, Ill.: InterVarsity Press, 1984. The responsibility of Christians in a time of world hunger, based on biblical testimony.

Taylor, John V. *Enough Is Enough.* Minneapolis: Augsburg, 1977. An English bishop presents a compelling theology of enough.

Wallis, Jim. *Agenda for a Biblical People.* San Francisco: Harper & Row, 1976. An evangelical perspective on the need to transform established Christianity.

Yoder, John Howard. *The Politics of Jesus.* Grand Rapids, Mich.: Eerdmans, 1972. A Mennonite theologian presents a radical approach for the Christian in today's society.

A Free-Market Response

Gary North

William Diehl's essay is difficult to deal with. If he had begun with a clear-cut set of biblical economic premises, or an economic model of how an economy functions, it would have made my assignment easier. But because there is an amorphous (mixed?) quality about his essay, my response may appear to miss the mark. I am having trouble seeing the target.

There is one fundamental presupposition that all three of my opponents share: a belief that the Bible does not provide explicit guidelines (or "blueprints") for the development of a uniquely biblical political economy. This presupposition has led all three of them to promote different outlines of what constitutes a truly biblical economic order. I can understand why readers might be confused. How can anyone know what is "truly biblical" if the Bible does not tell us what kind of economic order to promote? Diehl's statement is clear enough:

> The fact that our Scriptures can be used to support or condemn any economic philosophy suggests that the Bible is not intended

to lay out an economic plan which will apply for all times and places. If we are to examine economic structures in the light of Christian teachings, we will have to do it in another way. (p. 87)

Diehl could also have argued that Scripture can (and has) been used to support and condemn views regarding the family, church government, the mode of baptism, free will, predestination, the use of alcohol, celibacy, and a hundred other topics. Do men's disagreements over applied theology in these other areas also give us a legitimate reason for concluding that the Bible does not present answers—yes, even *blueprints* for these topics of discussion? Isn't Diehl's argument an argument for total relativism? Can it be limited to "mere" economics?

Later in his essay, he repeats himself: "There is no economic system which is inherently Christian in nature" (p. 101). All three authors begin with the same presupposition: The Bible does not give us a blueprint for the economic system. Then they all tell us what *they* like.

The reader may be tempted to ask himself: Why am I reading this book? If those who call themselves Christian social philosophers or Christian social scientists really can agree only on the starting point that the Bible does not tell us what a Christian social order should look like, and that the Bible also does not tell us anything specific about how a Christian social order can be constructed, *what possible hope is there for building a Christian civilization?* What concrete, specific difference would the gospel of Christ make to the way the world works if all men were converted to Christ tomorrow? More to the point, *how can we hope to maintain the prophetic tradition of the Old Testament?*

The prophets came before the whole society, rich and poor, powerful and weak, and called them all to repentance. The prophets cited biblical laws to remind the people of their *specific and general* transgressions. What should we cite, if biblical law is ruled out? The works of John Maynard Keynes, or the works of Karl Marx, or the works of Milton Friedman? Doesn't such a view of the *vagueness of the Bible* overthrow the possibility of prophetic preaching? If we hold such a view of the Bible's vagueness, how can we in good conscience announce, "Thus saith the Lord"?

Even more problematical is Diehl's statement that "over the

centuries it has been shown that Christians can live lives of faith within all kinds of economic structures. Therefore, it is important that Christians build into their economic systems those principles which are basic to the Christian faith" (p. 107). What principles does he have in mind? Freedom, justice, and responsibility. Problem: Diehl fails to give us *specific, concrete biblical rules* regarding what constitutes the substance of these three compelling words. Diehl's "economic principles" are verbal boxes without revelational content. They are little more than slogans—convenient grab-bags for every group to fill up with any social program they want and bring before the people in the name of Jesus, or Mohammed, or Buddha, or Lenin.

Yes, Christians can indeed live "lives of faith within all kinds of economic structures." We know from the writings of Alexandr Solzhenitsyn that Christians live "lives of faith" in the Gulag Archipelago. Now, if Christians can just get "freedom, justice, and responsibility" operating in the Gulag, will all be well? But if these three principles were imposed in the Gulag, could the Gulag survive?

Our initial response might be: "No, the Gulag would not survive." But this response is premature. Until these three words are *defined,* meaning until we can provide *explicitly biblical content* for them, how can we be sure that the Gulag wouldn't survive? After all, the Communist society which has created and sustains the Gulag system has always promoted its cause in terms of phrases such as "freedom, justice, and responsibility." This is one of the points Solzhenitsyn makes clear.

Let us depart for a moment from Diehl's presupposition, namely, that the Bible cannot provide us with explicit guidelines regarding the biblical form of economics. Let us assume that the Bible *does* give us explicit guidelines about the nature of freedom, justice, and responsibility. Could the application of *biblically defined* freedom, justice, and responsibility be imposed in the Gulag without destroying both the Gulag and the Communist civilization which created it and sustains it? Obviously, the whole Communist system would collapse. The whole Soviet system is morally corrupt.[1]

We have good reason to believe that the application of biblical principles to *all* corrupt or tyrannical economic systems would transform them from top to bottom. No aspect of society would escape the transformation, including the economy. Are we not entitled to ask, "Different in what specific, concrete, visible ways?"

Here is my "tip for the day"—or maybe even for the century. Whenever you hear the popular Christian buzz-words, "biblical principles," think to yourself, *biblical law.* If the proclaimed principles are not universally binding, both ethically and culturally, then they are not really principles; they are simply temporary slogans. *But if biblical principles are permanently binding, then they are laws.*

Don't let the person who uses these buzz-words wriggle away from this conclusion. Don't let him toss in a misleading extra qualifying adjective, such as "legalistic," to throw you off the trail. Don't accept as adequate a statement such as Diehl's: "The New Testament is filled with the good news that God does not want his children to be enslaved by a legalistic burden of the law" (p. 87). Beware of verbal smokescreens. They hide important ideas. The idea this particular phrase hides is *antinomianism*—hostility to biblical law.

Obviously, Jesus did not advocate "enslavement to legalism." But didn't he advocate mandatory adherence to universally binding ethical and cultural principles? If he did, then it is morally imperative that Christians specify precisely what these principles are, and then discover the ways that these binding principles should be applied, civilization by civilization, economy by economy, century by century. In short, Christians had better come to grips with R. J. Rushdoony's two-volume work, *The Institutes of Biblical Law* and Greg Bahnsen's *Theonomy in Christian Ethics.* (See my bibliography for full references.) Christian economics must be built upon the general principles ("spirit") *and* the specifics ("letter") of biblical law. This is why David Chilton used the works of both these scholars to write *Productive Christians in an Age of Guilt-Manipulators,* and why I am using them for my own multivolume study, *The Dominion Covenant.*

Diehl contrasts the spirit of the law and the letter of the law. This is a long-popular way to escape the specific requirements of God. Just consider this problem: honoring the spirit of God's prohibition against *adultery* without honoring the specifics. Are we "enslaved" by the "legalistic burden" of the actual specifics of the law? More to the point, *can we honor the "spirit" of the prohibition against adultery without at the same time honoring the specifics?*

I will be even more specific. All too often we are told that our behavior as Christians is bound only by New Testament ethics, not by the specific details of Old Testament law. "If the New Testament doesn't repeat the Old Testament law, it's not binding today." If this is taken as a principle of interpretation, then how do we deal with the problem of *incest?* There is no injunction in the New Testament against marrying your sister. This prohibition appears in the Old Testament (Lev 18:9). Some societies have allowed its kings to marry their sisters (Egypt as late as Christ's day, Hawaii until Christian missionaries put an end to this practice).

An even more graphic example is *bestiality.* There is no New Testament passage prohibiting people from having sex with animals, but there is an Old Testament prohibition (Lev 18:23). Are we to ignore Leviticus 18? On what moral or exegetical basis?

By abandoning the specifics of Old Testament law without a specific New Testament injunction to do so, how are Christians to deal with the *specifics of sin?* Beware of those who glibly (or deliberately) contrast the specifics ("letter") of biblical law and the general principles ("spirit") of biblical law.

What about Diehl's proposed "guided-market approach"? Above all, it is vague. I see no general principles in his essay that would tell us where we can find the proper "balance between freedom and justice." How do we decide between free market activities and State-directed activities in any given instance? Intuition? Is it all intuitive on the part of legislators and enforcing bureaucrats?

He says that "responsibility in the economic system demands that the concerns for freedom and justice be combined to produce optimum benefit to God's creatures and his creation" (p. 91). I agree, but *without biblical law as a guideline,* who is to say what the "optimum" really is? More to the point, the civil government possesses a *legal monopoly of imposing violence* on law-breakers. How can we limit the State so that "the concerns for freedom and justice" are, in fact, combined in a God-honoring, society-benefiting way?

Diehl confuses (or fails to clarify the distinctions between) *society* and *State.* "Where justice has been lacking, society must provide charity to meet the basic needs of nutrition, shelter, health care, education and income" (p. 91-92). He says "society," but he means the State.[2] What must be emphasized, as sociologist Robert Nisbet has done in his classic study *The Quest for Community,* is that State and society must be sharply distinguished.[3] Society is much broader than the State, a political institution. Nisbet is correct: The distrust of capitalism in the West, combined with the decline of influence of both kinship and traditional religion, has led to today's crisis, in which "the State has risen as the dominant institutional force in our society and the most evocative symbol of cultural unity and purpose."[4]

It is not the civil government which the Bible establishes as the agency of economic ameliorization, but other governments: the church, the family, voluntary associations, clubs, and other non-compulsory institutions. If this is what Diehl meant by "society," then I would have no quarrel with him, but it is not what he means, for in the following paragraph he begins his praise of Franklin Roosevelt, the President who saw better than any President before him the extent to which the State had become "the most evocative symbol of cultural unity and purpose." The Christian response is clear: It is the *tithe,* not the graduated income tax, which is established as binding by the Bible.

Diehl's essay is made up of bits and pieces that are not integrated into a coherent whole. Some of his observations are quite good. For example, inflation is indeed a tax. Furthermore, rising *nominal* (money-denominated) income, coupled with the graduated income tax, has pushed everyone into higher and higher tax brackets. The State gets more; taxpayers keep less. His observations on the social, economic, and political disaster that is Sweden are also appropriate. Anyone who thinks he is exaggerating should read Roland Huntford's book, *The New Totalitarians,* for the grim details.[5] He points to the thrift and future-orientation of the Japanese, as well he should. But the good bits in his essay are scrambled with bad bits. It will take an understanding of biblical law, as well as respect for the ethically and socially binding character of biblical law, to unscramble them. We have our work cut out for us.

Notes

[1]Konstantin Simis, *USSR: The Corrupt Society* (New York: Simon & Schuster, 1982).
[2]Later in his essay, he speaks of "the welfare of society." Here he is using the term "society" properly. But the economic system he proposes would primarily benefit the State—the political and bureaucratic apparatus—not "society."
[3]Robert A. Nisbet, *The Quest for Community* (New York: Oxford Univ. Press, 1952), p. 99.
[4]Ibid.
[5]Roland Huntford, *The New Totalitarians* (1972; reprint ed., Briarcliff Manor, N.Y.: Scarborough House, 1980).

A Decentralist Response
Art Gish

William Diehl argues that democratic capitalism is the best
approach to working at the values of freedom, justice and responsibility. I am unconvinced. It seems to me that Diehl's theological
approach is unbiblical and his social analysis shallow.

The basic flaw in Diehl's chapter is theological. He approaches
ethics by reducing the Bible to a few vague, general principles,
and then he tries to find some approximation of them in general
society. There are three serious problems with this approach.

First, Diehl's descriptions of freedom, justice and responsibility
are so general that they can mean anything. As stated, his principles can be used to support capitalism or socialism, pacifism or
militarism. On the basis of Diehl's general principles one can support or oppose the arms race. One could argue that the bombings of
Hiroshima and Nagasaki were acts of responsibility serving the
cause of justice and freedom. Vague principles like this are useful
only in justifying one's prejudices. They are of little value in hard
ethical thinking from a biblical perspective, for they strip the Bible

of its radical message of repentance and new life.

Although it is true, as Diehl states, that the Bible does not advocate one particular economic system for the world, the Bible gives a lot more detailed and specific instruction in ethics and economics than he is willing to admit. I was glad to see that he understands that the Bible forbids the charging of interest. Just that, if taken seriously, has a lot of economic implications.

Second, Diehl's whole theological approach too easily accepts the culture in which it is immersed, does not have an adequate basis for seeing the contradictions of the culture, and does not have any vision of an alternative to the status quo. This theology has a long history of cultural conformity, blessing worldly institutions and seeing the church as one of the supporting pillars of society. It is not surprising that Diehl easily accepts and defends the economic system in which he is living.

If the society in which we live is not the kingdom, then one would expect the Christian to have a radical critique of that society. Rather than in any way lessening our longing for or diminishing our vision of that kingdom, the imperfections of the world should spur us to seek that kingdom more fully.

Third, Diehl's approach to ethics starts with what seems possible in a fallen world rather than with Jesus and the new life to which he calls us. Diehl would come out at a different place if he were to start with Jesus and a vision of the new age, something Diehl leaves out.

There is no mention of the church (*koinōnia*) in Diehl's approach to ethics. There is no hint of a redeemed people who are living a new reality, no hint that the church might be living different values from the fallen world, or that this new life in koinonia might be the basis for any discussion of Christian ethics.

Christian faith is more than a religion or a set of vague principles. It is something to be lived out in every aspect of our lives. Jesus really is the way, the truth and the life. To be a Christian is to allow God's Spirit to transform every area of our lives. God wants to transform us in a more radical way than any of us ever imagined.

In addition to its weak theology, Diehl's economic analysis leaves much to be desired. Although Diehl probably considers himself a realist, his assessment of Western capitalism is rather unrealistic. In fact, his view of capitalism as a whole seems naive.

Other than introducing the great disparity between rich and poor, Diehl does not begin to deal with the social, economic and personal implications of the multinational corporations or the increasing concentration of economic power and control in the hands of a few.

Yes, capitalism has made tremendous economic and technological advances in this last stage of the era of plenty, the era of abundant, cheap energy. But how will capitalism deal with the realities of the new age of scarce, expensive resources? Capitalism has contributed to massive production of things (and waste and pollution), but it must be seen more as the problem than as the solution to our problems. Why does it take a deep recession to temporarily reduce inflation?

Has capitalism been so successful because it is inherently better or because it has exploited people and the environment? Has its material success been also related to political, cultural and geological factors? In comparing capitalist and noncapitalist economies, we need to take a historical perspective which will include the history of exploitation in those societies. We ought to avoid making the sort of mistake racists make. They see Whites outcompeting Blacks and assume White superiority, ignoring the history of slavery, prejudice and discrimination. Let's not be chauvinists in our economic analysis.

Suppose we compare any socialist country today with its previous condition while still under the domination of capitalism. If we compare the economies of China and India, we will see that China has done much more to eliminate poverty than has India. Compare Cuba with the rest of the Caribbean or Central America.

Because of its exploitation of the Third World, its Christian base of culture and its relative political freedom, the West is economically and technologically advanced. But this success in no way proves the superiority of capitalism.

Diehl recognizes that capitalism needs to be controlled. If unrestrained capitalism is bad, and if social control is good, then why not go the whole way and have people participate in making the decisions that affect them? Why not democratize the work place? In fact, why even hold on to that corrupt system that needs to be restrained?

Capitalism by its very nature involves exploitation, inequality and even slavery for those who do not have the power. If some can make it to the top of the pyramid, then of necessity others must be at the bottom. Inequality is an essential aspect of capitalism. The basic values, assumptions and shape of relationships in capitalism are in contradiction to God's kingdom. Capitalism is an expression of sin and should be rejected by Christians. We should never accept anything which contradicts God's revelation in Jesus.

Diehl began his chapter with a striking description of the great disparity and injustice of this world and a clear word of God's judgment on that injustice. But the main body of his chapter is an argument that things are pretty good after all. I wish he had carried his beginning to its logical conclusion. It is apparent that Diehl has a real concern for the poor and for justice, but he seems blind to the extent that injustice is caused and perpetuated by capitalism. Diehl assumes too easily that the capitalist system can solve our problems.

Is Diehl correct in his unsupported assertion that people can use the democratic process to reform the evils of capitalism? Although I believe we can (with much struggle and suffering) change the system, I would be more realistic than he is about how easily that change can take place. Diehl does not recognize that every reform that has been instituted was fought tooth and nail by the capitalist system and its government. Consider women's suffrage, equal rights for minorities or union bargaining rights. Those reforms took place in spite of the system, not because of it. There is also a difference between token reform and real change. Our system seems to be adept at making token changes.

Our government is controlled primarily by those with wealth and power. Government controls on the economy are for the most part supported by and serve the purposes of the corporate elite. Roosevelt's New Deal did more to save the capitalist system than to reform it. In fact, it can be argued that New Deal reforms only further entrenched the power of the capitalist elite. For example, farm programs hurt the small farmer and were a boon to agribusiness.[1] Big government was created by big business. They have been more allies than antagonists.

I am not aware of anything that Ronald Reagan has done to "get big government off the people's backs." He has given greater freedom to big business, hurt small business, increased government surveillance of citizens, eliminated local regulation of toxic nuclear materials, and reduced protection of the population and environment from the ravages of big business and the military.

I simply do not see what real reforms capitalism has brought. The present direction of government policy is toward increased militarization of the economy and society, increased social polarization, increased burdens on the lower eighty per cent of society, and economic policies favoring the rich and powerful.

Twenty per cent of the population owns eighty per cent of the wealth. Think of what that means. Eighty per cent of the population must struggle to divide up the remaining twenty per cent of the wealth. That inequality has remained fairly constant over the past century. No reforms have changed that. In fact, the situation is getting worse. From 1958 to 1970 the lowest fifth of male workers' share of wages declined from 5.1 per cent to 4.6 per cent, while the top fifth of male workers' share rose from 38.15 per cent to 40.55 per cent.[2] Reaganomics has done nothing to change this.

In 1981, U.S. corporations spent $82.6 billion in corporate takeovers. These takeovers created no new jobs and were not meant to increase productivity. It was money spent to increase the power of those corporations.[3] Barry Bluestone in his recent study has shown how the greed of the corporations hurts the economy and destroys jobs.[4]

The debate in the capitalist world at this point in history is between Keynesians, monetarists and supply siders. But none of them is asking the right questions or examining the basic assumptions of the capitalist system. They all want to increase production and consumption. But the world is finite, and these need to be reduced. None of the three speaks to the real needs of people, and all three are based solely on the unchristian motivation of self-interest.

Diehl's reference to one article on problems in Sweden is not enough to prove much to me. Doesn't Sweden have one of the highest standards of living in the world? But even if these problems he mentioned were so serious in Sweden, we would not necessarily need to assume that they are the result of a socialist economy. Actually Sweden is a capitalistic welfare state. We need to ask deeper questions. Why are Swedes not more motivated to work, if this is the case? Could it perhaps be a spiritual problem instead of an economic one?

A common argument against those who want more cooperation,

sharing and equality is that these values destroy initiative. It is argued that competition is needed to motivate people. Initiative can be based in greed and selfishness, or it can be based on love, on an infilling of God's Spirit, on a vision of a new order. Consider how in the past nurses worked with such deep dedication for low pay. This does not mean nurses should receive low pay, but it seems as though Christians could point to a better source of motivation than selfishness.

Diehl makes a good point when he criticizes "hired love." But if he is really serious about this point, he will have to reject capitalistic approaches to meeting human need. Isn't working in a capitalistic hospital, nursing home or day-care center providing "hired love"? The only alternative to hired love is koinonia.

Diehl is concerned with freedom, but his view could be called the trickle-down theory of freedom: The more freedom corporations have, the more free all of us will be. I don't believe it. The reality of our system is not people deciding the extent to which they will give up their freedom for the good of the whole, but rather a few people deciding the manner and extent to which they will try to curb other people's freedom.

For the Christian, freedom is based not in governments and structures but in Jesus. Governments can only seek to limit our freedom. They cannot grant us any freedom. We are free to the extent that we trust God for our security and are not intimidated by any of the world's structures. We are free to the extent we are able to act, to love, to live out God's call for our lives, to live out an alternative to the world's system.

Our capitalist system is based on freedom for the elite who control it. They decide what will be produced and how. Through advertising they will manipulate and create the desires and market for what they produce. The capitalist system hardly encourages people to be free in relation to God.

We could ask the same questions concerning responsibility. What is our responsibility before God? Does it include acting contrary to Jesus' teachings in order to defend the world's system? Does the capitalist system encourage responsibility, or does it tend to transform people into passive employees and consumers? How do power relationships created by capitalism relate to responsibility?

I know nothing about William Diehl, but on the basis of what he has written, I can guess that he has been living on a substantial salary. People who are free to travel, take vacations and eat in expensive restaurants will naturally like the present system. But Diehl is expressing his own class bias, not a biblical perspective. The Bible calls us to look at the world from the perspective of the poor, not of the rich, because that is how God views the world. If we view the world from the bottom, we will see things much differently than does Diehl.

Diehl's moving and sensitive call for simplifying our lives shows that he is a perceptive moral being. But I would challenge him to a deeper and more radical biblical ethic. We need to begin to think the unthinkable, to have visions of a new order, to dream of what could be; then we can begin to take those steps in our lives with our brothers and sisters.

To the extent that we begin to live in the new order of God's kingdom, we will find ourselves in conflict with the values and structures of the capitalist system.

Notes

[1]Jack Nelson, *Hunger for Justice* (Maryknoll, N.Y.: Orbis Books, 1980), pp. 132-57.
[2]Hazel Henderson, *Creating Alternative Futures: The End of Economics* (New York: Berkley Pub. Co., 1978), p. 71.
[3]Michael Harrington, "A Path for America," *Dissent* (Fall 1982), p. 408.
[4]Barry Bluestone, *The Deindustrialization of America* (New York: Basic Books, 1982).

A Centralist Response
John Gladwin

The basic method of argument employed by William Diehl I believe to be right. It is unhelpful as well as unbiblical to look to the Bible to give us a blueprint of economic theory or structure which we then apply to our contemporary life. We must rather work in a theological way, looking to the Bible to give us experience and insight into the kingdom of God in Jesus Christ. This then helps us discover values and methods of interpretation which we can use in understanding our present social experience. My questions about this chapter have more to do with the way the author has seen this at work for the questions addressed by us all.

The initial definitions of freedom, justice and responsibility are helpful. Clearly the gospel experience of entering into the liberty of Christ and its sense of liberation from those evil forces in the world which seek to make our consciences captive to their destructive and dehumanizing power is crucial. Actually it provides the needed ground for the discipline of justice in society. The individual who has discovered the key is able to accept restrictions on his life for the benefit they bring to others. To accept the obligations and responsibilities of social life is not, for Christians, destructive of their freedom in Christ.

I also agree with the author that no particular system of economic and social relations is to be elevated with the title *Christian* and also that *some* systems make better sense of our Christian understanding than others. My problem with the essay is that it offers too selective and uncritical an understanding of the model predominant in the United States. The comments made in favor of the Japanese experience and in criticism of the Swedish are too selective and establish little.

The picture given in this paper of the effect of publicly provided services is misleading. The suggestion made via the quotation of Sven Rydenfelt that the public provision of services is a type of "hired love" and a substitute for personal relationships and their responsibilities is grossly misleading. The provision of services is supportive of families and enables them to exercise love and responsibility. There is no evidence that the provision of pensions, homes for the elderly, schools for children and health care for the sick undermines the effect of love between persons. To the contrary, by relieving families of burdens heavier than they can often bear, such services enable parents and children to offer each other the emotional and personal support which they need at the different stages of their relationships. It also rescues the vulnerable from a dependency on their families, giving them the dignity of their own life rather than making them increasingly and inappropriately dependent on relatives. Such services are also vital for families who are either unable (through material or emotional deprivation) or unwilling to offer their parents or children the support to which they are entitled.

The welfare state was created as a support to people and to family life and responsibility. It provided a system through which the whole community accepted responsibility to meet basic and crisis needs and to rescue people from the uncertainties to which they had previously been subject. In the United Kingdom some people can still remember the anxieties they carried about their ability to meet doctors' bills or about what was to happen to them in old age or about support during times of unemployment.

The welfare state was a response to our hope that never again would people, especially the poorer groups in society, be left in such anxiety. It was a collective duty to provide so as to enable all citizens to live in freedom from fear of illness, homelessness, inequalities in education, old age and poverty. These are surely worthy goals for any society committed to the support of its citizens in their individual and family experience.

Again, I find the comments made on the Japanese experience selective. There are indeed lessons to be learned which we need to heed about economic development. Yet, to portray a culture which encourages mothers to be bound to the domestic world, both to their children and to their parents, as an example of a free society is surely stretching the meaning of freedom beyond any reasonable definition. A free-market economy may well be dependent on serious losses of freedom in other important areas of life.

The Christian gospel has always been a challenge to such cultural conservatism and has opened the way for groups of people to discover new vocations in new relationships as they discover their dignity in Christ. We may look at the rigid duties of Asian family structures with some nostalgia. They appear much less desirable to those who have to live by them and who suffer from their rigidities. The gospel offers new dignities to women and new responsibilities to men to see that those are acknowledged. Two of the most important achievements of responsible public welfare have been the freedom given to women and the opportunity for men and women to discover a more dignified form of partnership in the world. Any economic system which hinders this is open to serious question from Christian perspectives.

Public services and institutions are often attacked for being bureaucratic and inefficient. Such criticisms must be taken seriously. One of the most urgent tasks in the development of services today is to consider their organization and structures of accountability to the community. Yet I have to say that in my experience many voluntary and private agencies are out-of-date in their attitudes, unprofessional in their conduct and seriously mismanaged. That is not meant to question the vital contribution which such agencies can and do make. It is to say that questions about management and accountability apply to all organizations and that the world of private organizations is not always as good as their public relations departments would suggest. Moreover, one of the possibilities that the public management of services opens up is the possibility of setting vital professional standards of conduct. Whether services are provided privately or publicly, the state has a duty to see that basic standards are met. The vulnerable in our society have a right to the best service that can be provided. Well-meaning amateurism is not good enough if we are to properly meet our neighborly duties to the poor, the elderly, the sick and disabled. In Sweden and in the United Kingdom there may be problems with public services. They do, however, on the whole set a standard of practice which other agencies stretch to meet.

However, I was glad that this chapter introduced an international set of comparisons. It is good to listen carefully to a variety of experiences if we are to discover the best choices available to us today. That is one of the ways in which we might hear the Word of God for the shape of economic life in our society.

Decentralist Economics

Decentralist Economics
Art Gish

Suppose we based all of our economic decisions on the revelation of God in Jesus the Christ. Suppose Jesus were our starting point. Suppose the New Testament had more authority for us than what economists say. What would our economic lives look like? Where would these assumptions lead us?

Suppose also that Christian community, instead of our individual opinion, was the context for our discussion of economics. Suppose our answers came out of our life together in community. What difference would that make?

In this chapter we will try to do just that. We will consider the implications of Jesus' lordship and Christian community for economics. This will lead us in a direction quite different from the economic values of the fallen world. But that need not bother us much. We should expect Christian values and lifestyle to be different from the fallen world (Rom 12:2). We are simply called to be faithful, even when we do not understand what the results will be.

We could avoid a lot of confusion by simply seeing Christian ethics as discerning God's will instead of trying to find the lowest common denominator possible for the whole world. We do not need to answer what would be feasible for all humanity apart from God's Spirit. With God's Spirit we know all things are possible.

The call for Christians is first to get our own house in order, to begin to conform our own economic lives to the reality of the new age, to live a transformed life. The New Testament proclaims that in Jesus we see not only a clear revelation of God's intentions for humanity, of how it is that we as individuals are meant to live, but also the inbreaking of a new kingdom, a new social order, a new humanity. If anyone is in Christ, there is a whole new order (2 Cor 5:17). The power of sin and oppressive structures has been broken.

Of course, that is not true for the whole world. There is still plenty of alienation, oppression and suffering all around us. The kingdom has not come in its fullness. But it has begun to break in here and there. There are first fruits of that kingdom to be found in many places. The clearest evidence of that new humanity is a community of love and sharing, a community in which the vision that Jesus proclaimed has begun to take flesh in all relationships, including and especially economic relationships. This is what the church is meant to be: a new, transformed community.[1] So we can expect to see transformed economic relationships among God's people.

Those who participate in this relationship have experienced reconciliation not only with other people, but also with God. This has a lot to do with economics—basic activities like service, production, distribution and waste. We cannot talk of spiritual renewal without talking about its economic results.

Most of the world's economics has been divorced from God.[2] For Adam Smith, economics can function fine without a personal God. Smith's reliance on natural reason and self-interest is the material abdication of God's role in our lives. Concepts like *the free market* or *the dialectic of history* have replaced God and are now seen as ultimate. We can now put our faith in "the magic hand" instead of God. The problem is that, in separating life from God, people consider themselves free to manipulate and control history, nature and each other for their own purposes. When people think themselves sovereign, disastrous consequences always follow. When we forget that we are part of the creation, not the Creator, we are sure to "create" chaos out of God's good order.

Rather than seeing economics as an autonomous entity which doctrines such as laissez faire would imply, we can view economics as under the lordship of Jesus. Rather than seeing the economic order guided by the invisible hand of the market, we can see the need for communal decision making regarding the shape of our economic life. We can make economic decisions on the basis of the new age of Jesus Christ.

How liberating that can be! Our lifestyle can be a conscious result of our commitment to God instead of an unconscious acceptance of the culture around us. We can judge the world's systems by the norms of our faith instead of being made to fit into them. Our justification and sense of belonging can come from God instead of from the world's systems.

There are few issues which are amoral and can therefore be left to "experts" or systems to decide. Almost all economic decisions affect people's lives, particularly the poor. Decisions about interest rates or federal budgets then become moral choices. And anything which is seen as too important to be put under the lordship of Christ and the discernment of the Christian community has become an idol.

Economic questions are among the most important questions we can ask. And they are basic to biblical thought. There is no subject about which the Bible is more clear than economics. Jesus is recorded in the Gospels as having mentioned the subject of money and economics more often than any other subject. What he said was unmistakably clear, and it sounded just as unreasonable to people then as it does today.

It seems odd that in spite of all the biblical emphasis on economics, most church people today consider economic values and lifestyle to be a personal, private matter, completely separate from biblical faith. The unfaithfulness of the institutional church in the area of economics is equaled only by her apostasy in blessing violence and war.

The Old Testament Perspective
The Old Testament gives detailed laws regulating economic relationships. Although we need not feel bound by these laws, the general concern of justice and shalom found there is repeated in the

New Testament and is meant for us.

The biblical witness is clear. We are to be stewards, not owners, of what God created. "The earth is the LORD's and the fulness thereof" (Ps 24:1). "The land shall not be sold in perpetuity, for the land is mine; for you are strangers and sojourners with me" (Lev 25:23). The concept of private property cannot be reconciled to these teachings.

How different everything would be if we acted as stewards instead of owners! If the earth is the Lord's and we are stewards, then we can no longer see the creation as something we can manipulate and exploit in any way we choose, but rather as a gift to be received with gratitude and respect.

Stewardship is a long-term, not a short-term, view of economics. It can have no part in the philosophy of "Get all you can as quickly as you can." A life of stewardship stands opposed to the incentives of capitalism. They are short-term and hurt everyone, including the capitalist system itself—as when the quarterly statement becomes more important to the aspiring executive than long-term planning.

The Bible is also clear that what God created is good. The material world is not evil or somehow inferior to spiritual concerns. The goodness of creation is to be enjoyed by all. The Bible even goes so far as to promise prosperity to those who are righteous (Deut 7—8, 28). It is important to remember that this promise of prosperity is made to the collective people of God, not to greedy individuals who exploit others. There is a big difference between the wealth which is a gift of God and is shared, and the wealth which comes from exploitation.

With this promise of prosperity, however, comes the warning that wealth poses a great spiritual danger (Deut 8:11-20). Wealth can bring alienation from God and neighbor and can lead to enslavement. All through the Old Testament, when things went well for the people of Israel, they forgot the Lord their God and fell into captivity.

The promise of prosperity was dependent on social justice: "If you truly execute justice one with another, if you do not oppress the alien, the fatherless or the widow, . . . and if you do not go after other gods to your own hurt, then I will let you dwell in this place, in the land that I gave of old to your fathers for ever" (Jer 7:5-7).

God wants equality and justice. After the Hebrew people entered Canaan, the land resources were distributed equally among the various families and tribes. Archaeologists have found that as late as the tenth century B.C. all the houses were about the same size, indicating general economic equality. But by the time of Amos in the seventh century, there was a marked distinction between rich and poor areas.[3]

The Bible is clear about God's judgment on inequality based on exploitation (Amos 6:4, 7). In the Old Testament one of the most serious violations of God's covenant with his people was injustice and exploitation of the poor. In a time of great political and economic success for some, a time of expanding international trade, God sent Amos to announce that Israel would be destroyed, partly because of the exploitation of the poor that was going on.[4] Beneath the illusion of economic growth there was terrible misery and poverty caused by that growth. God allows the destruction of nations who oppress the poor. Sodom was destroyed partly because it did not serve the poor (Ezek 16:49-50).

The Bible portrays God as having a special concern for the poor. God identifies with the poor. God intervenes in history to liberate the oppressed poor. The Hebrew Exodus from slavery is only one example.

The LORD works vindication
and justice for all who are oppressed.
He made known his ways to Moses,
his acts to the people of Israel. (Ps 103:6-7)

The Bible portrays God as taking this whole matter quite personally. "He who oppresses a poor man insults his Maker, but he who is kind to the needy honors him" (Prov 14:31). Proverbs 19:17 puts it this way: "He who is kind to the poor lends to the LORD." Jesus said that what you do or do not do for the poor, you do to him (Mt 25:31-46).

There are over a hundred verses in the Bible that relate poverty to oppression.[5] There are only a few that list drunkenness or laziness as causes. The rich are considered responsible for the condition of the oppressed. Things haven't changed. The major causes of poverty in the world today are oppression and injustice.[6]

Not only does the Bible condemn the whole cycle of oppression and poverty and show that God liberates the oppressed, but the

Bible also calls us to establish justice.

> Hate evil, and love good,
>   and establish justice in the gate; . . .
> Let justice roll down like waters,
>   and righteousness like an ever-flowing stream.
> (Amos 5:15, 24)

The Old Testament also gives clear directives on how to relate to the poor. Rather than paternalistic handouts, the Bible requires social and economic justice. The rights of the poor are specified (for example, gleaning), and regular redistribution of wealth is called for.

Charging interest was prohibited. "If you lend money to any of my people with you who is poor, you shall not be to him as a creditor, and you shall not exact interest from him" (Ex 22:25; see also Deut 23:19-20; Lev 25:35-38).

Every seventh year was a Sabbath year in which all debts were to be canceled and all slaves freed (Deut 15:1-6). Any inequality that existed was to be remedied every seven years.

But the Old Testament law was even more radical than this. Every fiftieth year was to be the year of Jubilee, a time when all the land was to be redistributed (Lev 25). Here was a way of maintaining the original equality that existed when the land was first divided among the tribes. Imagine: all land redistributed with no compensation to the rich. Actually, people never were to buy the land. They were only supposed to buy a specific number of harvests before the land was again redistributed. Private property is not a biblical concept.

An important aspect of the Sabbath is the reminder that we are dependent on God. To stop work every seventh day and year challenges concepts and feelings of self-sufficiency. The point is that we are to trust God for our security rather than try to create that security ourselves.

The New Testament Perspective

In the New Testament we have the same themes as in the Old Testament, only they are stated even more radically and universally. Jesus was the message of the Old Testament made flesh. Jesus announced in his "Nazareth manifesto" that the Scripture was fulfilled in his own personhood:

The Spirit of the Lord is upon me,
because he has anointed me to preach good news to the poor.
He has sent me to proclaim release to the captives
and recovering of sight to the blind,
to set at liberty those who are oppressed,
to proclaim the acceptable year of the Lord. (Lk 4:18-19)

God's taking on flesh included liberating the oppressed and the poor. It was not an accident that Jesus was born in a stable and slept in a feeding trough. God became poor in order to identify with poverty and oppression and to liberate the oppressed. Note the difference in style between Jesus and most religious leaders today.

When Mary learned that she would give birth to the Messiah, she burst into singing. Here is what she sang about baby Jesus:

He has put down the mighty from their thrones,
and exalted those of low degree;
he has filled the hungry with good things,
and the rich he has sent empty away. (Lk 1:52-53)

The sign of Jesus' messiahship was that he identified with and served the poor (Mt 11:2-6). Jesus' teachings continue the Old Testament concern for social justice. Consider parables like those of the rich man and Lazarus, the rich fool or the good Samaritan. The same concern is shown in the following sayings of Jesus:

Blessed are you poor, for yours is the kingdom of God. (Lk 6:20)
But woe to you that are rich, for you have received your con-
solation. Woe to you that are full now, for you shall hunger.
(Lk 6:24-25)
Give to him who begs from you, and do not refuse him who
would borrow from you. (Mt 5:42)
Of him who takes away your goods do not ask them again.
(Lk 6:30)

Jesus said you cannot serve God and money. He didn't say we shouldn't do it; he said we couldn't. It is impossible. No one can serve two masters (Lk 16:13).

Jesus also said, "Do not lay up for yourselves treasures on earth" (Mt 6:19). That isn't hard to understand. Don't do it. Although simple to understand, it is not as easy to follow. Jesus did not say it would be impossible for the rich to enter the kingdom, but he did make it sound improbable. "How hard it is for those who have riches to enter the kingdom of God! For it is easier for a camel to go through the eye of a needle than for a rich man to enter the kingdom of God" (Lk 18:24-25). Jesus told the rich young ruler to sell all he had and give to the poor (Mk 10:21). That was shocking enough, but then in the following verses Jesus generalizes the command (Mk 10:23-31). The parallel in Luke 12:32-34 is an even clearer general command to give up private property.

Maybe we should stop at this point and ask if we really want to take Jesus seriously in relation to our lifestyles, or if we would rather spiritualize or somehow explain away the radical message he gives to us.

Remember, these are not just teachings of an idealist or even an inspired rabbi. We are talking about the Incarnation and the cross. Jesus embodied what he taught. He gave up everything for a cross, and we are called to take up the same cross. That call applies also to our economic lives.

Complete my joy by being of the same mind, having the same love, being in full accord and of one mind. Do nothing from selfishness or conceit, but in humility count others better than yourselves. Let each of you look not only to his own interests, but also to the interests of others. Have this mind among yourselves, which is yours in Christ Jesus, who, though he was in the form of God, did not count equality with God a thing to be grasped, but emptied himself, taking the form of a servant, being born in the likeness of men. And being found in human form he humbled himself and became obedient unto death, even death on a cross. Therefore God has highly exalted him and bestowed on him the name which is above every name, that at the name of Jesus every knee should bow, in heaven and on earth and under the earth, and every tongue confess that Jesus Christ is Lord, to the glory of God the Father. (Phil 2:2-11)

The way of salvation is the way of downward mobility. It is the way of the cross. It is the call to give up our privilege and power and to identify with the poor. But that is good news, not bad news. It is bad news only for those who worship Mammon. The upward way is the way of death. The cross leads to life. We have been called from death and slavery into life. "Truly, I say to you, there is no one who has left house or brothers or sisters or mother or father or children or lands, for my sake and for the gospel, who will not receive a hundredfold now in this time, houses and brothers and sisters and mothers and children and lands, with persecutions, and in the age to come eternal life" (Mk 10:29-30).

After the resurrection and the outpouring of the Holy Spirit at Pentecost, the early Christians were given the power to live out what Jesus taught them. It looked something like this:

And all who believed were together and had all things in common; and they sold their possessions and goods and distributed them to all, as any had need. (Acts 2:44-45)

Now the company of those who believed were of one heart and soul, and no one said that any of the things which he possessed was his own, but they had everything in common. And with great power the apostles gave their testimony to the resurrection of the Lord Jesus, and great grace was upon them all. There was not a needy person among them, for as many as were possessors of lands or houses sold them, and brought the proceeds of what was sold and laid it at the apostles' feet; and distribution was made to each as any had need. (Acts 4:32-35)

Here the Old Testament Jubilee was fulfilled. Only for Christians the Jubilee occurs not every fifty years, but daily in the ongoing lifestyle of the Christian community. Private property is abolished. The distinction between social classes is overcome (Gal 3:28). The gospel of Jesus Christ has become flesh.

We should note that the full community life experienced in Jerusalem was not an ill-fated experiment but became widespread throughout the early church.[7] Although we need not imitate every detail of the early church, if we are guided by the same Spirit, the shape of our church and economic life will not be much different.

If we look forward to the time when God's kingdom is fulfilled, when there will be justice for all, when love and sharing will characterize all relationships, why not begin living that way now? Why should we pattern our lives after the fallen world with its private property, competition and alienation? What should keep us from sharing our possessions, from living as brothers and sisters? Only our double-mindedness. But we cannot serve both God and money. The will to possess and the desire for community are opposites.

Christian Economic Values

We have looked at some biblical teachings on economics. Now we need to begin to apply that perspective to our own situation. Although the Bible does not advocate any particular shape our economic life must take, it does point in a definite direction. Any economic system that denies biblical values of justice, stewardship, sharing, equality, community and freedom is in rebellion against God.

One of the most important words in the New Testament to describe the life of the Christian community is *koinōnia*. No one English word can capture the meaning of this Greek word. It means to hold in *common*. It means communion, community, fellowship, partnership, connectedness, mutuality and solidarity. It means to participate in, to share, to belong. The one word, *koinōnia*, captures a lot of what our lives should look like, and it can be a guide for economics. Koinonia and Jubilee are the New Testament economic programs.

God created us for koinonia. It is only in koinonia that we can find true fulfillment in our lives. The desire for koinonia is probably in our genes. But this community is a gift, an expression of God's Spirit, a result of love—not a moral obligation or something we create.

Actually the most important reality of all is love. Love is the only thing that matters. Koinonia is an expression of love, of self-giving. Love does not calculate, expect return, look to self-interest or concern itself with profit. Love is a life of compassion and servanthood, revealed in concrete economics.

To participate in communion (koinonia) with Christ, to eat the bread and drink the cup, is more than a ritual to remember Jesus. To "do this in remembrance of me" is to become broken ourselves, to give ourselves for others. It is in giving ourselves that we find ourselves (Mt 16:25).

For the world, economics is a question of power. Probably the most important teaching of Jesus on the subject of power, economics and politics is found in Mark 10:42-45:

> You know that those who are supposed to rule over the Gentiles lord it over them, and their great men exercise authority over them. But it shall not be so among you; but whoever would be great among you must be your servant, and whoever would be first among you must be slave of all. For the Son of man also came not to be served but to serve, and to give his life as a ran-

som for many.

We are clearly told not to have power over others but to be servants. The economic and political implications of this are staggering.

This puts economics in a new perspective. If this is true, then our economic lives can start from a new foundation, a set of assumptions completely different from the fallen world's. In fact, we will see the whole purpose of economics in a new light. The purpose of economic activity in God's kingdom is not to acquire wealth and power, but to praise God and serve our neighbor. Time is not money but an opportunity to live, love and share. The goal is not profit but supplying people's needs, supporting a fulfilling lifestyle, teaching kingdom ways of relating to each other.

Economics in a Fallen World

The way of a people redeemed from the bondage of sin is quite different from the way the kingdoms of the world operate. The worldly kingdoms operate on the basis of power, profit, self-interest, complexity and expansion. The result is tremendous wealth and power for some, and misery for others—plus unimaginable destruction to the environment. The goal of the fallen world is not koinonia.[8]

The industrial revolution has brought in an age of fantastic centralization of power, enormous consumption of energy and resources, and great social disruption. This is equally true of private and state capitalism, bureaucratic socialism or corporate capitalism.

Concentrations of wealth and power in the hands of a few lead to neither freedom nor stability. The bigger and more centralized things get, the more authoritarian and undemocratic they become. Centers of power tend to use that power for their own ends. They become unresponsive to people's needs. They make it less possible for most people to have a sense of participation (koinonia), a sense of worth and meaning. They work to destroy values of responsibility, interdependence and partnership (koinonia).

Centralization of power is authoritarian, expensive, dangerous, fragile and unreliable. With any centralization of power come increased bureaucracies and military control to manage, protect and expand that power. Consider the interlocking of corporate, governmental and police power to protect a nuclear plant. Do we want a managed society ruled by an authoritarian bureaucracy primarily committed to the dictates of technology? Does this lead to koinonia?

Concentrations of power need massive police and military power to protect them and keep them in power. Without violence (or at least the threat of violence) they would soon collapse. The United States needs a strong military (although not as strong as we now have) to maintain our unjust relationship with the Third World.

But, as Dwight Eisenhower stated, "every gun that is made, every warship launched, every rocket fired signifies, in the final sense, a theft from those who hunger and are not fed, those who are cold and are not clothed."[9] This is true not only in that the resources for increased military spending are taken directly from the poor by cutting programs that meet human need, but also in the fact that military spending creates fewer jobs than the same investment in any other sector of the economy.[10] Military spending is a principal cause of inflation and deficit budgets. Military spending must be seen as one of the principal problems of the world economy.

Even more serious than diverting resources from meeting human need, however, is the function of the military to ensure that those in power stay in power, that the structures of injustice that cause poverty not be changed. This, rather than any concern for freedom or justice, is the primary reason for the build-up of the American military presence around the world. Cain's sin of killing Abel has now reached its logical conclusion. We are prepared to destroy the whole world for our own selfish purposes.[11]

The world economy is built on the exploitation of plentiful, cheap energy. That energy is limited. Thus the whole world economy is fast traveling down a dead-end street. Even now we are entering an age of scarcity, the end of the era of abundance and expansion. This is being revealed in repeated world economic crises. The rebellious world system is meeting its judgment. We cannot expect continued economic growth.

The simple truth is that there are limits to growth. We live in a finite world. We are not God. The world cannot much longer tolerate the idea of maximum production and maximum consumption. We are on a collision course with the limits of the environment. The philosophy of an ever-expanding pie which would provide larger portions for everyone is not based on reality.

Current economic thinking does not take into account the environmental costs of current activities to be paid for by future generations. If these real costs were added to the cost of production, things would have to drastically change. Much of what is produced would be too expensive for most people to afford.[12] But someone will have to pay sometime for our folly. Isaiah gave this warning a long time ago.

> The earth mourns and withers,
>> the world languishes and withers;
>> the heavens languish together with the earth.
> The earth lies polluted
>> under its inhabitants;
> for they have transgressed the laws,
>> violated the statutes,
>> broken the everlasting covenant. (Is 24:4-5)

Polluted rivers, smog-filled skies and eroded hillsides proclaim God's judgment on our sinful economic values and lifestyles.

We also need to consider the human costs of the world economy. Industrialization and centralization have meant urbanization with all its social disintegration, the uprooting of people from their communities and relationships. Growth of centralization and upturns in the world economy have meant increased economic and social suffering for the poor of the world.[13] Economic growth has been based on exploitation of the poor. As Francis Moore Lappé and Joseph Collins put it, "The root cause of hunger is the increasing concentration of control over food-producing resources in the hands of fewer and fewer people."[14]

Let us look at what happens in agriculture when small-scale peasant farming is replaced with mechanization, centralization and capitalist agribusiness in places like the Philippines. The result is not only greatly increased energy use per unit of harvest and reduced production per acre, but also less agricultural employment.[15] The peasants are forced off the land and are thereby denied employment, housing and food. They are then pushed into a swelling urban population and are rendered powerless and useless except as objects to be used for someone's gain. The land which once sustained them now produces luxury crops for people in the First World, products the former peasant farmers cannot afford to buy. The profits go to the rich, many of whom are American (for example, Dole, Del Monte). This pattern has been repeated in country after country. The "green revolution" has not been helpful to most of the world's people, partly because it was used by the rich to increase their power.[16]

Many argue that the forward march of technology will eventually resolve our current problems. Although we may benefit from the use of some technology, it is doubtful that salvation will be found in higher doses of it. Each new fix of technology requires increasing use of energy and resources and creates a whole new set of problems to be solved, many bigger than the original problems. It seems ironic that, as we advance further in science and technology, the survival of the world becomes more and more questionable.

Part of the sinful condition of the world's economy must be seen in capitalism itself. The free market is not free. It is rigged by a corporate elite who control the bulk of the world's economic and political power.[17] As a group, these elite are responsible to no one except themselves.

As Christians we need to make a complete break with the capitalist economy.[18] Capitalism stands in clear contradiction to biblical values. Profit and growth are its primary moral commitments. Private property, egoism, competition, materialism and greed are promoted. Capitalism stands opposed to koinonia.

The medieval church named seven sins as deadly: greed, avarice, envy, gluttony, luxury, pride and sloth. Capitalist economic philosophy has transformed six of the seven into virtues. Even sloth is permissible for the rich.

Adam Smith was wrong. Human egoism is not an adequate basis for economic development because private self-interest is seldom consistent with general social interest. When the self-serving elite control the means of production and distribution, we can expect that resources will be used for short-run profit rather than in harmony with the kingdom of God. It seems self-evident that a system built on internal competition will eventually destroy itself.

Capitalism has been quite able for a while with huge amounts of energy to produce inefficiently (in terms of energy use) a huge mountain of consumer goods which are available to some. But it has not been able to solve the problem of poverty because it is a large part of the cause of poverty.[19] Capitalism leads to the exploitation of the poor and weak by the powerful and rich. Investment, trade and aid are used to exploit Third World societies to keep them poor and subjugated.[20] The development of the capitalist world contributes to the de-development of the Third World.[21] The quality of life in Third World societies is lower today than it was a hundred years ago. The cause is exploitation, not population growth.[22]

The capitalist system is unconcerned even about those who cooperate with it and provides poorly for those who do succeed. Even those on the top are poorly rewarded, except for material affluence. Executives are all too familiar with anxiety, fear and neurosis. Peace, security, meaningful relationships and community are missing at the top. Capitalism does not encourage people to give and receive love. Koinonia, that most basic human need, is not part of the capitalist formula.

Applying Biblical Values
The only answer to the mess the world is in can be found in the good news of the kingdom of God. The world, to its own detriment, may not accept that good news, but we can. So let's start applying it and live it.

Jubilee.   One answer to the international economic mess is the Jubilee. To institute the Jubilee would mean immediately canceling all debts and radically redistributing wealth and power. Think of the burden that would be immediately lifted from the poor. The Jubilee calls us to share our resources with whoever needs them, to end any power one may have over another, to abolish boundaries of race, class and gender. Jubilee would mean unilateral disarmament. It would mean a whole new international economic order.

The entire system of money lending and interest must go. There is a striking similarity between the money lenders' credit system and slavery. Consider how the poor nations are perpetually indebted to the rich nations. This debt gives bankers the power to impose their rules on the indebted countries, thus further victimizing the poor.[23] When interest charges are included, the poor have to pay twice as much as the rich for the things they buy. The rich profit by putting their creditors (slaves) to work. Investments in poor countries usually benefit only a small, privileged minority within that country and drain the economy of that country through the huge profits reaped from those investments. Meanwhile, the poor are worse off than ever because those investments meant the loss of their land and livelihood.

Yes, the Jubilee would seriously disrupt, if not destroy, the present economic system. That is a good indication of how sinful that system is. But what can we say? The Jubilee was commanded by God and proclaimed by Jesus.[24] Why should we not implement it? Let's announce it among ourselves and then to the whole world. It is an essential part of the good news.

Redistribution of wealth and power must happen. And it will happen—either voluntarily or involuntarily, either nonviolently or violently. How it will happen will be determined to a large extent by the rich, although the poor will also shape the struggle by the choices they make. The church can also influence how change will take place by the nature of her involvement in the struggle.[25]

We need to understand that the problem of world poverty will never be solved until we stop keeping people poor, until we remove the conditions that perpetuate poverty. There is no need to wait. We as Christians can institute the Jubilee among ourselves, give up all private property, have everything in common, and start living the way God wants all the world to live. We can start being the church, the first fruits of the kingdom, an expression of the new creation.

Decentralization.   Increasingly I find myself moving toward the view that all human activities and structures need to be decentralized. An important reason for this is my understanding of the church as koinonia, with all its economic and political implications. My vision for society is no different from my understanding of what the church is called to be. I do understand that there are two kingdoms and that they are radically different, but we are called to live in God's kingdom and look forward to the day when the kingdom of this world will be the kingdom of our Lord (Rev 11:15).

The church is to be the primary context for our lives. The gathered body should be having more influence on the shape of our lives than all the other forces of the world put together. The church is not to be a mere reflection of the class interests of her members. The church is not to be an extracurricular activity, but the base from which all our activity originates. It is this vision that shapes all my thinking.

Koinonia implies decentralized, local, face-to-face, primary groups where the important activities and decisions of life are experienced, where each person is known, loved and honored, where we each bear each other's burdens. This implies a voluntary society, not a society based on coercion and imposed power.

I find myself moving toward a decentralized view because I am not convinced centralization is practical. Even if the National Association of Evangelicals took over our present economic and political structures, things would not be any better than they are now. The answer does not lie in getting more Christians into positions of power, for the structures themselves are part of the problem.

Empires have seldom lasted more than a century before pressures for decentralization have taken over. Even within strong empires, like the Roman Empire, most of life was decentralized. It was these decentralized units that were stable and survived after the empire crumbled. The unstable empire of the multinational corporations, like Babylon (Rev 18:2—19:8), will also soon crumble, although many people will suffer until it does fall. The Bible and history show us example after example of violent and corrupt regimes being destroyed either from the outside or from inherent internal weakness.

Decentralization seems to provide more possibilities for social justice than does centralization of power in the hands of a few. If everyone is able to participate (koinonia) in the decisions that affect their lives, there is less chance for tyranny than if the few rule over the many. People ruling over others is in itself wrong, according to Jesus.

It seems that all decisions should be made at the lowest possible level. All systems and organizations could be decentralized to the point that they could be controlled by those who are affected by them. As it is now, local areas have little control over what happens in their neighborhoods. The New England town meetings are one example of what could be. (It is not insignificant, by the way, that their roots are in the free church.)

It is true that local groups with individual class identity seeking power for themselves tend to end up as oppressive, selfish, racist groups concerned only with narrow self-interest. That need not happen, however, if the community is kingdom oriented, based on service and cooperation rather than power seeking, and if it is a community in which people can find answers to their fears. The experience of koinonia can liberate people to reach out beyond themselves.

One of the arguments for free-enterprise capitalism is that for freedom to be protected there need to be many centers of power. The problem is that capitalism works to destroy those centers of power in the push toward centralization. Society can be shaped in a way that makes it more difficult for any group to force submission of any regional population to tyranny. The more centralized political and economic structures are, the more vulnerable they are to sabotage, manipulation, blackmail or takeover.

Ecological concerns point us in the direction of decentralization. The centralized economy is extremely inefficient and dependent on massive amounts of energy and resources. It simply does not fit in an ecological, sustainable future.[26] Our present centralized economy is based on the use of nonrenewable resources. The use of renewable resources (solar, wind, organic waste) by nature needs to be decentralized. Consider, for example, the difference in social implications between solar and nuclear energy.

Solar	Nuclear
ecologically safe	threatening to the environment
democratic	bureaucratic or authoritarian
decentralized	centralized
flexible	inflexible
economical	expensive
simple	complex
safe	dangerous
sustainable	nonrenewable

A sensible, long-range solution to current economic problems such as unemployment is not in a reindustrialization based on outmoded concepts of high energy use and wasteful consumption. The answer is not in expanding an economy, which can only lead to disaster, but in creating a new economy based on realistic concepts of a sustainable future. The answer to unemployment is not to get people back into useless and destructive jobs. It is to put people to work at activities that meet real needs; and there is enough real need in the world to keep everyone busy for a long time.

While technology needs to be appropriate to the fragile nature of the planet and consistent with proper stewardship of the earth, it is even more important that it be appropriate to people's needs.

Continued investment in capital-intensive ventures will only widen the gap between rich and poor. Heavy capital-intensive investment will produce relatively fewer jobs than investment in work that is more labor intensive. The money needed to build a nuclear power plant would create many more jobs if it were invested in building solar collectors. Labor-intensive activities also use much less energy.

We would do well to reconsider Gandhi's idea of the spinning wheel. It may be that the spinning wheel itself is not the answer for us; but locally controlled, decentralized industry which makes work available to all is. The Amish with their simple farming methods may be ahead of, instead of behind, the times.

In New Covenant Fellowship, the community in which I am trying to live what I preach, we raise vegetables to sell. We use a minimum of machinery, most of the work being done by hand. We have found this to be economically competitive, ecologically sound, personally satisfying and a great way of sharing in fellowship.

In koinonia we are partners, not cogs on a wheel controlled by bosses who are dictators. Surely dehumanizing work is not what God wants for us. Work is meant to be a blessing. Work can be meaningful, give a sense of serving others, be creative and offer opportunities for self-expression. It need not be dehumanizing or alienating. In koinonia, even mundane tasks can be meaningful when seen as serving others. Work is a gift of God, not a curse. The curse of sin (alienation, boredom, unemployment) has been put on work, but we can work to remove that curse. If work is a blessing, it should be available to all.

Part of the process of our transformation is learning to work together cooperatively. The workplace can be a learning environment. How different this is from the world's system, with capital on one side and labor on the other, each with its own perspective, interests and fears! This results in conflict, usually with capital's having most of the power. This decreases productivity because of poor relations between workers and management.

The important thing is not whether the factory is controlled by capitalists or by the state. What does matter is the nature of relationships within the factory and the degree of participation (koinonia) in making decisions that affect the lives of those in the factory.[27]

Even the simple principle of worker participation in decision making points toward decentralization. This does not mean just having a crew decide who sweeps the floor, but also having real participation in shaping the policies, relationships and products of the business. In the realm of redemption all workers are partners (koinonia).

Some may wonder if all this is realistic. But is it biblical? If it is true, then it is realistic. Surely the present chaos is not realistic. Actually, much of what we have been discussing already exists in small ways, scattered here and there all over the world.[28] It is a sensible, workable alternative to chaos. There can be an economy which does not pit us against each other or against nature.

We already have an incredibly cooperative economy. Most people do what they are asked to do, work together and support each other in various ways. The problem is gross inequality in power. Some lord it over others. Still, it is amazing how employees cooperate with their employers in spite of oppressive working conditions. There must be some deeper motivation than just their paychecks.

At least seventy-one million Americans belong to some kind of cooperative. Think of all the cooperation and sharing that already exists among neighbors and friends, all the tasks that get done without pay. We don't need any centralized bureaucracy to keep that happening. What does need to happen is to encourage *these* activities instead of all the destructive activities.

Simple living.   If we take seriously the biblical witness and present realities, then a radical change in lifestyle is called for on the part of the affluent of the world.[29] Isaiah asks us, "Why do you spend your money for that which is not bread, and your labor for that which does not satisfy?" (Is 55:2).

I raise this not to make people feel guilty, but to share the good news that we can be liberated from our slavery and self-destructive habits. Our affluence leads to shallow and empty lifestyles and relationships. Our lifestyles have been destructive not only of the environment and the poor, but also of our own souls. I know of no group in the history of the world that ever became affluent without then losing their souls. Ancient Israel seemed unable to remember God in times of affluence. The Christian church seems to thrive better under persecution than under economic prosperity.

We can be liberated from all that. We can get a real sense of worth and identity from our relationships with God and with our brothers and sisters in koinonia, instead of the illusion of worth we get from owning and consuming things. If we know our true worth, we will not need to consider ourselves worth more than others and deserving of higher pay than others. There can be no true koinonia where some live on a higher economic level than others.

We can completely trust God for our economic security. We do not need to grab, exploit, hoard or defend ourselves. Such activities are based on fear and are unnecessary. The issues in economics and military armament are actually exactly the same. Do we trust God or build our own security? The problem is that the more wealth or armaments we have, the less secure we become.

The call of Jesus is to become poor, to identify with the oppressed, to cast our lots with the downtrodden. Real love leads us to become one with the homeless (maybe by opening our homes to them). This is the logic of the Incarnation. We are called to a life of poverty because of our deep identification with Jesus as our norm and example. He became poor, vulnerable, empty. He put his whole trust in God. He gave up all he had. Love calls us to give up all we have, too.

This need not be too frightening if we do it because we trust in God and if we do it in the context of koinonia. It is no sacrifice to give up what we have for something better. Faith and community lead to a liberated life, one that is simple rather than cluttered, ecologically responsible rather than destructive, and in harmony with the poor rather than exploitative.

There are enough resources in the world to meet everyone's needs. God has provided well for us. But there is not enough to go around on our present scale of greed. For example, the world's annual grain harvest could provide each person in the world with three thousand calories a day. Add to that all the beans, nuts, fruit and vegetables that are grown, and God's abundance is clear. But if we insist on eating a lot of meat, there is not enough to go around. It takes a lot of grain to produce a pound of meat. Two-thirds of the grain grown in the United States is fed to animals to produce protein for the rich First World, while the poor of the Third World go hungry.[30]

While some things, like food, can be provided for all, other things, like large country estates, by their very nature cannot be attained by all. There is not enough room in the world for everyone to be a land baron. Standing on tiptoe in a crowd may help one person to see better, but there is no advantage in all standing on tiptoe. Part of our economic problem is that people are striving for those things which cannot be shared by all. Any economic stimulation in this direction can only make things worse. We all will be better off if we don't always try to stand on tiptoe. Peter Maurin, founder of the Catholic Worker Movement, says this so well in his easy essay "The Case for Utopia."[31]

The world would be better off
if people tried to become better.
And people would become better
if they stopped trying to become
better off.
For when everybody tries to
become better off,
nobody is better off.
But when everybody tries to
become better,
everybody is better off.
Everybody would be rich
if nobody tried to become richer.
And nobody would be poor
if everybody tried to be poorest.

If we are to survive, we must turn from our idolatrous worship of economic growth. We need drastic de-development of the developed world.[32] Some people are saying that the GNP in the United States needs to be reduced by as much as ninety per cent. And then what would be left? Just those things and services which are needed for a good life. Many of these services, like those housewives and mothers have traditionally done,[33] are not even measured in the GNP. The GNP is mainly a measure of what it costs to maintain our exploitative system, not of things that are most important.

Social Change
So what does all this have to do with all the critical problems of the world? What difference does it make if I live simply, practice

the Jubilee and live in koinonia? How does my not eating meat help hungry people in Brazil?

My first responsibility is to be faithful, to live in the new age of God's kingdom. We cannot save the world, and I distrust anyone who thinks he or she can. History is in God's hands, not ours. Now I do believe that simply being faithful will have some effect. What effect, I do not know. That I leave to God. But God can use our response to the call of the new creation.

I also know that we are not serious about changing anything unless we begin to make those changes in our own lives. Making those changes in our lives can greatly reduce our sense of powerlessness and increase our sense of hope. Our living simply may not immediately help anyone in Brazil; but if we live simply, we may then have more sensitivity to the needs of people in Brazil and be better able to respond to their needs. If we are changed, maybe God can even use us for change in the world.

I have little hope in looking to the state as the source of repentance, justice or love. In fact, I see the state standing in the way.[34] Concentrations of power, with their own vested interests (be they rooted in the ruling or working class), are not the source of renewal and koinonia to which Christians should look. Since the state, which represents the interests of the powerful, is part of the source of poverty, I doubt that it will be the answer.

Although I do not see the state as the solution or seek to force the state to be Christian, we can speak truth to power and call the state to live up to its own professed ideals (liberty, justice, honesty and so on). To the extent that the state is involved in the economy, we can ask the state to not contribute to injustice. Our primary witness to the state may be negative. Instead of demanding that the state do this or that good thing, which we should be doing ourselves, we can ask the state to stop doing this and that bad thing.

The primary call of Christians is neither to change the structures of the old age which is passing away, nor to just change individuals and leave them as part of the old society. The primary task of the church is to be a new society (koinonia) into which we call people to enter through repentance. The Christian community is the alternative to the sick society. The mediating agent of God's saving grace is primarily the church. The church can create the alternatives, do the experimenting and take the risks with new and needed forms. After all, who would we expect to be in a better position to be open to God's Spirit?

The church can stop blessing worldly values which make oppression acceptable. The church can question the moral legitimacy of the corporations; it can proclaim biblical truth which will result in undermining the legitimacy of the powerful and the mighty. The church can follow the radical path of Jesus instead of being Sadducees who stay with the system of oppression and oppose radical repentance.

Since koinonia includes the participation of everyone involved, there is no blueprint for what this would look like on a global scale. New institutions must be developed from the bottom up as a process by the people involved. The more steps we take, the more clearly we will be able to see the next steps which are needed. We are talking about a process, not final answers. There is a need for experimentation with new types of economic activities and institutions in which people can participate in determining the shape and direction of not only their economic lifestyles, but the wider shape of social participation. There can be an economy which provides opportunity for all to participate, in which all can be cared for without paternalism.

This is not a retreat from the world. It is a creative way to be in the world yet not of the world. It is not enough to live the alternative and forget the world, however. We can both live the alternative and confront the world with the truth.

The best thing we can do for the poor is not to give handouts (although that is needed at times, such as after disasters), but to nonviolently fight the structures of injustice and oppression which cause people to be poor. We can change our lifestyles so that we no longer contribute to their oppression. We can also confront the structures of injustice with the nonviolent tools of truth and love. Such structures include both corporations which directly exploit the poor and others, like alcohol and tobacco companies, which destroy people more indirectly. We will look to find common cause with other groups seeking alternatives. Movements of the oppressed are quite significant. That is why those in power are ready to use such massive violence to suppress them.

Ultimately the only answer to world problems is to be found in Jesus Christ. Most of the world's suffering can be understood as a direct result of sin, especially corporate sin. As long as oppression and exploitation continue, there will be great human need. In the midst of that we can live an alternative, struggle against the powers of oppression, and give aid to those in need. But without repentance and the inbreaking of God's new order, the world's problems will never be solved. What we do can make some difference, however.

Followers of Jesus can begin to live in a whole new world. We can live a life of love, service, humility and simplicity, with a Jubilee economy. In koinonia we can begin to embody and live out the alternative.

Notes

[1]For a more comprehensive study of Christian community, see my *Living in Christian Community* (Scottdale, Pa.: Herald Press, 1979).

[2]For further discussion of this idea, see Wes Granberg-Michaelson, "At the Dawn of the New Creation: A Theology of the Environment," *Sojourners* 10 (November 1981):13-16.

[3]Ronald J. Sider, *Rich Christians in an Age of Hunger*, (Downers Grove, Ill.: InterVarsity Press, 1977), p. 62.

[4]For an excellent comparison of the political and economic conditions in the time of Amos with our own time, see Jack A. Nelson, *Hunger for Justice* (Maryknoll, N.Y.: Orbis Books, 1980).

[5]Tom Hanks, "Why People Are Poor," *Sojourners* 10 (January 1981):19-22.

[6]For detailed documentation of this thesis, see the excellent books by Frances Moore Lappé and Joseph Collins: *Aid as Obstacle* (San Francisco: Institute for Food and Development Policy, 1980); and *Food First: Beyond the Myth of Scarcity* (New York: Ballantine Books, 1978). Equally important are Jack Nelson, *Hunger for Justice*, and Ronald Sider, *Rich Christians*.

[7]For documentation for the widespread communalism of the early church, see my *Living in Christian Community*, pp. 68-80.

[8]Two aspects of the fallen world's failures at koinonia deserve note. First, people at the top of the world's principalities and powers have no limit to the atrocities they are willing to purposefully commit. The Jewish holocaust under Nazi Germany is not a singular example. It is matched by America's unrepented slaughter of six million Native Americans in its westward conquest. While major atrocities are being committed around the world today, history's greatest horror threatens to be only minutes away—the consumption of the entire planet in a nuclear fireball. See Howard Zinn, *A People's History of the United States* (New York: Harper & Row, 1980).

Second, while most of us have not been directly victimized by torturous oppression, the world's rulers nonetheless impose their power daily on the mass of working and poor people. Working people, faced with degrading unemployment, are offered jobs under conditions they have little control over—alienated not only from the full value of their work, but also from the very decision of what to produce. Working people feel defeated, out of control: "You can't fight city hall." Poor people's livelihoods are now bureaucratized with a myriad of rules that confront them every month. See Francis Fox Piven and Richard A. Cloward, *Regulating the Poor* (New York: Vintage Books, 1971).

[9] Quoted in Nelson, *Hunger for Justice*, p. 56.

[10] See ibid., pp. 82-86. See also Marion Anderson, *The Empty Pork Barrel* (Lansing, Mich.: Employment Research Associates, 1982).

[11] For a deeper look at a biblical approach to questions of violence and war, see Dale Aukerman, *Darkening Valley* (New York: Seabury Press, 1981); Ronald J. Sider, *Christ and Violence* (Scottdale, Pa.: Herald Press, 1979); John Howard Yoder, *The Politics of Jesus* (Grand Rapids, Mich.: Eerdmans, 1972).

[12] Environmentally sensitive production is not always vastly more expensive. By making material advantage (profit) the centerpiece of production planning, our society, to gain a few extra pennies, often makes decisions which harm the environment. We continue killing whales and using toxic chemicals to make lipstick, electronic gadgets and pesticides when alternatives are available at comparable costs.

In some cases it is actually cheaper to be environmentally conscious. With nuclear power, for example, utility companies are taking rate payers for a multi-billion-dollar ride, while suppressing drastically cheaper and safer solar technologies and cogeneration of heat and electricity. These cheaper energy systems, however, would decentralize control over energy and reduce our dependence on so-called utilities.

[13] Kirkpatrick Sale, *Human Scale* (New York: Coward, McCann & Geoghegan, 1980), pp. 129-42. Also see Lappé and Collins, *Food First*, pp. 220-29.

[14] Lappé, *Aid as Obstacle*, p. 10.

[15] Susan George, *Feeding the Few: Corporate Control of Food* (Washington, D.C.: Institute for Policy Studies, 1979).

[16] Nelson, *Hunger for Justice*, pp. 48-50, and Lappé and Collins, *Food First*, pp. 134-80.

[17] See Richard J. Barnet and Ronald E. Müller, *Global Reach: The Power of Multinational Corporations* (New York: Simon & Schuster, 1974); Noam Chomsky and Edward S. Herman, *The Washington Connection and Third World Fascism* (Boston: South End Press, 1979); and Holly Sklar, *Trilateralism: The Trilateral Commission and Elite Planning for World Management* (Boston: South End Press, 1980).

[18] For a Christian critique of capitalism, see my *Beyond the Rat Race* (Scottdale, Pa.: Herald Press, 1973), pp. 127-33.

[19] Nelson, *Hunger for Justice*, pp. 30-55; and Barnet and Müller, *Global Reach*, pp. 148-84.

[20] Lappé, *Aid as Obstacle*.

[21] Take, for example, the effects of colonialism on Third World countries. The effect of colonialism was to destroy the local economy. Before Britain took over India, there was a flourishing textile industry in Bengal. Through the use of

tariffs, Britain was able to destroy the textile industry in Bengal. Sider, *Rich Christians,* pp. 139-40.

[22]Nelson, *Hunger for Justice,* pp. 101-31; and Lappé and Collins, *Food First,* pp. 24-53.

[23]Nelson, *Hunger for Justice,* pp. 52-54.

[24]See Sider, *Rich Christians,* pp. 88-112.

[25]For suggestions of what we can do, see Lappé and Collins, *Food First,* pp. 491-513, and *Aid as Obstacle,* pp. 149-56.

[26]Although centralization may at first seem more efficient, it soon becomes less efficient and more wasteful than the less centralized system it replaces. For further reading on decentralization, see Sale, *Human Scale;* Jeremy Rifkin, *Entropy* (New York: Viking Press, 1980); E. F. Schumacher, *Good Work* (New York: Harper & Row, 1979); and E. F. Schumacher, *Small Is Beautiful* (New York: Harper & Row, 1973).

[27]For an excellent discussion of worker-owned businesses, see Robert Oakeshott, *The Case for Workers' Co-ops* (Boston: Routledge and Kegan Paul, 1978). This includes a discussion of the Mondragon group of highly successful worker-owned businesses in Spain. Also see Daniel Zwerdling, *Workplace Democracy* (New York: Harper & Row, 1979).

[28]In addition to the experience of Christian communities, there are many secular experiments with alternatives. See George McRobie, *Small Is Possible* (New York: Harper & Row, 1981).

[29]For a more detailed discussion of simple living, see my *Beyond the Rat Race.*

[30]Frances Moore Lappé, *Diet for a Small Planet* (New York: Ballantine Books, 1982).

[31]Thomas C. Cornell and James H. Forest, eds., *A Penny a Copy* (New York: Macmillan, 1968), pp. 16-17.

[32]Ivan Illich, *Energy and Equity* (New York: Harper & Row, 1974).

[33]This is particularly true of Third World women.

[34]See Ralph Miliband, *The State in Capitalist Society* (New York: Basic Books, 1969).

Select Bibliography

Barnet, Richard J. *The Lean Years: Politics in the Age of Scarcity.* New York: Simon & Schuster, 1980. Discusses political and economic implications of limited world resources.

Barnet, Richard J., and Müller, Ronald E. *Global Reach: The Power of Multinational Corporations.* New York: Simon & Schuster, 1974. An analysis of multinational corporations and their power.

Baron, Paul A., and Sweezy, Paul M. *Monopoly Capital.* New York: Monthly Review Press, 1966. A Marxist perspective on economics.

Bluestone, Barry. *The Deindustrialization of America.* New York: Basic Books, 1982. A study of how big corporations hurt local economies and create unemployment in their drive for profits.

Commoner, Barry. *The Closing Circle.* New York: Alfred A. Knopf, 1971. Combines arguments for social justice and ecological stewardship, showing one to be necessary for the other.

————. *The Poverty of Power: Energy and Economic Crisis.* New York: Bantam Books, 1977. Discusses problems of high energy use and possible alternatives.

Daly, Herman E., ed. *Toward a Steady-State Economy.* San Francisco: W. H. Freeman, 1973. An influential survey of the need to develop an economy consistent with ecological concerns. Calls for reduction of consumption and growth.

George, Susan. *Feeding the Few: Corporate Control of Food.* Washington, D.C.: Institute for Policy Studies, 1979. A study of corporate food control and its consequences.

Gish, Arthur G. *Beyond the Rat Race.* Scottdale, Pa.: Herald Press, 1973. Deals with economic issues in terms of lifestyle. An introduction to simple living.

————. *Living in Christian Community.* Scottdale, Pa.: Herald Press, 1979. A comprehensive study of what it would mean for the church to be a community. Deals with all the major issues of ecclesiology.

Harrington, Michael. *The Twilight of Capitalism.* New York: Simon & Schuster, 1976. A democratic socialist view of capitalism and economics.

Henderson, Hazel. *Creating Alternative Futures: The End of Economics.* New York: Berkley Pub., 1978. A good survey of literature and issues of ecology, justice and decentralization.

Illich, Ivan. *Energy and Equity.* New York: Harper & Row, 1974. A study of our use of energy and implications for the future.

Lappé, Frances Moore. *Diet for a Small Planet.* New York: Ballantine Books, 1982. Shows how food is related to social justice issues and how we can change our diets.

Lappé, Frances Moore, et al. *Aid as Obstacle.* San Francisco: Institute for Food and Development Policy, 1980. A critique of American foreign aid, arguing that this aid perpetuates injustice rather than working at the causes of poverty.

Lappé, Frances M., and Collins, Joseph. *Food First: Beyond the Myth of Scarcity.* New York: Ballantine Books, 1978. A thorough examination of international food issues, arguing that the root cause of hunger is the concentration of control over the production and distribution of food.

McRobie, George. *Small Is Possible.* New York: Harper & Row, 1981. Surveys various attempts at developing small-is-beautiful, decentralist economics.

Meadows, Donella H., et al. *The Limits to Growth.* New York: Universe Books, 1974. The controversial study by the Club of Rome. Argues for reducing use of world resources.

Nearing, Helen, and Nearing, Scott. *Living the Good Life.* New York: Schocken Books, 1970. The story of the Nearings' attempts at simple living.

Nelson, Jack A. *Hunger for Justice: The Politics of Food and Faith.* Maryknoll, N.Y.: Orbis Books, 1980. Shows how world hunger is the result of injustice. Based on both a biblical perspective and an examination of the multinational corporations' role in causing hunger.

Oakeshott, Robert. *The Case for Workers' Co-ops.* Boston: Routledge and Kegan Paul, 1978. An excellent survey of worker-owned business. Good discussion of the issues involved.

Rifkin, Jeremy. *Entropy*. New York: Viking Press, 1980. Applies the concept of entropy to many different social structures, arguing for drastic reduction of production and consumption.

Sale, Kirkpatrick. *Human Scale*. New York: Coward, McCann & Geoghegan, 1980. A thorough argument for decentralization of all aspects of society. Includes a historical survey and suggests what decentralization might mean for modern society.

Schumacher, E. F. *Good Work*. New York: Harper & Row, 1979. Argues for decentralization, appropriate technology and simple living.

——. *Small Is Beautiful*. New York: Harper & Row, 1973. The classic, influential book arguing for decentralization and appropriate technology.

Sider, Ronald J. *Rich Christians in an Age of Hunger*. Rev. ed. Downers Grove, Ill.: InterVarsity Press, 1984. A popular introduction to social justice issues with suggestions for steps Christians can take in working for justice.

Vasudevan, K. *Gandhian Economics*. Bombay: Bharatiya, Vidya Bhavan, 1967. An introduction to Gandhian economics, a side most people do not know of Gandhi.

Yoder, John Howard. *The Politics of Jesus*. Grand Rapids, Mich.: Eerdmans, 1972. Shows how social ethics can be rooted in Jesus and the kingdom of God.

Zwerdling, Daniel. *Workplace Democracy*. New York: Harper & Row, 1979. Shows how worker control of business could be possible.

A Free-Market Response
Gary North

Art Gish's essay gives us something detailed to sink our teeth into. Or put another way, his essay is like a swarm of bees. If we can swat enough of them away without getting stung, there may be some honey for our efforts when we're finished.

Gish, like the other two authors, is uncomfortable with Old Testament law. He cites some of these laws where convenient, but he is not ready to accept the Old Testament law-order—a consistent whole—as the governing system of law in New Testament times. He is unwilling to affirm that Jesus' reformulation of certain *applications* of *a few* of these laws (plural) did not in any way destroy the permanent, binding character of God's law-order.[1] He, like the other contributors, wants to speak of the "general concern of justice," but not of the binding character of Old Testament economic law. This is the heart of my objections to all three of the other contributors. I offer the same *general* objection, but varying *specific* objections, depending on the specific conclusions of each author.

Gish is not so emphatic as Diehl and Gladwin in his rejection of
the concept of a specific outline or blueprint for a Christian political economy, but he is generally in agreement with them:
    The Old Testament gives detailed laws regulating economic
    relationships. Although we need not feel bound by these laws,
    the general concern of justice and shalom found there is re-
    peated in the New Testament and is meant for us. (pp. 133-34)
    Although the Bible does not advocate any particular shape
    our economic life must take, it does point in a definite direction.
    (p. 140)
    Since koinonia includes the participation of everyone in-
    volved, there is no blueprint for what this would look like on a
    global scale. . . . We are talking about a process, not final an-
    swers. There is a need for experimentation with new types of
    economic activities and institutions. (p. 154)
The word "process" is a tip-off. Process philosophy, process theology, and situational ethics are all cut from the same evolutionary
cloth.[2] So is existentialism. This is not to say that Gish denies the
six-day creation; he may or may not. I am saying that he is import-
ing language from outside Christian orthodoxy when he appeals to
process rather than *permanent ethics which require a permanent
law-order,* created by God.
    If all he is saying is that we cannot know in detail what kind of
economic institutions will be constructed in the future, then I
heartily agree. It is my concern with the rising tide of compulsory
government bureaucracy which leads me to support free market
experimentation (entrepreneurship). I do not trust the judgment of
government bureaucrats to decide what products and services are
right for the world, now and forevermore.[3] I want *consumers* to
decide—always, of course, within the framework of biblical law.
    I am not advocating the legalization of prostitution, pornog-
raphy, or the sale of cocaine to eight-year-old schoolchildren in
exchange for homosexual favors. What I am saying in response to
Gish is that we *do* know the general outline of what an explicitly
Christian political economy would look like. We know, for example, that no branch of civil government could collect as much as
ten per cent of income from taxpayers in any given year, for such
levels of taxation constitute an affront to God (1 Sam 8:15, 17). All
the "process" in the world cannot alter this aspect of God's cove-

nant. And I suspect that it is precisely this kind of permanent restriction on the taxation policies of the civil government which Gish—as well as *The Other Side* magazine[4] and Evangelicals for Social Action (ESA)—would reject as "wooden exegesis."[5] If I am incorrect in my assessment of his views, then I will say so—just as soon as he publicly challenges *The Other Side* and ESA on this point concerning public finance.

I am in complete agreement with Gish's statement that "we could avoid a lot of confusion by simply seeing Christian ethics as discerning God's will instead of trying to find the lowest common denominator possible for the whole world. We do not need to answer what would be feasible for all humanity apart from God's Spirit. With God's Spirit we know all things are possible" (pp. 131-32). The issue, above all, is *ethics*. The problem is, we need the Bible to provide us with the details of our ethics. *This means biblical law.* What so few Christian social theorists are willing to admit is this: The New Testament is a *commentary* on the Old Testament, not its negation.

I also agree with Gish when he asserts that "economic questions are among the most important questions we can ask. And they are basic to biblical thought. There is no subject about which the Bible is more clear than economics" (p. 133). The Bible *is* clear about economics, and the wealth of material in the Bible which relates to economics would fill many shelves, which I am trying to do with my multivolume economic commentary on the Bible, *The Dominion Covenant.* But what may surprise the reader is the extent to which the contributors in this book do not agree about economics. If the Bible is so clear, why are the commentators so divided? The answer is found in the writings of the Christian philosopher, Cornelius Van Til: *It is a question of presuppositions.*[6] If we do not presuppose Old Testament law as morally binding, then we are faced with the horrendous task of spinning a theoretical universe out of our own entrails, the way a spider spins its web.

There are many strands of Gish's web that concern me. His underlying presupposition concerning market exchanges is what Ludwig von Mises calls the "Montaigne fallacy." Gish thinks that voluntary exchange is a case of "heads I win, tails you win." If I get ahead, I leave you worse off than before. *But you aren't worse off*—not unless you are eaten up with envy.[7] Only if I have lied to you (fraud) or have coerced you into giving me your wealth (theft) or have gotten together with other voters to take away your wealth ("economic democracy") are you worse off. As I stress in my main essay, *market capitalism is not a zero-sum game.* It is a means of achieving mutually beneficial goals through voluntary exchange and fully responsible ownership. It is a system of economic stewardship in which *consumers, as buyers or non-buyers, are sovereign.* There are two winners in a voluntary exchange.

It is not true, contrary to Gish (and also Marx, Lenin, and E. J. Hobsbawm), that "economic growth has been based on exploitation of the poor" (p. 143). Had Gish studied and absorbed the information on economic growth presented in the voluminous researches by Peter Bauer of the London School of Economics, he might not have made this unfortunate mistake.[8] Economic growth is the product of a world-and-life view which is favorable to future-orientation, thrift, risk-bearing, hard work, respect for contracts, honesty in financial dealings, education, and dozens of other essentially Western, Protestant attitudes. Max Weber was correct: There is a connection between the Protestant ethic and the spirit of capitalism.

Gish says that the Bible teaches that "the rich are considered responsible for the condition of the oppressed" (p. 135). Wrong. The Bible teaches that *oppressors* are responsible for the condition of the oppressed. The Bible does not say that all rich men are oppressors; it says that some of them are, and that if biblical law were respected and enforced, rich oppressors could not easily indulge in this sin. But most important, the Bible does *not* teach that the rich are responsible for the condition of poverty as such. I offer as evidence the book of Proverbs.

The Bible also does not teach that "God intervenes in history to liberate the oppressed poor" (p. 135). What the Bible does teach is that God intervenes in history to liberate the *righteous* oppressed, whether rich or poor. Did God liberate the poor who lived in Canaan? No. He had his people exterminate them. There were wicked poor people in Canaan, after all. They lived under the domination of "unrighteous structures," to use a popular phrase. God destroyed both Canaan's oppressed and Canaan's "unrighteous structures" when Joshua and the Israelites invaded the land.

The unrighteous poor are headed for hell, and God gives them a down payment (an "earnest"), in time and on earth, in order to warn them of their coming judgment. This is what Deuteronomy 28:15-68 is all about. But their poverty, which is an earthly curse, can become a means of calling them to repentance. On the other hand, the wealth of the unrighteous rich is an earthly blessing that condemns them in the future (Lk 16:19-31). It heaps coals of fire on their heads, to use an Old Testament and New Testament phrase (Prov 25:22; Rom 12:20).

If you remember nothing else that I have written, please remember this: It is a question of *ethics*, not net financial worth, which is the overriding social and economic concern of the Bible. This is why we are inevitably driven back to consider specifics of biblical law. This is why we must raise the question of the "blueprints."

Gish cites Matthew 6:19, "Do not lay up for yourselves treasures on earth." But his essay misses the point of Christ's warning. It is not *treasures* that are the focus of Christ's concern; it is the phrase *for yourselves*. We are God's stewards, and building up God's capital resources—a successful business, educated children, a profitable farm, or even a best-selling book on theology—is one of our assignments. The parable of the talents was not exclusively an economic parable, but the talents were units of money, after all. And it was better to have ten talents than only one at the end of the period.

Gish is mistaken when he says that "it is the call to give up our privilege and power and to identify with the poor" (p. 138). It is our task to seek influence, power, prestige, and capital in order to bring glory to God, respect for his law, and to identify with the *righteous*, not the poor as such.

Gish and his spiritual colleagues have made a fundamental theological error. They have confused *ethics* with *metaphysics*. They have confused one's historic class or status position in the plan of God with one's permanent *ethical standing before God*. This confusion led to most of the errors of economic analysis that David Chilton refutes, point by point, in his book *Productive Christians in an Age of Guilt-Manipulators*.

I have too little space to consider in detail other issues raised by Gish, such as his knee-jerk distrust of technology (which is overwhelmingly a *decentralizing* force today—microcomputers, solar power, and so forth),[9] and his implication, contrary to the Apostle

Paul's specific warning (1 Tim 4:3), that there is something morally suspect about eating meat. Ironically, we find that Gish wants to take away from Black Americans one of their delights, since Black Americans eat meat in greater quantities than White Americans do.[10] I find his hostility to factories somewhat amusing, since it is the factory which makes possible such mass-produced wonders as his typewriter and this paperback book. He offers no proof for his assertion that capitalism "is a large part of the cause of poverty" (p. 144). He claims that "current economic thinking does not take into account the environmental costs of current activities to be paid for by future generations" (p. 142). In fact, the technical literature on the economics of environmentalism is immense, stretching back to A. C. Pigou's *Wealth and Welfare* (1912). This error indicates that Gish has not studied economics very carefully.

His hostility to centralization and empire is altogether healthy. (I suspect John Gladwin will feel the heat of Gish's pen.) His fear of bureaucracy is warranted. I just wish he would come to grips with his own admission: "The Bible even goes so far as to promise prosperity to those who are righteous (Deut 7—8, 28). It is important to remember that this promise of prosperity is made to the collective people of God, not to greedy individuals who exploit others" (p. 134). Amen and amen.

Notes

[1]Greg L. Bahnsen, *Theonomy in Christian Ethics* (Nutley, N.J.: Craig Press, 1977).

[2]Ewert H. Cousins, ed., *Process Theology: Basic Writings* (New York: Newman Press, 1971); Delwin Brown, et al., eds., *Process Philosophy and Christian Thought* (Indianapolis: Bobbs-Merrill, 1971).

[3]On this point, see F. A. Hayek, *The Constitution of Liberty* (Chicago: Univ. of Chicago Press, 1960), chaps. 2, 3; Antony Sutton, *Western Technology and Soviet Economic Development*, 3 vols. (Stanford, Calif.: Hoover Institution Press, 1968-73); Leopold Tyrmand, *The Rosa Luxemburg Contraceptives Cooperative: A Primer on Communist Civilization* (New York: Macmillan, 1972).

[4]Gish was listed as an "associate" of *The Other Side* in the April 1979 issue.

[5]This was the phrase used against me by Ronald Sider in our debate at the Gordon-Conwell School of Theology in April of 1981. I asked him repeatedly to state exactly how large a percentage of a man's income the State has a right to extract, and to cite a passage in the Bible authorizing this limit. Dr. Sider repeatedly refused to answer my question. Copies of the tape are available from the Institute for Christian Economics in Tyler, Texas.

[6]Van Til's books are numerous. Two good introductions are *The Defense of the Faith*, 2nd ed. (Phillipsburg, N.J.: Presbyterian & Reformed, 1963), and *A Christian Theory of Knowledge* (Phillipsburg, N.J.: Presbyterian & Reformed, 1969).

[7]See Helmut Schoeck, *Envy: A Theory of Social Behavior* (New York: Harcourt, Brace, 1970).

[8]P. T. Bauer, *Dissent on Development* (Cambridge, Mass.: Harvard Univ. Press, 1972); *Equality, the Third World, and Economic Delusion* (Cambridge, Mass.: Harvard Univ. Press, 1981).

[9]Alvin Toffler, *The Third Wave* (New York: Random House, 1980).

[10]U.S. Department of Agriculture study; summarized in an Associated Press Story, *Tyler Morning Telegraph*, 18 December 1982.

A Guided-Market Response

William E. Diehl

What does it mean for the Christian to be "in the world" but not "of the world"? Christians can interpret these words from the Gospel of John in a variety of ways. At one end of the spectrum is the notion that Christians should distance themselves from all those aspects of worldly life which are not in accordance with their understanding of God's will for creation. I call followers of this position "clean-hands Christians." They are well aware of the fallen nature of both humanity and the institutions of society. They conclude that if they are to be true to their Lord, they must avoid all contact with them. The assumption is that if all Christians do likewise the institutions of our society will be forced to change.

At the other end of the scale are those Christians who are convinced that they should be totally immersed in the matters of the world in order to carry out their understanding of the will of God, but all the while affirming that they act as stewards of God and not as puppets of the world. I call such people "dirty-hands Christians." They are well aware that if God's love and justice is going to be felt in the world, they will have to dirty their hands by dealing with the fallen people and fallen institutions of society. The assumption is, as with clean-hands Christians, that if all believers do likewise, the institutions of society will be changed.

I am a dirty-hands Christian. I would classify Art Gish as a clean-hands Christian. Therein lies our difference.

Both of us have some problems with our position. While Gish can catalog a long list of people, ideologies and organizations which make for injustice in our society, his clean-hands philosophy restrains him from engaging directly in the swirl of worldly activities. His hope for creating a just society rests solely on the belief that if enough Christians follow his example the world will take note and be reformed. And, should the world not even notice, at least clean-hands Christians can point to a life relatively unsullied by godless influences.

For me the position of clean-hands Christians presents some real problems with respect to theology and strategy. At the same time, I must confess that we dirty-hands Christians must always struggle with trying to discern the will of God in any given situation and must constantly question our motives. Are we truly in but not of the world, or are we really owned by the world?

It seems to me that the Gish essay presents a viewpoint which is flawed theologically and doomed strategically. The essay argues convincingly that in both the Old and the New Testaments God's people are called to show mercy for the poor and to work for justice in the world. However, the connections which are made between the testimony of the Scriptures and today's economic systems are obscure. While the Bible does record the social and economic practices of God's people at given points in history, it does not provide us with simple solutions for twentieth-century problems. There is no such thing as Christian economics any more than there is Christian mathematics or Christian house painting. Yes, we do have Christians who are economists and mathematicians and house painters, but they call themselves Christian not because of a biblical directive for carrying out their work, but rather because of a relationship they have with God as revealed through Jesus Christ.

Art Gish says as much when he states that "the Bible does not advocate any particular shape our economic life must take" and then goes on to state certain principles which should be a part of

any economic order. Having said that, however, he devotes large
sections of the essay to showing how, in his opinion, the Bible rejects such systems as capitalism, the ownership of private property,
collecting interest on loans, industrialization and centralization.

For instance, we read that "a life of stewardship stands opposed
to the incentives of capitalism" (p. 134). For me there seems to be a
confusion of principles in such a statement. Christian stewardship
involves how I see myself in relationship to God. He is the owner
of "the world and those who dwell therein" (Ps 24:1). I use the gifts
he has given me to carry out his will. I came into this world with
no material things and I shall take none with me when I die. He is
the owner; he is the master. I am his steward.

However, if I am in rebellion against God, I see myself in a different relationship with him. I lay claim to being the owner of all
I possess. I am the master. Therefore I accumulate wealth and
power for my own pleasure, not to please God and serve my fellow
human beings.

Is capitalism the only economic system which offers one the
"incentives" of wealth, power and self-gratification? Hardly. Since
the rebellion against God is a universally human manifestation, it
can and does exist in every possible political and economic system. It seems to me, therefore, that a more proper phrasing of Gish's
sentence would be that "a life of stewardship stands in opposition
to the incentives of capitalism, socialism, communism, fascism or
any other ism."

But the author is really saying more. He cannot see how the biblical concept of stewardship can exist in a capitalistic system.
Specifically, can a steward of God own property? Of course; it's
done all the time. As I write these lines I am looking out the win-
dow into our yard filled with blossoming flowers. I live in a society
which has given me legal title to that yard and the home in which I
live. I "own" them, and yet I don't own them. Within the political
and economic framework of my environment I have legal title to
material things. But at the same time I recognize that I am a steward
of my material goods on behalf of God, who most certainly is the
owner.

In fact, I submit that the biblical concept of stewardship has a
greater significance in an economic system which grants private
ownership than in one of a collective or state ownership because

I cannot concede to God ownership of what my society says I do not own in the first place. The beautiful feature of the koinonia which the author so highly esteems is that it is a voluntary surrender of self and possessions. Can there be Christian stewardship in a capitalistic system? Of course.

"Private property is not a biblical concept," says Gish (p. 136). He supports this statement with references to Old Testament law. As readers will observe, Gary North uses the same Old Testament law to support exactly the contrary view. I have trouble with both authors' being so certain that the Bible supports their own economic philosophies. By being selective one can find Scripture citations to support virtually any position one might hold on virtually any issue. For example, the Gish essay makes the flat statement that "charging interest is prohibited" (p. 136). In support of this position we are offered Exodus 22:25 (which is quoted) and Deuteronomy 23:19-20 (which is not quoted). Jewish law did prohibit charging interest to other Jews, but permitted it when dealing with others. Deuteronomy 23:20 clearly states, "You may charge interest on a loan to a foreigner but not on a loan to a fellow-countryman" (NEB). That is selective use of Scriptures.

Furthermore, the essay does not report on commonly accepted historical information relative to certain Scripture passages. For instance, while the laws concerning the Jubilee year are indeed radical, historians tell us that there is no evidence that the Jews ever practiced them.

Frankly, I think the Old Testament books do sanction private ownership of property with certain limitations as to its use. Leviticus 27 outlines the ways in which the Israelites can give property to the Lord. In fact, verse 19 provides a means for "redeeming" land which had previously been given to the Lord Why would such rules exist if there were no generally accepted rule for private ownership?

How does the New Testament treat private ownership of property? As I mentioned in my response to the North essay, there is little said in the New Testament which clearly supports the absolute right to private property. On the other hand, little is said which would deny that right. The New Testament does not seem to consider the issue of holding private property. Yes, the book of Acts does relate how the early church members pooled their resources for community use, but the motive seems to be koinonia rather than biblical imperative.

Gish's New Testament references seem to confuse the issue of *having* money and *loving* money. Jesus is quite clear about the evil of worshiping one's possessions, of worrying about them, of letting them get in the way of keeping God first in one's life. We are reminded that we cannot *serve* God and Mammon. In many personal encounters and in his parables, Jesus frequently deals with people's personal possessions, but the issue seems always to be the love of possessions rather than the holding of them. Money and land are not evil in themselves; it is only when we place them ahead of our love of God and our neighbor that the evil arises.

What about the statement that it is easier for a camel to go through the eye of a needle than for a rich man to enter the kingdom of God? Some commentators explain this text by suggesting that Jesus was saying that most rich people have already succumbed to the love of money and are therefore doomed. Perhaps, but I see Jesus making a different point here. In Jesus' time money talked in much the same way it does today. A rich man could get almost anything he wanted. But one thing a rich man cannot do with his wealth is to walk into the kingdom of God. Entrance into the kingdom of God is solely within God's hands and is a freely given gift. Jesus underlines this point in response to the disciples' question of who then can be saved. He replies, "For men it is impossible, but not for God; everything is possible for God" (Mk 10:27 NEB). Rich man, poor man, beggar man, thief: As astonishing as it seems to us, the grace of God is available to all who accept the gift.

Here is the nub of my problem with my friends who are "radical Christians." It seems to me that their theology is largely one of works righteousness. By doing or not doing certain things, one thereby comes into a right relationship with God which then assures one of salvation. I think Gish is following this way of thinking when he writes, "The way of salvation is the way of downward mobility" (p. 138). I agree with our need for downward mobility. I believe downward mobility in a society as affluent as ours is pleasing in the eyes of God. I advocate it. But to say that moving downward in our style of living is the "way of salvation" is to contradict the theology of unmerited grace.

Would a proper analogy be, "It is easier for a camel to go through the eye of a needle than for a downwardly mobile person to enter the kingdom of God"? I think so. Why? Because salvation is God's action; not ours.

So much for the biblical and theological aspects of the Gish essay. What about his strategy for attaining economic justice?

"Koinonia and Jubilee are the New Testament economic programs," we are told (p. 140). Reference has already been made to Jubilee which, by the way, is not a New Testament economic program. What about koinonia?

I share Gish's passion for koinonia. There is no question in my mind that koinonia is the ideal state of relationships among Christians. It has been through koinonia that our family has grown in the Christian faith. For over twelve years my wife, Judy, and I have been part of an ecumenical koinonia group known as FOCUS. For those twelve years we have come together virtually once every week. It has been somewhat like a house-church in that our families share the experiences of worship, study, fellowship and service, mostly within our homes. We have together gone through the experiences of birth and death, marriage and divorce, sickness and health, joy and sadness. We have come to know and love each other in ways I had never before experienced in the church.

We are also members of another koinonia group, one which consists of members of the same congregation. This group has been together for eight years and has also developed into a remarkable extended family of loving, caring people. I think all of us are at our best when we are in koinonia.

But koinonia is not magic. It has not repealed the truth of original sin. Being in koinonia has not transformed us into sinless people with no selfish impulses. It has not prevented differences of opinion from arising—and occasional heated debates. It has not prevented sickness or unemployment or problems with teen-agers or strains within marriages. There have been times when our koinonia groups have come together in prayer and action on behalf of one of our members, only to find that we have been unable to meet the need. So it first needs to be said that koinonia is no guaranteed route to a sin-free humanity.

Second, I have real problems trying to picture what global koinonia would look like. The author properly describes koinonia with such words as "communion, community, fellowship, partnership, connectedness, mutuality and solidarity" (p. 140). For most of those words to have meaning, people must be in proximity to each other, both physically and emotionally. How does one experience koinonia in a city of one million people, in a nation, in the world? Certainly Gish owes us more than the statement, "Since koinonia includes the participation of everyone involved, there is no blueprint for what this would look like on a global scale" (p. 154). If he really believes koinonia can exist on a global scale, we are at least entitled to some models of how this would be, visionary though they might seem.

When my sisters or brothers are hurting because of a famine in Bangladesh or a drought in Africa or unemployment in Detroit or a housing eviction in the South Bronx, there must be some system that brings resources to those needs. We can debate whether it is capitalism or socialism or communism or any other system which best delivers economic justice, but to advocate a nonsystem seems irresponsible. Koinonia, on a global scale, without any blueprint, is a nonsystem. Because it is a nonsystem it can hardly be called a "New Testament economic program." Utopia it is; an economic program it is not.

In this essay one can detect some of the whimsy of E. F. Schumacher's *Small Is Beautiful*. Much emphasis is placed on the decentralization of institutions, on having the control of life in the hands of small, localized groups of people. There is no doubt in my mind that some of our institutions and organizations are too large. Some functions of society can be carried out on a smaller scale to the benefit of all. But small is not beautiful in all instances.

For example, Gish points out that "there are enough resources in the world to meet everyone's needs. . . . For example, the world's annual grain harvest could provide each person in the world with three thousand calories a day" (p. 151). The problem of world hunger is not simply a matter of our greed, as the author suggests, but also a problem of poor distribution. Much of the world's grain is grown in temperate climates, from about the thirty-fifth to the fiftieth parallels. Greed didn't decide this; the earth's climatic conditions did. How then do we get that grain into the mouths of people living in tropical regions—by bicycles and rowboats? The huge tonnages of grain which must be moved from one part of the earth to another require railroads and ships. To build trains and ships we need steel mills and shipyards. To power those trains and ships we need oil refineries and pipelines. While cottage industries may make sense for some products, like clothing and furniture, we simply must have large organizations to accomplish other tasks.

We must admire Gish's passion for economic justice. If only more people showed his concern and commitment for the poor and the disadvantaged, we'd surely have a better world. But the best of intentions and the purest of motives are not enough if we do not consider the complexity of the problem we are addressing. Our global economy is unbelievably complex and does not lend itself to simplistic approaches. Regrettably, Gish does not appear to be as conversant in economic philosophies as I would have hoped. While he can identify the pains of the system we have, he has not diagnosed root causes other than to talk of greed and oppression. Christians are called to work for economic justice while at the same time acknowledging the fallen nature of humans and their institutions. It is entirely possible that there is a radically Christian approach to economics but, having read such authors as Ronald Sider, John Howard Yoder and Jack Nelson, I have yet to find one who is persuasive.

Art Gish, with his vision of koinonia and Jubilee, has given us a glimpse of economic utopia. For that we can thank him. But we need to deal with the distressing economic conditions of the here and now. For those of us who call ourselves dirty-hands Christians, that means dealing with imperfect people and imperfect institutions. It means making difficult trade-offs in a complex, global community. It means having to make decisions when there are no clear best choices. All of that might sound depressing and hopeless except for one fact: We are a called and redeemed people of God. And with God "everything is possible."

A Centralist Response

John Gladwin

The vision shared in this chapter of a just and sustainable economy founded in Christian koinonia confronts us with the claim of the kingdom of God on our social relationships. Here we are presented with a contrast between the corrupt and destructive systems and structures of a fallen world and the possibilities of a new approach given to the people of God.

Much of the analysis of this chapter will be shared by others—including many who do not share our Christian faith. Resources are squandered, the poor are exploited, power is centralized in the hands of the few, and our world is threatened by the expensive and terrifying weapons of mass destruction. The competitive and acquisitive world in which we live seems a far cry from the sort of life to which Jesus called his disciples (and us by implication).

My problem with the chapter concerns the way such insight is used in the theological context. The answer pursued is for Christians to abandon all efforts at participating in the life of the world and instead to set up outposts of the kingdom of God in the church.

We need to become church based in communities practicing economic koinonia. This is the classic sectarian case for making the church an alternative to the world.

Only a selective reading of the New Testament could support such a picture of the church. The New Testament church is not portrayed to us as ideal communities of believers who practiced an alternative economy to that of the world. While New Testament Christians supported one another in a hostile world through the sharing of resources and generosity in times of need, they did not seem to abandon their vocations in the world. They continued with their marriages (unless their unbelieving partner sought separation and divorce), they practiced their professions (even Paul made tents from time to time), and they accepted the usual duties of life in society. They were called to be communities of mutual encouragement, edification and support, but not alternative societies increasingly divorced from the concourse of life in society.

The failure of this chapter to discuss important Christian doctrines which might rescue it from the strict polarization of the church and the world into which it falls is the key omission. There is no discussion here of the doctrine of creation, with its implication that God both loves and cares for his world and that he calls Christians to share in loving and caring for the world. The Christian doctrine of common grace, in which we recognize the gifts of God common to all people and to be used in the service of all people, is also not discussed.

The assumption in the chapter that unbelieving people are not able to contribute to the well-being of the world is unbiblical and unrealistic. Thus the chapter fails to appreciate the great contributions which are made by others and which Christians ought to be supporting in society. There is no proper discussion of the institutions which God has provided for the common benefit of all people, institutions such as marriage, work, the state and law. That people abuse God's gifts is no reason for abandoning those gifts. The abuse of marriage is no reason for celibacy. The abuse of politics is no reason for Christian withdrawal into sectarian alternatives. Rather, if we believe that these institutions are given to us by God, then they are a reason for us to be involved in constantly seeking to recall them to their true purpose.

The chapter rightly recognizes that it is not possible to use the

Bible in a literal way for discovering blueprints for modern life. Yet it seems at times in its discussion of Old Testament practice and New Testament example to want to call us to follow in the same pattern of life. It is important to sort out how the Bible is to be used in these discussions.

The question we face is, How are we to live obediently to the gospel in our situation, knowing how the biblical people of God were called to live obediently in their situation? Any serious discussion must come to terms with our unique place in history if it is to make sense of our calling in the kingdom of God. Regret for our situation or rejection of our history is no way to approach the question and find an answer. We have to accept the place God has put us in and then seek to discover the judgment and the hope of the kingdom of God for it. That is the essentially radical task of the church. And I fear that, for all its many useful insights, this contribution brings us no further forward in finding an answer.

IV
Centralist Economics

Centralist Economics
John Gladwin

This chapter is based on a number of assumptions. The first concerns the Bible and the form of government. I will maintain that Scripture offers no blueprint for the form of modern government. This means that I will resist any idea that decentralized or privatized versions of the management of the economy and the provision of services are necessarily more Christian than the centralized solution. The argument for centralized work is a political and economic one, and it must be established within the bounds of Christian principles for human concern.

Second, I will argue that an analysis of the problems we face necessitates some form of centralized solution if we are to fulfill our biblical duty to our neighbor in distress. No amount of emotional response to this thesis in the form of labeling it communistic or socialistic will shift the strength of the case.

The Biblical Idea of the State and the Modern State
Scripture offers us two important perspectives for thinking about

social activity. First, it reminds us that God provides the state for our good. No reading of Romans 13:1-10 could justify any other statement. The state, therefore, is not to be thought of as either evil in itself or a necessary evil. It is provided by God for human benefit —to reinforce good conduct and to make evil conduct unprofitable. In carrying through that task, government, which is the central institution giving unity to the state, is fulfilling a divine vocation.

Second, Scripture warns us that we live in a fallen world and that human disobedience corrupts human institutions. Even the good institutions of God's provision—marriage, family, work and social life in organized society—are corruptible and corrupted. That God has provided government in society for our good, to be a help and supporter of people in meeting their vocations, does not mean that particular governments will be true to their calling. They can possess an office and power from God and still abuse it, corrupt it and overturn God's purposes for it.

This is the biblical pattern of thought in which God's creation and human disobedience work against each other and drive us to seek for resolution. The Christian message is that God himself has found the way forward in the story of salvation. We are not forever caught on the dilemma of our creation coupled, because of disobedience, with our subjection. There is hope, and this hope is given in all its richness in Jesus Christ. Even the structures of a world made subject to decay wait with eager longing for the experience promised in the resurrection of the crucified One from the dead (Rom 8:18-25).

The task of interpreting these theological themes in the modern age is never easy, and it is even less so when we consider them in the context of the meaning of the modern state. The modern state with its form of government cannot be found in Scripture. It cannot be found in the days of St. Augustine or Aquinas or even in the time of Luther or Calvin. They did their reasoning of the gospel in a different social and political context. We may turn to Scripture to help us shape a Christian frame of mind and to study its procedure, even as we look at the content of these men's thought. All of this is necessary to a full theology for the present. What we may not do and still remain loyal to our calling is repeat what earlier Christian thinkers said as if no fundamental changes had taken place in the form of the state or in the character of modern government.

Scripture does, however, provide us with encouragement to continue with the task of interpreting the meaning of the knowledge of God for the place and calling given to us in the present. This is how Scripture itself proceeds. There is in Scripture no blueprint of the ideal state or the ideal economy. We cannot turn to chapters of the Bible and find in them a model to copy or a plan for building the ideal biblical state and national economy.

Even the people of God in the Old Testament—whose form of life is the nearest the Bible ever brings us to a model for a political economy—move through a variety of social forms in the different parts of their history. We find them first a mobile tribal group and economy, then a developing nation in a predominantly land-based and rural economy, then a successful and expanding kingdom with growing urban life and a more sophisticated economy, and finally a reconstituted, city-based state in the midst of great imperial movements in the Greco-Roman world. If we took some of the basic forms of economic and social life and looked at them at different points in the biblical history, we would be surprised by the diversity present there. If we examined money, taxation, employment, land distribution, slavery, family structure, the roles of men and women in the economy and so on, we would be struck by the rich variety of Old Testament experience. Some of it was commendable, and some of it would be shameful of any social order.

All the forms in which social and economic relationships are structured are to be judged against the righteousness revealed in God himself. The calling of all forms of government, when set in the religious context of biblical faith, concern good and evil as understood in the righteousness of God. Governments are to promote the good, enable the good, support the good and encourage the good. They are to avoid the evil, make evil unattractive, undermine its influence and make it difficult and undesirable.

Because of this high and moral calling, governments and authorities do not "wield the sword in vain." Thus we may consider the performance of the institutions of our modern society and the modern political economy and see how much they do support good things and discourage evil things. We may consider the detail of policy—how modern taxation systems affect family experience, how they assist or destroy the life of the poor or vulnerable sections of the community. In looking at such detail we shall discover areas where the modern state encourages or discourages people from the good and strengthens or weakens them in the face of evil. These general areas of moral concern which undergird political life home in, in a specific and disciplined manner, on areas of policy and social procedure.

Scripture encourages us in this process. God's Word comes straight at areas of specific experience and passes broad judgment on the social order in the light of these. In Amos we are taken to the marketplace, and we see the corrupt abuse which robs the weak of justice on the scales (Amos 8:4-6). In his opening sermon recorded in chapters 1 and 2, Amos specifies inter-nation behavior and records the judgment of God on nations for specific acts of policy in their mutual relationships. He even gives the specific detail of the desecration of the bones of the king of Edom by Moab (2:1-3). The general concern for righteousness expressed in good and evil breaks out in specific examination of policy and processes. In our present, different setting the same task awaits us. We can look at specific areas of poverty and discrimination and find the judgment of God homing in on the whole social order. We are all implicated by what is present in our society.

The Rights of the Poor

Economic provision to meet the needs of the poor is an important biblical area in which the state has responsibilities. These are not matters which can safely be left to individual mood or whim. The structural framework of law and social values must make clear provision for defined needs. This is especially so for the poor, for slaves and hired servants, for widows and others in distress, and for those who sojourn in the nation. The law places obligations on the whole community toward such groups. The presence of these matters in the law helps to establish custom and so helps create and reinforce social patterns of behavior. The framework provided in the law is founded in justice and aims at maintaining and supporting justice in the community.

The Bible fully understands that the natural man, left to his own devices, is selfish and shortsighted. He will not do what his neighbor's need demands of him unless some pressure is placed on his conscience and some practical provision is made for him to act on.

He needs to be reminded of his duty, he needs pressure on him to meet his obligations, and he needs processes of enforcement when he fails in his duty. In the absence of such he will drift into situations in which he is tempted to exploit the weak, to deny the poor their rights and to forget the needs of those in distress. The rights of the weak and the poor need protecting. There is no natural protection for them in human society, and they have no substantial resources of their own to defend their rightful interests. They need the law and the force of authority to act on their behalf.

Good law in economic affairs, therefore, is designed to maintain a state of justice in economic relationships. It can support the good in human life by encouraging the strong to meet their obligations and by coming to the aid of the weak when their right is under threat. It can promote justice and act as a bulwark against the growth of injustice.

An example of the way in which biblical law achieved this can be found in its provisions over the land. Land was a basic and vital resource to the new nation of Israel. The tribal and family groups all needed access to land to provide for themselves and to contribute to the needs of the community. Thus, when the people settled in the Promised Land it was carefully apportioned among the tribes and families of Israel (Num 33:53-54). We must remember that in the Old Testament the land was given to Israel, not as a matter of right, but as a gift from God. It was their land only because God had been gracious to them and given it to them. They held it in trust from him.

The law in the Old Testament not only talked about the distribution of land on arrival in the Promised Land, but also about how justice was to be maintained in the possession of it once the people had settled. Because of the variety of experiences which the people would have, the original, fair distribution of land would gradually be disrupted. The fortunate and strong would accumulate more while the unfortunate and weak would lose what they had and sink to the status of hired service or even slaves. Therefore, the law provided for redistribution of the land at regular intervals.

Whether the famous Jubilee principle (Lev 25) was ever practiced does not alter the fact of its presence in the law of God. God saw a need for a redistributive principle whose aim was to restore justice and peace (one of the purposes of the Sabbath provision in Scripture). So, built into the law surrounding this essential matter of land rights in a rural economy, we find provision for fair distribution and for the maintenance of this state of justice. The operations of the free market in land sales and its impact on people are not trusted in Scripture!

We can learn a number of things from this. First, that people who recognize God's claim on their lives must seek to live in just and mutually supportive relationships in the community. Second, justice involves an equitable provision of resources for all the families which make up the community. Justice is not done where there are gross and deepening disparities in social experience. Third, injustice is a constant threat to the community. Injustice can happen not just through deliberate misdemeanor, but also through the unfortunate developments of life in a fallen world. Death, illness and disaster can ruin families and leave them overly dependent on others. So provision must be made against the injustices which so easily threaten to destroy society and its harmony founded on equity.

Fourth, the Old Testament provisions made against injustice and with a view to restoring justice with peace have two levels to them. First, there are immediate relief provisions: the poor may glean after the harvest is taken, strangers are to be welcomed, hired servants are to be paid immediately and so on. Second, there are structural provisions designed to get at the root of the problems and to seek resolution. These include the Jubilee provision for the redistribution of land, the release and provision of resources for slaves, and the access of the needy to the courts for redress when their rights are taken away by the strong.

It might be suggested that this Old Testament concern with society, its land and its laws, gives way in the New Testament to the spiritual things to which it points. An incident in the life of Jesus might help us grasp this nettle and resolve the question. In Matthew 26:6-13 we read the story of the woman who poured an expensive jar of ointment over Jesus. The disciples were indignant and protested at the waste. Such a treasure might have been sold and the large proceeds given to the poor. But Jesus rebukes them, saying that she had anointed him for his burial and that they would always have the poor with them, while he would soon be gone. In no sense in this story is Jesus undermining the biblical obligation to the poor. The gospel does not weaken the command of God in the Old Testament. He is rather celebrating the spontaneity of her love and the appropriateness of what she has done in the light of his coming and imminent death. She had but a fleeting chance to show her love. They would still have the poor to respond to long after his ministry was complete. The story does not trivialize the poor or Jesus' attitude toward them. It celebrates generous love and the joy of the presence and work of Jesus. The poor are still with us today, and they remain a demand on our action.

When we consider the actions of states in their duty to good behavior and in opposition to evil, it is clear that some pass the test better than others. In the Old Testament the closer Israel stuck to the demand of God's law, the closer it came to encouraging good living and undermining evil forces. Yet many are the instances of that nation's forgetting its responsibilities. The poor were exploited, the weak overrun, and the vulnerable oppressed. The duty of the state to protect their interests was forgotten, and power was used in selfish and corrupt ways. Good people and good living were threatened, and evil people and evil ways were promoted in the community.

Thus, whatever form Old Testament society took—whether mobile agrarian community or a settled and more complex nation state—there remained tests to be put against its life to see how well it enabled the good and resisted the evil. What provision it made for the poor and vulnerable was one of the most important of such tests. A community which is callous to the poor and which, in effect, leaves the weak and vulnerable without adequate protection and recourse to justice is under the judgment of God for its failure in stewardship. We learn in Scripture that God himself is the greatest defender of the poor and the needy. It is he who comes to the rescue. It is he who looks with displeasure on the strong and the rich in the world when they fail to follow in his steps of action for those in human need.

Poverty and the Modern State
One of the most pronounced features of social order in the twentieth century has been the growth of the state. This is not an experience limited to Marxist states with their centralist and bureau-

cratic form of political order. It is also true of liberal democracies. Industrialization, urbanization and the growth of sophisticated systems of communication have made it easier as well as more necessary for the state to play a larger part in social organization.

One has only to think of what ease of travel has done to the capacity of the state to enforce its way on larger and larger areas of community life. In the early eighteenth century it could take up to six days to travel a distance of two hundred miles. Under such conditions the power of government was much more restricted. Today we are living through yet another communications revolution which will improve the means by which the state can achieve its will. Control of nationality and passport matters, enforcement of taxation and the maintenance of records about citizens are made much easier by recent technological innovation.

The whole business of administering government involves huge expenditure and vast networks of employment. The sophisticated needs of the modern defense industry make large inroads into the national economy and create important centers of power inside the state. The state is the largest employer of people and the largest source of wealth for all who depend on it for business and employment. All of this is true whether or not the state is involved in any large way in welfare provision and the central distribution of resources to places and people of need within its bounds.

It is accepted in this essay that all of this presents us with important problems concerning control of power and accountability in power. It is also accepted that, unless we address such problems in a political manner, we may well experience a drift away from democratic forms of accountability and involvement. The problem of the power of the state is a severe one. Yet I will resist the temptation to try to reverse the course of history. There is no foreseeable future in attempts at fundamentally reducing the size and power of the state. Such radical solutions could threaten the whole basis of much modern civilization and lead us into anarchy rather than to better order. We have the modern large and powerful state, and we are going to have to learn to live with it, to provide for its problems and to maximize its benefits.

There are benefits in the modern state. The loss of such sophisticated organization might break the back of the order on which our urban industrial society works. We may not, for example, think much of the standards of modern policing in our society. But the removal of an organized police service founded on statutory duties and standards of conduct and operation might lead to even greater injustices in the enforcement of order in our society. We may complain about traffic regulations and the organization needed to maintain and enforce them. But we would certainly be worse off without them.

A large state is required for the style of life we possess at present. The alternative may be chaos or a relapse into a form of society lacking in good communication and founded on rough justice. In these days of large and powerful business organizations, we need a strong state if any semblance of standards is to be enforced with regard to business conduct and the employment of labor. England has trouble as it is maintaining the standards for working conditions laid down by statute. A weakening of the central government would contribute to further erosion of enforcement. In the end the workers in the office and on the factory floor benefit when the state comes in to see that employers maintain agreed conditions of work and employment. The same applies to the citizen who enters the store to purchase goods. He or she also needs to know that proper standards of trade are not only present but enforceable.

Our sophisticated social order requires that people have access to a wide range of experiences and services basic to their participation in society. Health, education, family support, communications, housing and employment are some of the things which are basic to life in our society. The state has a duty, therefore, to see that citizens have sufficient access to these things to enable their full participation in the community. The withdrawal of the state from any of these spheres might increase the liberties of those strong enough to care for themselves, but at the same time reduce the choices of those most vulnerable to misfortune and abuse.

The dreams of a stateless future belong to Marxist and anarchist mythology, not to a proper assessment of human nature as seen in the biblical tradition. The exact role of the modern state in relation to economic life is dependent on our analysis of the nature of economic life and its effect on people. In this essay I will look especially at poverty. I will argue that unless central government takes a leading role through structural change and large provision, the problem of poverty will never be adequately met.

The Nature of Poverty

What are the causes of poverty? A number of answers have been suggested. One which has sometimes found credence among a Christian public keen to emphasize personal responsibility is that poverty is mainly due to personal imcompetence. This can either be individual incompetence or some notion of an inherited cycle of inability to take responsibility for one's life and affairs. The poor, it is suggested, breed poverty through genetic deficiency. If this is the root of the matter, then recovery must lie both in a recovery of stronger individual responsibility in society (and so a lessening of welfare provision and central support) and through a gradual mixing of society to overcome cycles of inherited deprivation.

A second answer lies in the suggestion that widespread poverty in the world is due to the collapse of values, especially among the rich. If the rich understood their duty, they would voluntarily provide for the poor. We have lost the driving force behind charity. Thus the answer lies in a recovery of values which stress the responsibility of the rich to meet the needs of the poor.

A third answer suggests that poverty is caused through the failure of modern social institutions to meet their obligations— businesses in their duty to employees, banks in their duty to charity, other financial institutions in their reaction to poverty, and so on. Thus the answer might be in legislating to encourage institutions to meet obligations.

It is, of course, possible that there are truths in all these approaches. We are not necessarily in a situation where we have to choose one understanding and reject others altogether. However, all these ideas make one assumption which modern studies of poverty would strongly deny. They assume that there is nothing basically wrong with the structure of the social order and its economy. The problem lies with individuals or institutions.

A brief glance at the problem would make us doubt whether any of these ideas really accounts for the nature of poverty in our modern society. The vast majority of the poor do not end up where they are because of personal incompetence. They are born into it. Sizable proportions of both wealth and poverty are inherited in our liberal democracies. Even before they leave the womb the poor are at a disadvantage. The capacity of mothers to meet the needs of their babies is put under strain by their own poverty and the demands made on them to be able to survive. The babies of the poor are more exposed to health risks and have fewer support services available to them. The children of the poor, already falling behind the children of the rich in their bid for a place in society, are then subjected to the worst education, to cramped and poor housing, and to the constant frustration of their gifts and ambitions.

An economy which depends for its survival on regularly driving groups into unemployment and leaving them with reduced social benefits is dependent on poverty. At one time it was thought that, in a capitalistic and liberal democratic society, poverty would be eradicated by growing wealth—the rich would pull the poor out of poverty through continued growth. Few would believe such theories today. A society which survives on the deep distinctions between different groups in terms of wealth and income is built on a principle which institutionalizes poverty. Gone are the days when it was thought that poverty could be undermined without a change in the structures of social order and economic life.

The rich feed off the poor—not through any personal callousness or sin but because we are all bound together in a social system that works in that way. What we need, therefore, are not sermons directed at the rich to make them more charitable or directed at the poor to make them more diligent, but a discovery by both rich and poor of biblical values which will bring them together in common fellowship in the pursuit of justice. The solution must lie in a common search for a form of order which more truly affirms the creation, resists the Fall and offers more substantial hope.

If we judge that poverty is a result of the way society functions and comes out of the structures of modern economy, then we are bound to conclude that unless more fundamental measures are taken all the above suggestions will but scratch the surface of the problem. The main argument for centralist economic management is that the problems of our economy are structural rather than superficial, that they need the involvement of central, democratically controlled management.

In our present society some poor people can escape by their own efforts—with a bit of luck thrown in for good measure. They are a tiny minority. These are the few to whom the system points to show that poverty is not its fault. Again, other poor people will escape through the generosity of the rich and of good institutions. They too will be a minority, and only the margins of poverty will be touched. Some poverty will be relieved by a group's tackling pockets of it in places of great stress. These measures will always be welcome, but they hardly touch the root problem. Unless the community as a whole, in both national and international terms, makes better structural provision for economic relationships within a settled and just political order, neither personal effort nor charity will ever do more than offer some marginal hope to the poor.

We can often see the situation best by considering it in a context other than our own. Consider, for example, poverty in the developing world. Here, hard though it sometimes is for us to accept, we have to say that voluntary charity through relief and development agencies is but a drop in the bucket when set against the extent of the problem. Unless these good and necessary deeds are backed by the good work of state governments, little progress can be made at cutting back on the vast and terrifying scale of poverty in the modern world. In spite of the work done voluntarily, the poor, in their millions, will continue to die in destitution. Why? Because there poverty is not due to lack of Western charity but to a whole range of forces at work from the past and in the present in the very structure of international and national economies. Tackling the disease of poverty cannot be done without a major contribution from central authority, both at national and international levels.

There are no fundamental differences between the developed and developing world in the causes of poverty which both experience. It may come as a surprise to some to realize that Western economies include a sizable experience of poverty. Certainly Western problems differ in extent from those of the rest of the world. Comparatively, the West is rich. Yet within its experience of riches there lurks a severe experience of poverty for many. Poverty in our societies is to be found in both rural and urban settings. Even though it may predominate among certain groups, it can be found at different levels throughout modern liberal democracies. Worse, in the turbulent, recessionary climate of the 1980s it is on the increase.

The Need for Large-Scale State Activity
When we look at poverty in our own society, we are looking at an accumulation of enormous problems—unemployment, poor

health, bad housing, inadequate education, family crisis and stress, social deviancy and so on. When we consider the scale of the problems, it is clear that a piecemeal approach will not only not help serious resolution in the long term but it may well increase deprivation in the short term. Trying to improve housing without improving the financial capacity to maintain the homes and the families within them is shortsighted. Grand new housing schemes for the poor end up as the slums of the future. In some of the cities of the United States and the United Kingdom housing built to relieve slums twenty years ago is now being demolished as unfit for habitation.

When we look at this bundle of enormous social and economic problems, we cannot trust the unfettered activity of a market economy. A free market can only make sense when there is reasonable equity of opportunity and built-in mechanisms to maintain that equity. In a society which leaves the essential ingredients of social life to the fortunes of private practice, the strong will usually win the lion's share of provision and the weak will be constantly driven to grab the crumbs left after the strong have taken their fill.

If health care is left to the market, the rich will always be able to afford coverage, whereas the poor will be left unable to meet the costs. If education and housing are left to the market forces, again those in positions of strength in the social order will always corner the best provision and leave the second-rate to the weaker sections of society. No Christian assessment of the social order will ever dare trust human nature, without incentives, to be altruistic and generous. Even government itself is under pressure to ignore the demand to adjust social systems to make better and more equitable provision. In liberal democracies governments are often dependent on the support of the established middle-class groups and so have strong disincentives from hemming in such groups in the cause of greater social justice. All forces of our society—including the political forces of democratic societies—militate against the needs of the poor and the weak.

Yet there is no escape from the need for large-scale state activity if our society is to move into a more equitable future at social and economic levels. Central government activity has to take on many forms. First, there is the need for immediate provision for the poor. There must be tax-funded schemes to provide security for the un-

employed, the sick, the homeless and those in family crisis—
irrespective of their personal position. Every society must have
some central and fair provision guaranteed to the needy. There
is a Band-Aid activity for the state to pursue.

Second, the state can provide an environment of legal protection against abuse of the poor by the rich. Such provision must be
enforceable. These provisions in modern society protect workers
against careless and callous employers, protect special groups
against the operations of prejudice on the grounds of sex, color
or religion, and help define the boundaries of individual freedom
lest freedom become a means of license to injustice.

Third, the modern state with its power in the economy can seek
through legal and economic measures to change the structures of
both social and economic relationships. There can be a deliberate
endeavor on the part of government to create a greater commitment
to justice and fairness in the social order. By taxation there can be
redistribution of wealth. By positive discrimination there can be
improved and more equitable provision of fundamental resources
for the poor in housing, education and jobs. In terms of basic resource needs, the state can work on the principle, "From each according to his ability, to each according to his need." Thus the
social system can be made to work so that those who prosper by it
make a significant contribution through a planned economy,
enabling the weak to recover a responsible and supported form of
life in the community.

By such means government can play a major part in tackling
poverty. By *poverty* we mean the experience of those groups in
society who have become far removed from the rest of society in
which they live. The poor are those whose economic and social
experience puts a considerable distance between them and the
average experience of members of society. While they are a minority, they are frequently a large and significant minority made up of
the elderly, single-parent families, the unemployed and the sick.
Significant groups of people in these sectors of society are poor.
Immediate state relief, legal protection of rights, and measures designed to redistribute wealth and so alter the balance of power in
society: All three are central to the alleviation of poverty. That is
why the state must play a key role in this matter.

Government alone in our society has the power and the resources to attempt such programs. There are no other institutions or individuals with any hope of achieving by their efforts what can be achieved through the will of government when it is so persuaded. Even governments will not attempt the exercise without conflict. A naive reliance on the good will of central government will not lead to change. Government will only act in these ways when under pressure to do so. Only the successful joining of forces of all who would seek such change with those rare moments in history when the door opens to allow radical actions can lead to change being initiated through central activity. This is why the weak and the poor have to use their collective power to constantly defend their rights against all centers of power and to work for a day when authority will bend to their needs and aspirations. Industrial and political groupings and organization are essential to bringing government to that point where it will turn its power and resources to affecting the structures of the economy and social order in favor of groups who have benefited least from the previous order. That it is possible to achieve some such change without violent political upheaval in the state is witnessed to in those moments in the twentieth century when for brief periods government has worked in some cooperation with the interests of the poor and the vulnerable.

In between such moments of change the poor are dependent on what charity government and others send their way; they look to people and groups of good will to point to a more hopeful future by the quality of their concern and the imaginative nature of their activity. The presence of such people encourages communities of the poor and disadvantaged to go on pressing by what means are at hand to seek for a change in the order of affairs and for authority to heed its voice and become a handmaid for justice in the world.

If we have to say that there is no easy way for central government to be persuaded of the need for its action, we must also say that there is no serious route to resolution without central authority and the force of the state being turned to serve the needs of justice. The size and power of the modern state make it unavoidable in the management of the economy for justice. For Christians this must mean that there is no by-passing the central political structures of the social order in seeking to work for a better future in which the form of the state and its economy more readily encourages the good life and undermines that which is evil. If we are to remove some of the greatest stresses on families and households, if we are to encourage vocational and community-oriented living, we must see that the form of the social order as managed by the state and the shape of the economy work to these ends. Poverty institutionalized into the structure of our society is a killer of goodness and a promoter of evil. That God is able to turn even this disaster to our good is no recommendation of our tolerance of it; it is rather an incentive to work continuously to attack its roots so that its evil consequences may be avoided.

In Scripture there are no good reasons why we should not call on the state to play its part. In our analysis of poverty and our modern experience of life in society today, we have every reason to call on the central power of the state to come to the aid of the weak and the poor and to help us adjust our lives to the boundaries of justice and peace. It is time Christians raised their voices to call for a greater participation by government in the management of the economy, in the provision of equitable services, and in the adjustment of our social relationships so that those most at risk in today's world are supported in the fabric of law and social order.

What Does This Mean for Us?

Centralist solutions lead to political activity. While it is not my purpose in any way to undermine the contemporary concern for lifestyle issues, it is my concern to stress that these can only have real strength when they are allied to political positions and action. Christian lifestyle in the modern world, if it is to address the problems of poverty and inequality, cannot avoid the arena of contemporary politics. We need to be involved in pressure groups, we need to be building support for programs, and we need to be capturing the heartlands of political opinion and organization. An enormous task awaits us in persuading governments that they have a crucial role in attacking poverty and distress in our society.

We must not be ashamed to espouse policies which require a larger contribution from the wealthy to the public purse for the benefit of the poor. We must work on the detail of such programs so that they reflect, both in content and structure, the most humane principles of social order. We must work on our education with a view to the wider education of the church and of our neighbors.

We must help build up the disciplined collective strengths of the poor and of working people through strong and effective political and industrial organization. As Reinhold Niebuhr demonstrated earlier this century, the structures of power in our society will not yield to the niceties of liberal reason. They will have to respond to strength in the cause of justice. (See his *Moral Man and Immoral Society*.)

Our personal lives must carry the mark of integrity with our cause. Ostentatious living in an age of want is an affront to conscience. In our personal relationships and stewardship we must witness to the motivation of our hearts. We must help our society see the way of Christ, who was not ashamed to shed the wealth and position of heaven to share fellowship in the poverty-stricken world of human life. The more excellent way of love must be lived by us as we call for our society to learn the way of service—of yielding power and property in order to respond to the humanity of those caught in the stress of our modern economies. In such ways we can bring the light of the gospel into the complex world of economic theory and practice.

Select Bibliography

Atherton, John. *The Scandal of Poverty: Priorities for the Emerging Church.* Oxford: Mowbrays, 1983.

Hay, Donald. *Christian Critique of Capitalism.* Grove Ethics Books. New York: Grove Press, 1975.

——— . *Christian Critique of Socialism.* Grove Ethics Books. New York: Grove Press, 1982.

Holman, Robert. *Poverty.* London: Martin Robertson, 1978.

Niebuhr, Reinhold. *Moral Man and Immoral Society.* New York: Scribner, 1960.

Preston, Ronald H. *Religion and the Persistence of Capitalism.* London: SCM Press, 1979.

Sheppard, David. *Bias to the Poor,* London: Hodder and Stoughton, 1983.

Tawney, R. H. *The Acquisitive Society.* New York: Harcourt Brace, 1948.

——— . *Equality.* Totowa, N. J.: Barnes & Noble, 1980.

——— . *Religion and the Rise of Capitalism.* New York: Mentor Books, 1954.

Temple, William. *Christianity and the Social Order.* London: SCM Press, 1950.

Willmer, Haddon. "Towards a Theology of the State." In *Essays in Evangelical Social Ethics,* edited by D. Wright. Exeter: Paternoster, 1978.

Willmer, Haddon, ed. *Christian Faith and Political Hopes.* London: Epworth, 1979.

A Free-Market Response

Gary North

Let me suggest the following academic exercise to the reader. Pretend you are the teacher of a twelfth-grade civics class. You have assigned a term paper on a controversial topic. One student submits a paper which consists of a series of assertions. He offers little or no substantiating evidence, no references to any other studies related to the topic, and no logical development that indicates that his assertions follow from his premises. His chief premise is, in fact, the very conclusion which his essay was supposed to prove. In short, the paper asserts what it is supposed to demonstrate. What grade would you give the student? Would you be generous and suggest that he rewrite his paper?

John Gladwin's essay begins with an assumption. He is forthright about his commitment to the following principle of biblical interpretation:

> There is in Scripture no blueprint of the ideal state or the ideal economy. We cannot turn to chapters of the Bible and find in them a model to copy or a plan for building the ideal biblical state and national economy. (p. 183)

This is Gladwin's most important operating assumption—at least his most important *admitted* operating assumption—and it is at the heart of my objections to virtually everything in his essay. This operating presupposition is what he needs to prove through an appeal to the Bible, but he does not even attempt to show that Scripture teaches it. He simply asserts that it is true. Assertion is not exegesis.

I totally reject Gladwin's operating presupposition that the Bible offers no blueprint for political economy. I am devoting the bulk of the academic side of my career to disproving it. The first volume of my multivolume economic commentary on the Bible, *The Dominion Covenant: Genesis,* devotes considerable space to a consideration (and refutation) of Gladwin's assertion. The second volume, *The Dominion Covenant: Exodus,* is presently in manuscript form, and the bulk of its nine hundred pages also deals with it. There is an old rule of logic: "A universal negative is refuted by a single positive." I have presented a lot more evidence than a single positive.

What Gladwin is justifiably worried about is simple enough: the form of political economy which is described in the Old Testament as morally binding—and which was never explicitly repudiated by Jesus or the apostles, as Bahnsen has demonstrated so forcefully[1]—is not the form of political economy which he personally prefers. He admits as much in the opening lines of his essay when he writes that "Scripture offers no blueprint for the form of modern government. This means that I will resist any idea that decentralized or privatized versions of the management of the economy and the provision of services are necessarily more Christian than the centralized solution" (p. 181). Ah, yes: not "necessarily more Christian." Here is the old neutrality argument: "neither more nor less," *until* we get to Gladwin's conclusions, and *then,* lo and behold, we find that all the neutrality is gone, and the morality of Jesus is lined up behind central planning. Franky Schaeffer is correct when he rejects any and all such appeals to the myth of neutrality.[2]

Here is a rarity in Gladwin's essay, an *argument,* however brief: (1) the Bible offers no blueprint for the form of modern government; *therefore,* (2) we must resist decentralized or privatized versions of the management of the economy. Gladwin apparently suspects that if Scripture did, in fact, offer a blueprint, it would present a privatized or decentralized version of management. As a matter of fact, Scripture *does* present just such a blueprint, in the sense of presenting a series of permanently binding social and economic laws, and this blueprint *does* describe a privatized and decentralized form of economy. What the Bible proclaims is a system of *self-government under biblical law*, which I have described elsewhere.[3]

Are we not being asked by Gladwin to believe (or eventually conclude) that his centralized planning solution is really "more Christian"? If not, then why did he write the essay? If so, then there must be some criteria that are explicitly Christian that testify to the moral preferability of the centralized system. And if these criteria exist, then they constitute some sort of guideline, or to use Gladwin's word, a "blueprint."

Always be suspicious of someone coming in the name of Jesus Christ who tells you that the Bible does not provide blueprints. You can be reasonably certain that you are about to be told that he has a "new, improved interpretation" of the topic under discussion which is in accord with the "ultimate concern" of the Bible, or the "moral perspective" of the Bible, or the "overall sentiment" of the Bible, or whatever the latest buzz-words are that people prefer to use *when they are trying to avoid a discussion of the explicit teaching of the Bible.* Some of Gladwin's preferred buzz-words are these:
1. "the bounds of Christian principles of human concern"
2. "the righteousness revealed to us in God himself"
3. "the good" (Plato lives!)
4. "structural framework of law and social values"
5. "needs of justice"
6. "gross and deepening disparities in social experience"
7. "spontaneity of love"
8. "the light of the gospel"
9. "the most humane principles of social order"
These phrases sound wonderful, but social commentators who come to us in the name of Christ must learn to restrain themselves in their use of pat phrases. When the phrases also happen to be the stock phrases of liberal humanism and theological liberalism, they should be qualified (reinterpreted) by means of biblical exegesis.

Liberals today have a tendency to use these phrases in much the same way that adherents of Eastern religions use their "mantras": a continuous, almost hypnotic repetition of familiar words that communicate nearly zero content to outsiders who do not share their faith. Such repetition may help them emotionally; it does not do anything to solve specific social problems.

If Gladwin had demonstrated exegetically that his stock phrases were legitimate summaries of the Bible's explicit teaching, then I would have no strong objection. But *repetition is not explanation*, any more than a string of assertions constitutes argumentation, and as far as I can determine, these stock phrases are not the product of biblical analysis. More to the point: Gladwin's explicit rejection of the use of the Bible in discovering permanently binding patterns and structures for economics and civil government makes it difficult for me to conclude anything else than the obvious, namely, that *these stock phrases are little more than baptized humanism and liberalism*—and only lightly sprinkled at that. Why, then, does he come to us in the name of Jesus Christ? Why bother to baptize socialism (or any other system)? If the Bible provides no blueprint, why use it as a theological cloak for any social system?

The reason there is a market for a book like this one is that people are increasingly aware of the preposterousness of any version of Christianity which comes to people and claims that "the Bible has the answers to all of life's problems," and then refuses to offer any specific, concrete answers to specific, concrete social and economic problems. How seriously can any thoughtful person take a world-and-life view which openly declares that it has no explicitly Bible-based answers for this world, but which simultaneously parades itself as a perspective which is relevant—even exclusively relevant—to this world because of its commitment to the Bible? American fundamentalism has tried to play this game for a hundred years.[4] It hasn't worked.[5]

Gladwin defends central economic planning by means of the very same assertion that fundamentalists have used to justify their own social inaction, namely, that the Bible does not provide specific guidelines regarding social issues. Theologically speaking, it is just as David Chilton has described it: the case of the missing blueprints.[6] Chilton was speaking of Ronald Sider and the Evan-

gelicals for Social Action, but the general principle of interpretation is the same: the Bible supposedly does not provide specific
rules and regulations that govern social, political, and economic
affairs. Thus, Christians can believe just about anything in these
areas (and they generally do).

What about my specific objections to Gladwin's perspective?
First and foremost is my commitment to the general biblical principle of original sin. By concentrating power in the hands of any
person or institution, men destroy freedom and create tyranny. The
political kingdoms of the ancient Near East, most notably Egypt,
were theocratic kingdoms that were ruled by supposedly divine-
human figures.[7] Israel was the great exception to this form of civil
government.

Egypt had central planning under Joseph, as a judgment on
Egypt.[8] Such a planning system was never allowed by biblical law
in Israel. Indeed, Samuel warned the people against a civil government under a king who would extract a tithe (ten per cent) in taxes
(1 Sam 8:15), which was only half of what Pharaoh had extracted
from the Egyptians (Gen 47:24), and only about twenty per cent to
twenty-five per cent of what virtually all Western industrial states
today confiscate from their citizens. Unfortunately for Israel, the
Israelites paid about as much attention to Samuel's warning as
Gladwin does. Just try to run a centrally planned economy with a
tax system based on a flat (non-graduated) income tax of under
ten per cent, with no other taxes allowed. It is impossible.

The Bible sets forth the outline of a political economy which
will enable most of the poor to become increasingly successful
and ultimately self-supporting. The Bible does not call for massive,
compulsory wealth redistribution; it calls for the poor tithe, gleaning, voluntary charity, and hard work on the part of the poor.
Where are Gladwin's biblical citations? They are glaringly, con-
spicuously absent. Where is his exegesis? There is none.

He writes: "The Bible fully understands that the natural man,
left to his own devices, is selfish and shortsighted" (p. 184). Indeed, this is precisely what the Bible teaches. *Who does Gladwin
think will be running the massive bureaucracies of a centrally
planned state, angels?* He would deliver the economy into the
hands of an agency which possesses a monopoly of violence, the
civil government.

What we need is *countervailing power*, a decentralized system of legitimately sovereign institutions that "stand in the gap" when any agency arrogates to itself power that must not be entrusted to any fallen man. The alternative is totalitarianism.[9] Could Stalin and Hitler, or even Pharaoh, have done what they did without a central planning apparatus?[10]

The oddest feature of his presentation here is that it conflicts with many of the anti-centralization, anti-civil government arguments in his book. For example:

> The ownership of the larger part of wealth and property by the few is a disincentive to responsibility. The attempt to answer this by centralizing ownership and control does little to solve the problem because it does nothing to renew responsibility throughout the whole community. It is not surprising, therefore, that we suffer from problems of vandalism when property is controlled either by a few private owners or remotely by government.[11]

Are you confused? Gladwin's essay presents the case for a massive bureaucratization of State economic power, yet his book admits that such a solution leads to failure. Gish comes in the name of decentralization, yet he presents a case for political control over economic decisions which seems to be essentially centralist and socialist. And Diehl thinks today's mixed-up and disintegrating economy is the best that Christians can legitimately expect.

Those who want refutations, point by point, of Gladwin's assertions (they are not arguments) regarding the ability of central planning to achieve the stated goals of the planners, can refer to the notes of my essay. For an illuminating case study of what central planning has done to hamper the economic opportunities of an important minority group in the United States, see Walter Williams' book, *The State Against Blacks*.[12]

I shall be charitable to Gladwin and say only this: *Case not proven.*

Notes

[1]Greg L. Bahnsen, *Theonomy in Christian Ethics* (Nutley, N.J.: Craig Press, 1977).

[2]Franky Schaeffer, *A Time for Anger: The Myth of Neutrality* (Westchester, Ill.: Crossway Books, 1982).

[3]Gary North, *Unconditional Surrender: God's Program for Victory*, 2nd ed. (Tyler, Tex.: Geneva Divinity School Press, 1983), pt. 2.

[4]George Marsden, *Fundamentalism and American Culture: The Shaping of Twentieth-Century Evangelicalism, 1870-1925* (New York: Oxford Univ. Press, 1980).

[5]James B. Jordan, ed., *The Failure of the American Baptist Culture* (Tyler, Tex.: Geneva Divinity School, 1982).

[6]David Chilton, "The Case of the Missing Blueprints," *The Journal of Christian Reconstruction* 8 (Summer 1981): "Symposium on Social Action," published by the Chalcedon Foundation, Vallecito, Calif.

[7]R. J. Rushdoony, *The One and the Many: Studies in the Philosophy of Order and Ultimacy* (1971; reprint ed., Fairfax, Va.: Thoburn Press, 1978), chap. 2.

[8]See my book, *The Dominion Covenant: Genesis* (Tyler, Tex.: Institute for Christian Economics, 1982), chap. 23.

[9]Robert Nisbet, *The Quest for Community* (New York: Oxford Univ. Press, 1952).

[10]F. A. Hayek, *The Road to Serfdom* (Chicago: Univ. of Chicago Press, 1944).

[11]John Gladwin, *God's People in God's World* (Downers Grove, Ill.: InterVarsity Press, 1980), p. 178.

[12]Walter Williams, *The State Against Blacks* (New York: New Books, McGraw-Hill, 1982).

A Guided-Market Response

William E. Diehl

Of the other three essays presented in this book, I find myself closest in harmony to the thoughts expressed by John Gladwin—but not close enough to accept his solution. In building his case for a centralized solution, Gladwin has not fully examined all the theological implications. He has overlooked some economic realities of existing centralized systems, and he has failed to provide us with models, real or theoretical, of how his proposed system would work.

Some fifty years ago advocates of centralized economic management compared the evils of a free capitalistic system to the ideals of a government-controlled system and, quite frankly, their claims were appealing if you really cared about justice and poverty. However, in the past half century the world has been able to observe the functioning of a rather broad variety of centralized systems, and we have discovered that idealism does not readily convert into realism. Experience has shown that we must be much more modest about the ability of a centralized economic system to fulfill our fond desires for a just society.

206 Wealth and Poverty

Let's first look at the theological content of Gladwin's essay. While one can scarcely disagree with that theology which the essay gives us, the problem is that it is selective and therefore incomplete.

Gladwin states, "Scripture offers us two important perspectives for thinking about social activity" (p. 181). The first perspective is that God provides the state for our good (Rom 13:1-10). I agree. Second, we are reminded that Scripture warns us that we live in a fallen world and that human disobedience corrupts human institutions. Again, who can possibly disagree? (It is interesting to note, however, that as the essay unfolds, it does appear that the author feels centrally controlled systems are more immune to corruption than are free societies.)

But are these two points the sum and substance of biblical perspectives on social activity? I would suggest that there are at least two other biblical principles which must be considered: freedom and the responsibility of the individual, which we sometimes call stewardship.

God has given us the great gift of freedom. The wonderful story of creation spells it out for us. God gave man the freedom to disobey, and man quickly exercised it. That is the basis of the fallen world to which the author points us. But God's concern for the freedom of his creatures keeps reappearing over and over again in the Bible. The Exodus brought freedom from political captivity. The Jubilee year, to which Gladwin makes reference, was a freeing from economic captivity. The teachings and sacrifice of Jesus Christ were a freeing from legalistic captivity. For there to be true love, there must be the capacity for rejection. God graciously gave us that capacity. He did not create puppets. He gave his creatures free will.

Therefore, any economic system must be examined with respect to the degree to which it provides for one's freedom. The Gladwin essay is liberal in its examples of how unbridled freedom in the hands of self-centered people can create injustice. But is there no injustice in a centralized system which is so tightly controlled by self-centered people that there is an absence of freedom?

Another thread which constantly runs through the Bible is individual responsibility. When Cain cries out, "Am I my brother's keeper?" we all know the answer. There is nothing in Scripture which suggests that collective social activity exempts the individual from responsibility. Jesus constantly challenged people about their individual responsibility to care for others.

The danger of carrying centralized government to the extreme is that it leads people to feel absolved of individual responsibility. If the central system takes care of everything, then my only responsibility is to vote. If people are hungry or hurting, it's the fault of the system and of no concern to me. Jesus does not tell us why the priest and the Levite passed by in the parable of the Good Samaritan, but it is interesting to note that both of them were members of the centralized institution of the Jewish society of that day. Could it be that they abdicated their individual responsibility to the half-dead traveler because they had implicit faith that "the system" would somehow care for him? Whatever the reason, the point of the parable, of course, is to stress the individual responsibility we all have. Any centralized system of managing society which causes people to absolve themselves of a personal responsibility for others is not in keeping with our Judeo-Christian teachings. So much for the theology.

I wish the Gladwin essay were more specific in describing the degree to which centralized government should "change the structures of both social and economic relationships" (p. 194). Does Gladwin envision a system in which a market operates within certain limits, or is there no place for free-market forces to act? The essay does not say. At times the reader has the feeling that the author is seeking a structure in which market forces operate but with greater centralized government control than we now have. If this is his vision, then he and I differ only in matters of the degree of control. But at other times one has the suspicion that he really sees no place for the market system and is simply unwilling to be so bold as to say so. For the purposes of advancing the debate, I will assume that the latter case is true; the comments which follow are presented accordingly.

What are some of the real problems of centralized systems? First, centralized systems do not readily adapt to changing forces in the economy. That is especially the case now that we are in a truly global economy. Unfortunately, too many of us still think in terms of our own domestic economy and fail to see that global events have a greater effect than do local events. Our first awakening to this fact came in 1973 when the OPEC nations agreed to cooperate in establishing the price of oil. The effects of this one action were felt around the world within months. It is fascinating to trace the way in which the oil crisis changed world patterns in trade, industry, banking and even agriculture. We are still feeling the ripple effects. The Communist-bloc nations, with their ponderous central planning systems, did not respond quickly to the sharp run-up of energy costs. For some time the U.S.S.R. continued to sell oil to its satellites at pre-1973 price levels. The result was that in world markets Eastern-bloc exports were priced at pre-1973 levels while their imports were priced at post-1973 levels, creating highly unfavorable balances of trade. Tightly drawn five-year plans do not readily yield to economic surprises, to the detriment of a nation.

At the same time, however, one must say that the nature of our global economy is such that the philosophy of a totally free market will not work either. World governments are involved in the shaping of their economies more than at any time in the past. Nations have discovered that an aggressive world trade policy can do much to strengthen a weak condition at home. We have moved into a mercantilistic age.

Former special trade representative Robert Strauss writes,

Increasingly it is governments, not market forces, that are determining the direction and content of trade flows. American workers and farmers now compete with 20th century mercantilistic stages—nations whose governments have formed alliances with corporations, farmers, and workers, not to maximize profits, but to maximize exports. The American farmer is not competing with the European farmer, but with $7 billion of agricultural subsidies of the European Economic Community. The American aerospace worker is not competing with the European aerospace worker, but with France's policy of export credit financing. And American computer technicians are not competing with their Japanese counterparts, but with the predatory pricing policies of the Japanese computer industry working with the Japanese government in targeting high-tech advancement.[1]

Comparisons between nations with centralized management and those which operate with the market system show some convincing evidence of the weakness of the former. The flaws in centralized management can be seen in comparing the Soviet management of its agricultural industry with that of the United States. Any comparison between U.S. and Soviet agriculture must take into consideration some differences in their resources. The Soviet Union enjoys a significant advantage over the United States in total arable land. With 500 million acres being farmed, Soviet farmers plant almost fifty per cent more land than the 350 million acres used by American farmers. On the other hand, the United States enjoys the advantage of more favorable rainfall distribution and a more favorable climate. Whether these offsetting factors give both nations an equal potential for food production is difficult to say, but they are relatively close to each other in overall agricultural resources.

The November 1982 issue of *Worldview* compares the two farm systems as follows:

The Soviet Union employs a farm labor force of 26.1 million. Of this group over 26 million are farm workers directed by 46,800 farm managers, who in turn are directed by Moscow. By contrast, the U.S. farm labor force totals only 3.7 million. Some 2.4 million are managers of family farms, mostly owner-operators; fewer than 1.3 million are hired workers.

Individual farmers making day-to-day decisions in response to market signals, changing weather, and the conditions of their crops have a collective intelligence far exceeding that of centralized bureaucracy, however well designed and staffed. For example, the Soviets already knew in 1982 how much phosphate fertilizer they were going to use in 1984 because it was spelled out in the 1981-85 Plan. An American farmer in 1982 will not know how much phosphate fertilizer he will use in 1984 until he tests the soil in the spring of that year and decides what crops to plant. At that time the fertilizer manufacturer will be expected to meet the farmer's demand. Indeed, the fertilizer firm's success depends on its ability to do so. But it is the farmer who determines how much of what kind of fertilizer is used, not the fertilizer manufacturer or a planning office in Washington. . . .

In their single-minded focus on the expansion of food production, the Soviets have neglected storage, packaging and transport. Their press is filled with examples of the resulting waste: grain harvested but without a storage place; fields red with ripe tomatoes but without crates to transport them to market;

potatoes left to rot because farm to market roads are impass-
able. An expert in Soviet affairs, Marshall Goldman observes
that "the dearth of marketing facilities is a reflection of Marxist ideology which regards marketing as a nonproductive,
even parasitic activity."[2]
Some nations with centralized economic management have mod-
erated their ideologies to the extent of granting their farmers small
plots of land on which they can grow whatever they wish for their
own use—capitalistic, free-market style. Without exception the
productivity of the small, privately held acreage far exceeds that of
the larger state-controlled farms.

The same pattern applies when one compares industrial production between nations with a tight central control and those
which permit the market system to operate. Without exception, the
more a nation's industry is planned and controlled by central
government, the less efficient is that industry and the less competitive is it in world markets.

As one who advocates a democratic capitalistic system in which
market forces can operate but with some guidance by central
government, I must admit that the core problem is deciding how
much government intervention is "enough." In the past five years
we have seen several instances in which Western European nations have overstepped the line of cooperation with their industries and moved into control of them with disastrous results.
The British steel industry is one example. France is another.

In February 1982 the Ministry of Industry in France assumed
absolute control over five of that nation's largest companies and,
in so doing, expanded its control to more than thirty per cent of the
nation's industrial activity and fifty per cent of its industrial investment. There is no evidence that productivity in any of the
state-controlled industries has improved. French industrial and
agricultural products are competitive in world markets only by virtue of heavy government subsidies, which is the mercantilistic
trend referred to earlier. In February 1983 the Organization for
Economic Cooperation and Development issued a sixty-two-page
report on the overall effectiveness of France's shift to more centralized government control of the economy. While there were some
benefits from the shift, the report concludes that the overall effect
was negative. One of the key conclusions from the report reads,

"The Socialist attempt to stimulate the French economy through wage boosts, higher social benefits and other government subsidies backfired badly. The measure increased consumer purchasing power, as planned, but imports, rather than French goods, benefited most. The rise in imports widened France's trade deficit sharply. At the same time the increase in French wages exacerbated inflation and made French goods less competitive abroad."

The centralized government management of a nation's economy simply does not work for two basic reasons. First, individual initiative is given little expression. There is something within all humans which cries out for the freedom of self-determination. Give the Russian farmer a few acres of land of his own, and watch him blossom. The second reason is that there is simply not enough human wisdom around to "manage" any economic system, especially a global one. Economics has been called a dismal science for good reason. Not only have we been unable to understand fully all the forces at work within an economy, but we have no way of planning for the "surprises" of droughts, floods, wars, political events, new inventions and all the other occurrences which ebb and flow through the stream of civilization. Our most sophisticated computer programs are unable to give us solid forecasts of the future because we have no way of providing them with the list of surprises. It is difficult for us as highly intelligent creatures to admit that there are certain things which we cannot manage, no matter how hard we try. We need to be modest about what we can do; in economics it is not possible for us to play God.

In addition to his plea for a greater participation by government in the management of the economy, Gladwin also makes frequent mention of government's role in providing needed human services and a more equitable distribution of wealth. As my essay indicated, I too see a role for government in this area; but I suspect that Gladwin desires significantly greater government intervention in these matters than I do.

Anyone who has worked with human service agencies which are under direct federal control or which receive heavy federal funding have had firsthand experiences with many examples of inefficiency and ineffectiveness. I was a member of the board of directors of a legal services agency during the period that we went from private funding to full public funding. While our budget quickly grew to three times the size it had been under private funding, our client load increased only marginally. The federal requirements for investigating and validating client eligibility, for maintaining client records and for reporting staff activities soaked up huge amounts of staff time. We were less efficient. Moreover, the client eligibility regulations did not provide for the flexibility we once had to deal with injustices. Why should a hard-working mother be denied free legal services simply because she has finally worked her way up to an income level one per cent above the maximum established for eligibility, especially when the problem she is dealing with is sapping her financial resources? Under private funding we had the flexibility to deal with exceptions to our rules. Under central government control we were less effective. Admittedly, flexibility opens the door to possible discrimination against certain groups, but it is the role of board members and society at large to guard against such injustices.

We have also seen numerous examples of how, in a perverse way, programs designed to help the poor or disadvantaged end up creating a dependency relationship. Not only is central government unable to plan, direct and administer programs which take into account the many variables of cultural backgrounds, value systems and personal differences of people, but the huge bureaucracy which is needed to deliver programs depends for its continued existence on having clients. Without intention the huge federal structures for implementing human service programs create a client dependency which will ensure survival, and often growth, of the delivery system.

We need to look for more creative ways for central government to induce the private sector and the market system to provide for the delivery of more human services than is the case today. Federal contracting with the private sector for delivery of programs is one way, but perhaps more promising is the trend toward a greater use of vouchers, tax incentives and local development programs.

That the Gladwin essay does not give us specific examples of a centralized society which comes close to his ideals speaks for itself. Those nations which have tended toward strong central, governmental management of society provide proof enough that the surrender of individual freedoms to the state does not yield a just, humane or well-fed society.

From a purely philosophical and theological standpoint, there are grave reservations we should all have about a society so highly centralized that individual initiatives and freedoms are subverted. But when one adds to this the abundant evidence that centrally controlled societies do not function well in a global economy and are neither efficient nor effective in the direct delivery of human services, it is clear that the expectations of the Gladwin essay are much too visionary.

Notes

[1]Robert Strauss, "The Mercantilistic Threat to World Trade," *Wall Street Journal* 200, no. 103 (24 November 1982):26.
[2]Lester R. Brown, "U.S. & Soviet Agriculture: The Shifting Balance of Power," *Worldwatch Paper* 51 (October 1982).

A Decentralist Response
Art Gish

I find myself in many ways attracted to Gladwin's position. Of the other three writers, he is most aware that there is serious injustice in the world, that there is something critically wrong with present structures and that more drastic solutions must be found. He seems to have a deeper understanding than North or Diehl of how sin has taken flesh in our social structures. I admire his concern for social justice. He clearly shows how capitalism doesn't have the sanction of Scripture.

Gladwin is right in his analysis that individual acts of charity and the good will of capitalistic corporations can never be expected to solve the massive problems of the world. Individual acts are too small and scattered, and monopoly capitalism is so much a part of the problem that it can hardly be expected to save and transform itself. Salvation must come from beyond ourselves.

I find something attractive about the notion of centralized planning and control to deal with the massive, complex and almost overwhelming problems of social justice. What more efficient way of dealing with them than through a benevolent state that has the power to enforce justice, environmental protection, redistribution of wealth and rational planning to meet the needs of all humanity? Sounds good.

But Gladwin's position also sounds a little naive. Isn't he aware of the extent to which the state is a tool of the multinational corporations and the capitalistic elite? Isn't the state more concerned with order than justice? Isn't the state part of the problem? My perception is that the state historically has resisted movements for social change and empowerment of people. The civil-rights movement of the 1960s in the United States was fought every step of the way by centralized government. Gladwin never answers the questions of who will control the centralized structures and how they will be controlled. These are critical questions.

One of the basic problems in the world is that people have been made to feel powerless (actually they aren't) and hopeless, cut off from participation in making the decisions that affect their lives.

Maybe there is a need for centralized authority. I don't know. But I do know that it is an extremely dangerous thing unless subject to and accountable to decentralized centers of power and decision making in which all people can meaningfully participate. Therefore, it is more important to decentralize and work on the local level. It may be that we will still need some centralized decision making, but first we need decentralization of power and decision making. We already have too much centralization of power. First we need to enable people to make decisions regarding the shape of their own lives. Gladwin also recognizes this need. On page 195 he states,

> A naive reliance on the good will of central government will not lead to change. Government will only act in these ways when under pressure to do so. Only the successful joining of forces of all who would seek such change ... can lead to change *being initiated through central activity*. This is why the weak and the poor have to use their collective power to constantly defend their rights against all centers of power and to work for a day when authority will bend to their needs and aspirations. (Italics mine)

With the exception of the phrase in italics, his sounds like a decentralist argument to me. If the people are able to collectively mobilize and change government, why do they need to remain dependent on centralized control? Why not take that power and use it to shape a new life in which they can have meaningful participation?

Maybe Gladwin's position could be restated in such a way that we could both agree. The answer to the world's problems must be worked at in collective, common, public action. The question between us is how centralized or decentralized that action must be, to what extent people are able to participate in those structures, and to what extent people are given a sense of participation (koinonia), involvement and voice in what happens.

This history of centralized planning and control is not encouraging. It has been and continues to be corrupt, inefficient, expensive and wasteful. With centralization comes increased bureaucracy, complexity and specialization. It becomes so complex a system that human control of it becomes increasingly difficult. This results in increased social costs: alienation, personal maladjustment, communal disruption and environmental damage. Add to this the perceived need for increased military and police to protect that centralized power and the wars that inevitably result, and the cost becomes overwhelming.

The history of Israel can be instructive for us. For three hundred years they did fine under the decentralized system of the judges. But shortly after the establishment of centralized government (the monarchy), the kingdom split. There were government oppression and corruption. The Bible for the most part takes a rather negative view of centralized government. First Samuel 8 warns against the repressive outcome of centralized government. Revelation 13 describes the centralized state as a beast to be resisted. The state is referred to as Babylon. Nowhere in the Bible is the state looked to as the source of renewal, community or salvation. Even in Romans 13:1-7 the state is given only a minimal role.

Gladwin seems fatalistic in his description of the growth of the modern state and its power over people's lives. Yes, through modern technology the state is now more able to achieve its will, conduct surveillance over its citizens and control people's lives. But why does Gladwin maintain the impossibility of reducing the power of the state? What is wrong with reversing history? That is the call of the prophets and the meaning of repentance, is it not?

The civil-rights movement in the United States reversed a long history of discrimination; and chaos did not result, as some had feared.

There are alternative futures. To be unaware of them is to lock ourselves into a narrow world view and relinquish our freedom. Gladwin is probably right in his statement that "a large state is required for the style of life we possess at present" (p. 189). But maybe there is something wrong with our style of life. Maybe there are alternatives which could lead to liberation and koinonia.

Gladwin seems to have a fear of chaos and anarchy, and so he puts much emphasis on maintenance of order. Because of this he accepts the violence and militarism of the state. I wonder if he also accepts the nuclear arms race.

The problem with Gladwin, Diehl and North is that they all are essentially humanists who believe it is we who must create and impose order. When it comes right down to practical issues, God cannot be trusted for our security. We must create our own security and impose our order (disorder?) on the world.

This humanist idea that we are in control of history creates more concern for me than fears of what would happen if order were not imposed. It is my sense that, over the long haul of history, governments have created more problems than they have solved. Instead of being God's servants and accepting their orders (ordination) from God, they have rebelled against God and created chaos. They now threaten the whole human race with extinction. I distrust any group of people who think they have the answers and are willing to impose their answers on others. I especially distrust them if they think they are acting on behalf of God.

We should learn from history that, in the long run, all human attempts to impose order end in dismal failure. Instead of imposing order on the poor, we might first get off their backs and allow them space to find their own order. Order is the result of justice.

Where in the Bible is the suggestion that Christians should use the state to impose order on the world? The call of the New Testament is clear. Get out of the present system. It is about to collapse. Although we continue to live in the world, we are not of it and do not pledge allegiance to its structures or flags. The Bible anticipates no ideal state or economy apart from the new creation. The call of the New Testament is not to reform the old order, but to become part of the new order.

The basis of the state has not changed throughout history. Its basis is still violence: the threat of the sword and prison. The problems of the world cannot be solved with violence and coercion. Forcing the scoundrels to be good is not the answer. Resorting to the use of violence and coercion is a denial of the way of the cross.

Gladwin seems to argue that we can employ one evil to overcome another. The end justifies the means. Even if the state is evil, we have to have it to protect our way of life (or is it our way of death?). A way of life that cannot be maintained by voluntary cooperation, that needs a powerful state to force people into its mold, is not worth preserving.

The problem with Gladwin is that he does not begin with Jesus. Although he has a deep understanding of injustice, he lacks a vision of God's kingdom, the new order that is offered to us which we can begin living now. The New Testament offers us a vision of the future far more radical than either the Marxist or anarchist dreams.

Gladwin has inklings of this alternative. On page 191 he writes, What we need, therefore, are not sermons directed at the rich to make them more charitable or directed at the poor to make them more diligent, but a discovery by both rich and poor of biblical values which will bring them together in common fellowship [koinonia] in the pursuit of justice. The solution must lie in a common search for a form of order which more truly affirms the creation, resists the Fall and offers more substantial hope.

That says it so beautifully. Amen! I would encourage Gladwin and each reader to think about the fantastic implications of this statement.

We need a vision of the church as the liberated people of God. We must first call the church to repentance and a life of justice. Then the church can call the world to repentance and justice. But how can we call the world to something the church is not ready to accept?

Gladwin is right in challenging us who are concerned about lifestyle to also think and act politically. Unless we do take political action and resist oppression and injustice, our concerns for lifestyle will soon become self-righteous, pharisaic legalism.

It is important, however, that our politics be the politics of God's kingdom, not Caesar's. It is essential that our action be based in

God's redeeming love, not in any will for power. Our tools in that struggle are spiritual, not carnal. They are definitely political, but not the politics of worldly power. They are tools like love, truth and suffering.

Our primary weapon is the cross—defenseless, suffering love. That may seem like foolishness in the eyes of the power seekers, but Christians know that the cross leads to resurrection. If we are serious about social justice, we will lay our lives on the line, give up our privilege and become vulnerable, looking to God as the only source of power to overcome the injustice of the world.

We creatures are not called to save the world, to enforce virtue. That is God's prerogative alone. But we *are* called to be faithful, to live the new, radiant life of the kingdom of God—here and now. We can point to a new social order based on the sovereignty of God's truth and love.

Postscript
Robert G. Clouse

Christianity must be a message of spiritual renewal as well as hope and comfort to people in situations of deprivation and hunger. The preaching of the gospel cannot be limited to a private transaction between the believer and Christ. Gospel witness in its fullness includes the call to a life of discipleship expressed in loving service to others through economic, political and social means.

The problem is, just how can this be done? There seem to be few clear statements in the Bible on many of our most pressing contemporary economic problems. The answer is complex, but as one scholar suggests,

> The way out is not . . . by a flight from Scripture to sociology or psychology. What is needed is a dialog with Scripture, in which we aim to hear its basic affirmations and intentions and then apply these to our situation and time, in light of our best understandings. Theologically, this approach can be termed an ethic of discipleship, in distinction from an ethic of imitation. . . .

With regard to the use of possessions ... discipleship says
something like this: "No one rule applies. Every disciple of Jesus
is called to unselfish giving and sharing; the needs of the poor
cry out for help, the exploitation of the rich for condemnation.
Let this be reflected in the way you live and the way you give."[1]
What are some specific principles that shall guide us in our attitudes toward wealth and poverty?

First, we must put the highest priority on sharing what we have
with others. This may be done through individual actions, volun-
teer associations such as churches and civic clubs, and government programs. The amount of giving will vary from individual to
individual. Jesus asked some people, such as the rich young ruler,
to surrender all their possessions (Mt 19:16-30; Mk 10:17-31;
Lk 18:18-30) while others, like Zacchaeus, were not called on to
abandon everything (Lk 19:1-10). Zacchaeus returned the goods
he had illegally taken and gave half of his money to the poor. This
story of costly discipleship should challenge each of us to live in a
generous manner toward others rather than follow the example of
the rich fool who lavished everything on himself (Lk 12:13-21).

A second response to poverty and riches on the part of Christians in the industrialized lands of the world should be to simplify
the way they live. Christians are to be separate from the world. This
ought to include adopting a countercultural attitude toward the
consumer-oriented lifestyle of Western civilization. Although
Christians disagree as to how radical our approach to lifestyle
should be, we may find that rejecting the graver examples of consumer manipulation would restore believers to a happier Christian
life. As Tom Sine points out:

> If our national intake of alcohol, valium, and assorted other
> chemicals or our statistics on mental health problems, suicide,
> and stress-related illness are any indication, we aren't enjoying
> "the good life" as much as we think.
>
> I suspect one of the major reasons we are belatedly discover-
> ing high consumption isn't all that satisfying is that, contrary to
> popular opinion, humans are primarily spiritual and social—
> not economic—beings. We have been conditioned to believe
> that ever-increasing consumption of goods and services will not
> only make us happier but will increase our self-worth and power.[2]

A more simple lifestyle might mean a smaller house, less expensive transportation or a change in vocation. These differences might help us live longer, healthier lives, and they would sensitize us to human need. Also, according to some people at least, in a world of limited resources, reduced consumption conserves resources for others.[3]

A third assignment for Christians who wish to respond to current economic problems must involve speaking for the poor. In the mind of Jesus, the supreme example of God's purpose was an interest in the poor (Mt 11:5). In the sense that Jesus used the term *poor*, it meant not only those with little or no resources but also the brokenhearted, the captives, those who mourn and those who are oppressed in a general sense. They are the ones who must depend on God, for they have no status or power of their own.[4] In Jesus' day the religious establishment discriminated against people such as these. First-century Judaism would not allow them to change their way of life in order to be forgiven. Other religious teachers of his time laid burdens on these prostitutes, widows, orphans, tax collectors and sick people, but Jesus invited them to come to him and find acceptance and rest (Mt 11:28).

Many of us must confess that we do not share Jesus' view of the poor and the oppressed. Actually there seems to be an attitude of contempt for the poor among many American Christians. As a former social worker states, "We find greater tolerance in our hearts for the Mafia and for those involved in white-collar crime— after all, they keep their yards up and they're obviously successful in their work—but we seem to hate the welfare mother who is struggling to simply keep life together."[5]

Often the poor and exploited find more sympathy among unbelievers, such as Marxists, than among Christians. The situation leads one theologian to observe:

> Why do atheistic systems like Marxism prosper among the oppressed far more than Christianity? Is it because the poor have known only a church captive to its culture, or even worse, one lending its justification to a system that perpetuates gross injustices and inequalities? Where is the prophetic voice of Jesus in the church that says with courage and integrity, "Blessed are you poor" and "Woe to you rich." Are we all too silent because we have lost so much of our integrity, or because we do not want to prophesy against ourselves?[6]

Championing the cause of the poor will lead us to labor for justice
and a greater degree of equality for all people. Evil can be understood in the traditional way as involved with individual persons,
but it may be found in social structures as well. These "principalities and powers" benefit the well-to-do and the powerful, and they
prevent social change that would aid the powerless. A poem by
Vinicio Aguilar from Central America catches the attitude of those
mistreated by unjust structures:

Where was god, daddy; where, where, where
when the commissioners
    broke the fence,
    burnt the farm,
    destroyed the harvest,
    killed the pigs,
    raped Imelda,
    drank our rum?
HE WAS UP THERE, boy.
Where was god, daddy; where, where, where
when because we complained
    the state judge came and fined us
    the bailiff came to arrest us
    and even the priest came to insult us?
HE WAS UP THERE, boy.
Well, then, daddy; we must now tell him plainly
that he must come down sometimes
to be with us.
You can see how we are, daddy,
with no fields sown, no farm, no pigs, nothing, and he
as if nothing had happened. It isn't right, you know, daddy.
If he's really up there
let him come down
Let him come down to taste this cruel hunger with us
let him come down and sweat
in the maize-fields, come down to be imprisoned,
let him come down and spew on the rich man
who throws the stone and hides his hand,
    on the venal judge,
    on the unworthy priest,
    and on the bailiffs and commissioners

who rob and kill
the peasants;
because I certainly don't want to tell my son when he
asks me one day:
HE WAS UP THERE, boy.[7]

If Christians do not work to bring social and economic justice to the people of the world who suffer from such wrongs, they have a useless gospel. We may not solve all of the problems, but we must try to approximate the vision of God's coming world which differs so radically from our own. As the seer John explained:

And I saw the holy city, new Jerusalem, coming down out of heaven from God, prepared as a bride adorned for her husband; and I heard a loud voice from the throne saying, "Behold, the dwelling of God is with men. He will dwell with them, and they shall be his people, and God himself will be with them; he will wipe away every tear from their eyes, and death shall be no more, neither shall there be mourning nor crying nor pain any more...."

And I saw no temple in the city, for its temple is the Lord God the Almighty and the Lamb. And the city has no need of sun or moon to shine upon it, for the glory of God is its light, and its lamp is the Lamb. By its light shall the nations walk; and the kings of the earth shall bring their glory into it, and its gates shall never be shut by day—and there shall be no night there; they shall bring into it the glory and the honor of the nations....

Then he showed me the river of the water of life, bright as crystal, flowing from the throne of God and of the Lamb through the middle of the street of the city; also, on either side of the river, the tree of life with its twelve kinds of fruit, yielding its fruit each month; and the leaves of the tree were for the healing of the nations. There shall no more be anything accursed, but the throne of God and of the Lamb shall be in it, and his servants shall worship him. (Rev 21:2-4, 22-26; 22:1-3)

Notes

[1]Walter E. Pilgrim, *Good News to the Poor: Wealth and Poverty in Luke-Acts* (Minneapolis: Augsburg Pub. House, 1981), pp. 167-68.

[2]Tom Sine, *The Mustard Seed Conspiracy* (Waco, Tex.: Word Books, 1981), p. 81.

[3]The point is reinforced by such writers as Fred Hirsch, who explains the paradox of affluence, namely, that it is unsatisfying when widely spread. Beyond certain basic needs such as food, clothing and shelter, there are what he called "positional goods" which are relatively scarce. In this category he placed the enjoyment of scenery, the pleasure of suburban living and holding leadership positions. Here the problem arises that "if everyone stands on tiptoe, no one sees better." The positional good depends on scarcity and takes time to acquire. It makes people less concerned with others and acts as a stimulus to wage inflation. To look upon economic advances as individual achievement is to set up expectations that cannot be realized. See his *Social Limits To Growth* (Cambridge: Harvard Univ. Press, 1976).

Other helpful books that deal with lifestyle decisions are the following: David M. Beckmann, *Where Faith and Economics Meet: A Christian Critique* (Minneapolis: Augsburg Pub. House, 1981); David M. Beckmann and Elizabeth A. Donnelly, *The Overseas List* (Minneapolis: Augsburg Pub. House, 1976); Larry L. Rasmussen, *Economic Anxiety and Christian Faith* (Minneapolis: Augsburg Pub. House, 1981); James A. Scherer, *Global Living Here and Now* (New York: Friendship Press, 1974); Robert L. Stivers, *The Sustainable Society: Ethics and Economic Growth* (Philadelphia: Westminster Press, 1976); and John V. Taylor, *Enough is Enough: A Biblical Call for Moderation in a Consumer-Oriented Society* (Minneapolis: Augsburg Pub. House, 1977).

[4]For information on global poverty see Michael Harrington, *The Vast Majority: A Journey to the World's Poor* (New York: Simon & Schuster, 1977); for the biblical material notice Richard Batey, *Jesus and the Poor* (New York: Harper & Row, 1972); Conrad Boerma, *The Rich, the Poor and the Bible* (Philadelphia: Westminster Press, 1979); and Allen Hollis, *The Bible and Money* (New York: Hawthorn Books, 1976).

[5]Sine, *Mustard Seed Conspiracy*, p. 55.

[6]Pilgrim, *Good News to the Poor*, p. 174.

[7]Quoted in Stephen Travis, *I Believe in the Second Coming of Jesus* (Grand Rapids: Eerdmans, 1982), pp. 241-42.